Starting a Business
in

howtobooks
Send for a free copy of the latest catalogue:
How To Books
Spring Hill House, Spring Hill Road,
Begbroke, Oxford OX5 1RX United Kingdom
email: info@howtobooks.co.uk
http://www.howtobooks.co.uk

Starting a Business
in
Italy

How to set up
and run a
successful business
in the Bel Paese

Emma Bird and Mario Berri

howtobooks

Published by How To Books Ltd
Spring Hill House, Spring Hill Road
Begbroke, Oxford OX5 1RX. United Kingdom
Tel: (01865) 375974. Fax: (01865) 379162
email: info@howtobooks.co.uk
www.howtobooks.co.uk

British Library Cataloguing in Publication Data
A catalogue record for this book is available from the British Library

ISBN 13: 978 1 84528 128 1
ISBN 10: 1 84528 128 4

Produced for How to Books by Deer Park Productions, Tavistock
Cover design by Mousemat Design Ltd
Typeset by Pantek Arts Ltd, Maidstone, Kent
Printed and bound in Great Britain by Bell & Bain Ltd, Glasgow

Contents

Acknowledgements

To Mum and Dad for always believing in my dreams however improssible they seemed.

Emma:

Thanks to everyone who has played a part in my Italian adventures: to Nan for keeping me in Cadbury chocolate supplies, to Siobhan Clifford for being my partner in crime while aupairing in Naples and Abruzzo, to Camilla Falcioni for being my Anglo-Italian link and to Tamara Molinas and Simone Semprini for adopting me during my year in Bologna when my Italian was awful and to Tamara for her *amicizia* (friendship) ever since. Thanks to Elinor Hodgson for her inspiration, wisdom, friendship and timely emails from the other end of Sardinia, to Stephanie Scotto for inspiration and Emma Southwell for being a fab friend and for giving up her valuable time to proofread the book when she could have been out enjoying herself. Thanks to expats Max Ingold, Dave Marsh, Morgan Cox, Graham Lane, Nicola Schroeder, Valerie Ryder, Sylvie Michelotti-Leder, Aimie Louie, Sally Jones, Simon Curtis, Sam Morgan and Jonathan McGuiness who generously agreed to talk to us and share their secrets. Without them this book could never have been written. Thanks to Margaret Eaglestone, Nikki Read, and everyone else who took the idea for the book from concept to reality. Finally thanks to Mario for his technical knowledge, support and encouragement throughout.

Mario:

I would like to acknowledge seven people: Paolo Carloni for having been an inspirational manager when I first started in the corporate world in Milan, for encouraging me in my professional career and for becoming a great friend, too. Marco Trionfo for always being there. Barbara Gaion for being a true friend ever since we met in Glasgow and for being like a sister to me. Sabina Morreale for her great pieces of advice. Roberto Puzzanghera and Diletta Pia for going above and beyond the call of friendship and for everything they've done since we moved to Sardinia. And to Emma for making me realise my potential and value of my Italian business knowledge.

TAKE MORE OF YOUR MONEY WITH YOU

If you're starting a business in Italy it's likely that the last thing on your mind is foreign exchange. However, exchange rates are constantly moving and as a result can have a big impact on the amount of money you have to start your new life in Italy.

For example, if you look at the euro during 2005 you can see how this movement can affect your capital. Sterling against the euro was as high as 1.5124 and as low as 1.4086. This meant that if you had £200,000 you could have ended up with as much as €302,480 or as little as €281,720, a difference of over €20,000.

To ensure you get the most for your money it's a good idea to use a foreign exchange specialist such as Currencies Direct. As an alternative to your bank Currencies Direct is able to offer you extremely competitive exchange rates, no commission charges and free transfers*. This can mean considerable savings on your transfer when compared to using a bank.

Buying Options

Spot Deal – This is the *Buy now*, *Pay now* option and will give you the best rate available right now and guarantee it.

Forward Contract – This is the *Buy now, Pay later* option and allows you to fix a rate for anywhere up to 2 years in advance.

Limit Order – You set the rate that you want and the market is then monitored. As soon as that rate is achieved the currency is purchased for you.

*Over £5,000

Information provided by Currencies Direct.
www.currenciesdirect.com   Tel: 0845 389 1729
Email: info@currenciesdirect.com

Introduction

We decided to write this book together after setting up How to Italy, our company which provides practical and inspirational advice for people wishing to live in Italy. Every day we receive letters from all over the world from people looking to move to the Bel Paese. According to statistics from the Transitions Abroad portal, Italy is the destination most readers want to move to. In most cases, there is just one problem: how to find a job and earn enough money to live *la Dolce Vita*.

Once you have a job, employees in Italy enjoy some of the best perks in Europe, but actually getting the job is the hardest part. Unfortunately, as those of you who have tried know, it's not just a case of updating your curriculum vitae (CV), translating it into Italian, sending it off with a slick *lettera di accompagnamento* (covering letter) and waiting to hear back from your potential employer. In Italy, you have to be super qualified, with a degree in the field you want to work in. Of course, it also helps if you know someone who already knows someone in the company you hope to end up working for. Unless your network extends to both expats and Italians who are already in Italy, finding a job is not a straightforward process.

ONE THOUSAND NEW BUSINESSES LAUNCH EVERY DAY IN ITALY

By setting up and running your own business in Italy, you overcome all of these obstacles because you are working for yourself.

If you do take the plunge, you will be in good company. In the preface to the Corriere Lavoro 2004 edition of *Mettersi in proprio: idee, strumenti e storie*, Walter Passerini makes the claim that more than 1,000 new businesses are launched every day in Italy. This backs up research carried out by Union Camere, the governing body of Italy's *camere di commercio* (chambers of commerce), in 2003, which put the number of businesses in Italy at a staggering 5.8m.

Whereas in other countries people look at entrepreneurs as risk takers and daredevils, in Italy this is not the case. Eavesdrop on the conversations going on in an Italian pizzeria on a Saturday evening and at least one is bound to centre around a new business idea and the possibility of turning the dream into reality.

SILVIO BERLUSCONI

Italy has a long-standing tradition of producing entrepreneurs, but probably the most famous of them all is Silvio Berlusconi. He came from a modest background (his father was a bank clerk) and started wheeling and dealing as a schoolboy during the Second World War when he used to collect waste paper in the street, compress it into balls and resell it to people as fuel for their stoves. The now billionaire and the richest man in Italy also admits to having been paid to do the homework of the richer boys at his school in Milan and, later, to take photos at weddings and funerals.

From there, Berlusconi paid his way through university by singing on cruise ships and when he was just 27, he conceived the plans to build Milano2, a town of 4,000 units outside of Milan and where his television company, Mediaset, now has its headquarters. He got around the problem of private television channels only being allowed to operate at local level by setting up a series of local TV stations across Italy and simultaneously broadcasting the same programmes at exactly the same time throughout the country. If that wasn't enough, he has penned the lyrics for an album of love songs, he owns Mondadori, Italy's largest publishing house, and the football club AC Milan. He also formed his own political party, Forza Italia, and has twice been the Italian prime minister. In the April 2006 elections his party earned the largest share of the vote overall, but his centre-right coalition, Casa della Libertà, lost out to rival Romano Prodi's centre-left coalition, Unione, by 25,000 votes in the lower house. The fact that the election result was so close and that Forza Italia brought home the majority of the votes despite early exit polls putting Prodi in the lead, shows that Berlusconi's slick, charismatic image continues to prove a hit with the Italian public.

Of course, we are not suggesting you copy Berlusconi. Our point is that in Italy being an entrepreneur is a way of life and anyone can do it. Naturally, you will have to cut through the red tape and overcome many obstacles, but by setting up your own business you will be joining millions of other like-minded souls.

The bad news is that one of the most challenging aspects of setting up a company in Italy is that easy-to-read material isn't as readily available here as it is in other countries. Type 'setting up business' into Google's UK search engine and it will throw up www. businesslink.gov.uk, www.entrepreneur.com, www.bytestart.co.uk and www.bstartup.com, along with a plethora of other useful sites. Try the same with the Italian translation '*avviare impresa*' and you do not get a comprehensive list of material. What you get instead are sites attempting to sell you their services to help you set up a business. As a consequence, you (or at least Emma did), end up getting quite confused, scratching your head and wondering where to begin your mammoth search for information.

OUR OWN JOURNEY

When it came to writing *Starting a Business in Italy*, we rewound to the beginning of our entrepreneur journey in Italy. In Emma's case that was when she was teaching English ful time in a private language school after giving up her journalism career in Milan, and in Mario's case, it was when he was made redundant. How we ever came to set up a business in Italy is a bit of a mystery considering our two very different perspectives. Although Emma had never worked in the corporate world, she viewed the challenge through her expatriate eyes and realised it was the only way she would ever be able to make a living in Sardinia. Emma was ready to commit herself 100 per cent to the challenge even though the light bulb in her head hadn't yet started flashing and she had no idea what she wanted to do. A *dirigente* (senior manager), Mario was far more cautious. He wanted to find another senior management position and didn't believe he should risk everything to set up on his own. Given that Emma was only earning €900 per month teaching English, Mario didn't think both of us should risk launching our own start-up without a steady income to fall back on. But then Emma started ordering business books off Amazon and would leave them strategically lying around the house or would pack them into the beach bag. A couple of months later, Mario had secured his first clients.

HOW TO ITALY

The conception of How to Italy took a little longer – just over a year longer to be precise. Emma was still determined she was going to become a businesswoman in Italy and 15-minute breaks between one English lesson and the next were spent brainstorming potential ideas. She used to list her skills and experiences, what she wanted to do and what she could become an expert in. Out of the blue, Emma landed a corporate relocation contract with an American company. She had no idea where it would take her, but she knew it was the first step on her journey to become an *imprenditrice* (female entrepreneur).

In the end, How to Italy was born completely by accident. In fact, we almost missed the lamp bulb flashing in our heads altogether. By 2004, Emma had resumed her writing career and was freelancing for magazines and newspapers and writing on her favourite topic: living and working in Italy (of course!). One of her commissions was a piece on living in Sardinia, which was published on the Escape Artist website. The next day when Emma turned on her PC, her inbox was full with emails (342) from people asking for her advice on living and working not only in Sardinia, but also in Italy. The same thing happened a further four times but, far from jumping on the bandwagon and realising she had a unique selling point, Emma secretly got annoyed with this deluge of emails because she simply did not have time to reply. It was only in September 2005 when she started to send out emails with her consultation rates that she realised people were actually willing to pay for concrete advice on finding work in Italy. It was a revelation.

XVI / STARTING A BUSINESS IN ITALY

But even then, How to Italy still wasn't a proper business. Consultations were done as and when people requested them, but there was still no strategy in place. Then, one Sunday afternoon when we were at the beach, we started talking about the consultations Emma offered and how we could add value to them.

We realised that Mario's senior management experience as a financial and administration manager for various Italian companies, coupled with his ability to speak fluent English, complemented Emma's expatriate experiences of living in Abruzzo, Bologna, Cagliari, Milan, Naples and Olbia.

THIS BOOK

There are so many regional characteristics in Italy that it is impossible to define a typical Italian. The Milanese for example certainly feel much more at home doing business with their Swiss or French counterparts than they do with southern Italians. However, given that space does not allow us to list the regional differences every time we make comparisons between Italy and other countries we have had to make certain generalisations in *Starting a Business in Italy*.

The book provides a step-by-step guide to launching your start-up and includes our experiences along the way. We've also included interviews with other expatriates who have already turned their dreams into reality and are busy running companies in the country. But what we are not doing is writing this guide through rose-tinted specs and not all the case studies have a happy-ever-after ending. We wanted this book to be a comprehensive nuts and bolts guide. With that in mind, we felt we also had to include the cautionary tales of expatriates who moved back to their home countries after their business ventures failed.

In each chapter, we have included useful websites for you to find out more information and Mario provides his Pearl of Wisdom to give you added insight into the situation in Italy.

If you still find yourself slightly daunted by the prospect of setting up your own business, it is only natural. After all, you are plunging into the unknown. But think of it as an adventure, think of all the *gelati* (ice cream), wine and cappuccinos you will soon be enjoying when you are not running the company, and bear in mind the words of Nereo Rocco, one of Italy's most famous football players-turned-managers. '*Chi ha paura, resti nello spogliatoio*' he used to say – 'He who is afraid should stay in the locker room'.

What more can we say

The labour market in Italy

There is no doubt about it. Italy knows how to work its magic. Whether you have spent a few days or a few weeks in Italy, the chances are you never realised a person could fall so in love with a place. But now it's happened and you are planning on upping sticks and moving to the Bel Paese.

We don't blame you, either. After all, with the laid back lifestyle, stunning scenery, generous hosts, tasty food and wine which also happens to be good for you, lots of sunshine and a mild climate, a cultural and historical richness that other countries can only envy, a good health service, job security, and property that is still cheaper than in the UK despite prices shooting through the roof in the past few years, what more could you ask for?

DISADVANTAGES

But here comes our first word of warning: it's not all *Chianti* and *cappuccinos*, olive and lemon groves, *vino bianco* and *vino rosso*. Living in Italy also has some disadvantages but what country doesn't?

Here they are:

◆ English is rarely spoken so a good level of Italian is absolutely essential if you plan to live anywhere apart from major cities such as Milan, Rome and Florence. If you don't speak Italian and you aren't prepared to learn, the solution is simple: don't even think of starting a new life here. We know plenty of expatriates that have to be accompanied to the toilet in bars and can't even order a meal in Italian at McDonalds (and no, sadly, we're not making that up) because they cannot be bothered to make the effort. If you would rather speak English move to the Costa Del Sol or another expat enclave.

◆ Bureaucracy rules. Italy is the land where new rules and regulations are invented all the time, but no one bothers to inform anyone else. You will run around in circles for days, weeks and months (in some cases, years) as you figure out just what exactly you are meant to be doing. You'll find out more about this in Chapter 2: Key figures and insitututions.

◆ There are three Italys: the north, the centre and the *mezzogiorno* (this literally means 'midday', but is also the term used to refer to the south of Italy, Sicily and Sardinia). While the north is highly advanced and has lots of opportunities for skilled workers and professionals, high employment rates in the south, along with the peculiarities of the Italian labour market, mean there are very few jobs available to expats.

And therein lays the problem. You need to accept from day one that, unless you want to be in the metropolis, even with all the best will in the world, it's going to be very, very difficult to find a job in Italy that: (a) pays well; and (b) gives you stability.

So how are you going to beat the system? Do you really need to ask? By setting up your own business of course!

EMMA'S STORY

Still not convinced? Take it from Emma, she didn't think she would have any difficulty in finding a job when she moved to Cagliari in Sardinia back in June 2003. She had had visions of relaxing after a hard day's work by topping up her tan on whiter-than-white sandy beaches and swimming in the turquoise sea. She was convinced it was going to be a charmed life and infinitely better than the rat race she had left behind in Milan and prior to that in Liverpool. She was definitely being over-optimistic.

Of course, part of Emma's dream came true: from May through to October, there really were postcard-perfect blue skies every day and she really could sunbathe as much as she wanted. But there was just one problem: she didn't have a job, and not for want of trying, either. Realising that the TEFL (Teaching English as a Foreign Language) industry shut down completely over the summer, she knew she was going to have to be proactive. She wrote her CV and accompanying letter in Italian (by this time, she was fluent in the language so didn't have a problem) and sent it to every single temping agency in Cagliari. She followed this up with phone calls and even went in to see the consultants in person. But nothing. Not even a glimmer of hope.

Why? Lack of qualifications or work experience weren't to blame. Emma had worked in various shops both at home and abroad so could lay claim to being a *commessa esperta* (experienced shop assistant). Plus, she had also worked in a hotel and restaurant, doled out fish and chips in takeaways, been an admin assistant and carried out international research for a publishing company. She could also touch-type pretty quickly and spoke French and

Italian fluently along with a smattering of German. She wasn't fussy that summer. She would have done anything and everything as a way of making money. Mistakenly, Emma thought that the work experience and skills accumulated over the years would have come in handy.

Italians graduate late

So what was the reason? She was accused of inventing what was on her CV. Emma had just turned 26 when she moved to Italy and already had a fairly full CV. This may be normal for an American, Brit, Australian or New Zealander in their mid-twenties. But it wasn't normal in Italy. Whereas the average young European graduates from university at the age of 22, the Italian average is 28 and it is not uncommon for Italians to graduate in their early thirties without any professional experience whatsoever (source: *Fondazione Marco Biagi*, June 2005). Whereas most young Europeans, Americans and Canadians are looking to get on the first rung of the career ladder, young Italians make the most of their long summer holidays by lying on the beach to perfect their golden tan. Emma was not given any respect by the people interviewing her as they clearly thought she was little more than an ambitious liar. That day ended with her sobbing over a campari and soda in a Cagliari bar convinced she would never ever find a job. In fact, that summer she never did.

MARIO'S STORY

Mario graduated from the University of Cagliari with a degree in *Economia e Commercio* (Business and Economics) when he was 24. He immediately took a low-paid job as a clerk in an accountant's office while preparing for his state accountancy exams. A year later he moved to England to perfect his language skills, but when he moved back to Sardinia he couldn't find a job so he had no choice but to head to Milan. There, he found work immediately as an accountant for the multinational Brill Manitoba SpA. After seven years working in management positions for multinationals in Italy and abroad, he was headhunted back to Sardinia in 2003 to become the finance and administration director of a large supermarket chain.

But after 15 months of working for the company, he suddenly found himself redundant because the parent company in north Italy wanted to transfer the whole of the administration department to their own offices. He was made several job offers but none of the companies in Sardinia were willing to recognise his *dirigente* (senior management) status because they wanted to keep their costs down.

Case study

Simon Curtis, 40, is a British-trained GP who was a partner in a busy practice in Oxford before moving to Italy with his family in 2003. He continues to jet back to the UK to teach fellow GPs on the latest research findings relevant to general practice. In 2004, he set up Doctor Curtis, a private medical practice aimed at expats in Tuscany and Umbria.

Emma: Why did you set up your own practice? Surely working in the Italian state system would have been easier?

Simon: That's what I thought, too. I naively thought it would just be a case of getting my qualifications translated, learning Italian and applying for a job in the **Servizio Sanitario Nazionale**.

▶

Emma: So what happened?

Simon: Someone told me just how many people are unemployed in Italy and how there simply aren't enough jobs for doctors to go around. Unlike the British system, anyone can apply to do medicine in Italy and that means thousands of new doctors every year.

Emma: But surely with all your qualifications, you would have been given a priority placing.

Simon: Unfortunately not. Plus, I would have been waiting for years. I needed a job straight away.

Emma: Okay, I get your point. How did you beat the system?

Simon: I didn't want to teach English or change my job because I love being a doctor. I realised that if I wanted to stay in Italy and continue to practise medicine my only option was to set up on my own.

Emma: And was it easy?

Simon: It involved lots of bureaucracy in order to get my qualifications recognised and actually be able to practise. Plus, I had to find premises, learn Italian medical jargon and how the system operates here – and find clients.

Emma: I hope it's been worth it though.

Simon: Absolutely. Back in the UK, GPs are choked with paperwork. In the UK, you have ten minutes to see each new patient and you are forced to think 'how can I wrap this up?' and move on to the next one. But in Italy there is no time limit, so I can really get to know the patient and what is really bothering them. I never thought I would be able to set up my own business in a foreign country. If I can do it, anyone can.

THE ITALIAN LABOUR MARKET – A SORRY TALE

As you may be starting to gather, the job situation in Italy makes for grim reading. Italy is similar to the UK in many respects: both countries have similar sized populations (Italy 57.7m, UK 59.5m), similar economic power and a similar GDP (gross domestic product). But despite Italy's status as one of the world's most industrialised and prosperous countries, the economic situation is stagnant and there are just not enough jobs to go around.

Let's have a look at the statistics.

The Italian Labour market

According to ISTAT, the Italian Institute of Statistics, unemployment in Italy in 2004 was 8.2 per cent. Each region's own unemployment rate as a percentage of the regional population, rather than the national population, was broken down as follows:

The north	4.5 per cent
The north-west	4.7 per cent
The north-east	4.3 per cent
The centre	6.5 per cent
The *mezzogiorno*	15.0 per cent

Among the young, unemployment figures can shoot up to as high as 50 per cent. Nevertheless, there is some room for hope as the unemployment in 2001 was a much higher at 9.4 per cent.

Protected workforce

Even these statistics do not tell the whole story. Italy has three main *sindacati* (trade unions), which are all politically affiliated:

Confederzione Generale Italiana del Lavoro (CGIL), the Confederazione Italiana Sindacati Lavoratori (CISL) and the Unione Italiana del Lavoro (UIL). These lobbies are Italy's real policy makers on employment law. Confidustria is the Italian Employers' Federation and counteracts the force of the other three unions. Under these current laws, employers are highly reluctant to take on new workers because they are afraid of absorbing high employment costs. Employers are expected to pay the employee's social security payments, plus annual bonuses and other benefits which can add up to an extra 40–45 per cent on top of the worker's salary. In addition, Italy's workforce is the most protected in Europe and you can read more about this in Chapter 21: Taking on staff.

Permanent contracts

Permanent contracts are like gold dust – very valuable and extremely rare especially after the *Riforma Biagi* came into force in 2003, which aimed to reform the rigid labour market by introducing more temporary contracts. It is not surprising that Italians hang on to jobs that they hate all their life in order to be guaranteed good working conditions. This is especially true of the jobs within the state sector, where employees are generally frustrated and are only motivated by the salary and high job security.

Proof of this stagnant workforce comes from sociologist Ivano Bison who, in 2005, published his findings into the career prospects of his compatriots. More than 90 per cent of graduates enter employment at the level they eventually leave and more than two thirds of the entire workforce remains in the same position for their entire working lives.

Lavoro in nero or 'working under the table'

In order to get around the strict labour laws governing the nation, Italian employers sometimes offer work *in nero* or under the table. Alongside Greece, Italy suffers more than other European countries.

The reasons for the *economia sommersa* (hidden economy) are as follows:

- excessive taxes and employee contributions;
- lack of legislation surrounding the labour market;
- the diffusion of micro and macro companies which are unlikely to ever implement laws;
- low-level education and lack of training contributes to a low technological innovation;
- a general acceptance of the situation.

Back in June 2005, the then Italian Prime Minister Silvio Berlusconi admitted as much. He told Confindustria, the Italian Employers' Federation, that the Italian economy was held together by 40 per cent of Italians (that is 2 in 5) working illegally in some capacity or another. That figure rises to 1 in 3 workers in the *mezzogiorno*.

So what exactly does the *economia sommersa* consist of? This illegal employment takes many forms: from employers not giving workers contracts and paying them entirely in cash or employers paying part of a salary legally and the other part in a wad of banknotes, to second jobs whose earnings are never declared to the Italian tax authorities. The advantage is that you pay less tax (or none at all), the disadvantage is that you will not be able to access the *Servizio Sanitario Nazionale* (equivalent of the British NHS) or be able to apply for an Italian mortgage. You could lose your job at any moment or have an accident at work and not be protected. And it doesn't matter even if you are highly skilled and can speak Italian well. As a foreigner, don't be surprised to be offered work *in nero*.

Teaching English

Of all the jobs available to native English-speakers, teaching English is perennially popular. But, unless you are well off and don't need to make a living, forget it. Most schools only offer you a contract from October or November through to May or June if you are really lucky. For a full-time teaching position, you will most likely be given a *lavoro a progetto* (contract for a specific project) and your monthly take-home pay will be around €900 per month. But in the summer months you will not receive holiday pay so, unless you have an alternative source of income, you might have to look for a summer job.

Having to work in summer school

If you have moved, or are thinking of moving, to Italy to escape the 9–5 grind of the rat race, the chances are you do not want to be heading back for six months in the summer to teach at a summer school in order to make ends meet. The other major problem of the *lavoro a progetto* is that you have no job security. At the end of the fixed period, the contract cannot be renewed until the new academic year. Also, unless you have a particularly nice employer (Emma did), you will not be paid for sick, holiday or maternity leave. If you happen to have an accident or need time off work for whatever reason, the chances are you will be left seriously out of pocket.

Entering the state system

Many expatriates think they will be able to enter the state set-up as a teacher, doctor or dentist. Most dentists are private in Italy and anyone can attend medical school. As a result, there are thousands of newly qualified dentists each year looking for a place in the state system. To even be in with a chance you need to sit a state-run *concorso* (exam) which will then classify you in the *graduatoria*. This list grades each person and you will not be given a job until everyone above you has been given a job. Don't be any under any illusions: as a foreigner (EU or non-EU) you will come way down the list, even if you do have impressive credentials. Some foreigners are currently challenging this law.

ITALY IS THE LAND OF *IMPRENDITORI*

Setting up your own business allows you to skirt around the unwritten employment regulations which dominate the job scene in Italy.

Aside from a small collection of blue-chip corporations, the backbone of its economy is the small shops and family-run concerns. In fact, there are more *imprenditori* (entrepreneurs) in Italy than in any other country in the EU. Here in the Bel Paese, it seems people are almost born with a permanent desire to set up business that other countries can only envy.

For many, it is also the time to try something new: to become a full-time consultant or to turn a hobby into a full-time business.

Since Italy is lacking in so many services readily available in other countries, there is a wide range of business possibilities for foreigners with an outsider's perspective on what is missing from the market. For possible business ventures, see Chapter 3: Finding the idea.

Things going wrong

At least half of all new companies in Italy fold one year after they first start up. But you shouldn't be discouraged. Many new start-ups in Italy are by people who don't have any experience in the world of work and who have charged in without fully looking at all the things that can go wrong. In the majority of cases, the situation goes wrong when the business has not been planned properly (see Chapter 5: The business plan). In his work as a temporary manager, Mario can count on both his hands the numbers of companies he has been involved with which had no idea of how much profit and loss they were making or that the situation was worse than they thought.

Mario's Pearl of Wisdom

When I first decided to become a consultant, I was asked to develop a new business with other consultants. Because they had different skill-sets to me, I jumped at the opportunity. It seemed ideal. But after several meetings and writing a business plan, I realised that the reason for this invitation was because this new company would have replaced their old company which had a lot of debt and low profitability. If I had said yes, I would have been partly responsible for that debt. Before rushing into doing a business venture with other people, make sure you really trust them and that no one is taking advantage of you.

So here you are at the end of this chapter. If you are still reading, then you must be pretty determined to set up your own business – congratulations. You won't regret it. Now we've presented you with the negatives, here's the good news: setting up your own business in Italy will bring you freedom and a new way of life. So, when you are ready, let's get rolling.

2

Key figures and institutions

If you are anything like us, we expect you are itching to find out the ins and outs of setting up your own business in Italy. But before we get you to start planning your new business, you need to be familiar with the institutions you will be visiting a lot over the coming months and years and with the people who can help you negotiate this minefield.

When Mario was based in Germany with IT Holding, he regularly flew to Milan for meetings at the company's head office. One evening, he was sitting in the pub and got talking to Richard, a Brit who had lived in Italy for three years. When Richard found out that Mario was a *commercialista* (trained chartered accountant), he started talking about a problematic work scenario.

Several years earlier, Richard had started up his own business as a software engineer. Not knowing anything about Italian tax requirements, he asked an English-speaking Italian friend, who had spent five years working for a firm of accountants, for help. But his friend didn't have sufficient knowledge of the Italian tax system either and after 18 months, the *Agenzia delle Entrate*, the Italian tax office, sent him an *avviso di accertamento* (summons). In this letter, they told Richard that they had verified his accounts and he was being charged with *evasione fiscale* (tax evasion) to the tune of €25,000. Richard had no choice but to find the money from somewhere. He also had no legal recourse because he thought he could trust his friend and had therefore not bothered to draw up a legally-binding contract.

At the risk of sounding alarmist, this is not a one-off situation. Moving to a new country can be exciting and feel like an adventure but, at the other end of the scale, it can also be confusing and downright scary. When you don't know how the system works, it is only natural to feel grateful to the people that offer you help even if you don't know much about them and whether or not they are competent at their job. You automatically lean on them and trust them more than you should.

Emma knows all about this. When she moved to Milan and her Italian was rusty, she met an estate agent who went out of his way to be friendly to her. As a result, she ended up signing a housing contract which proved extremely difficult to get out of. Her Italian wasn't good enough at the time to understand the technical jargon. What she should have done was to find an English-speaking lawyer who could have negotiated a much better contract for her.

KEY FIGURES

Figure 2.1 below shows a list of job titles and their descriptions:

Figure 2.1

Notaio	Public notary
Ragioniere Commercialista	Certified accountant
Dottore Commercialista	Chartered accountant
Consulente del lavoro	Consultant specialised in employment issues

Notaio
www.notaio.org

When you purchase property, this act must be legally recorded in the public register by the notary. Unless you are a *lavoratore autonomo* (a professional belonging to a professional association or providing services such as consulting), you must appoint a notary to register the creation of your company. A notary is legally bound to advise you of the possible costs you will incur and should give you advice on the best and most economic procedure to follow in order to finalise the act.

Normally, the accountant and notary work together and your accountant will arrange this for you. You, your associates if you have any, and your accountant will meet the notary in their office. Your accountant will have provided the notary with all the relevant documents in advance so that no time is wasted during the *appuntamento* (appointment). The *notaio* will read you the memorandum of the company and ask if it has been understood by you and your business partners. If there are any problems, the accountant will intervene on your behalf. You and your associates must then sign the documents in front of the notary. Note that if you are buying property either for your own use or business purposes, you will also have to sign a *contratto preliminare* (preliminary contract) which means the vendor is legally bound to sell you the property. In this situation, a notary's costs are fixed by Italian law.

Ragioniere commercialista and dottore commercialista
In Italy, tax laws change all the time and the tax return forms are complicated. Having a good accountant on board from the start is

essential as they will be able to guide you on company structure and fill out all the forms on your behalf so that all you have to do is sign them. Thanks to email and all-in-one printers, photo-copiers and scanners now being affordable, you do not need to work with an accountant in your town. Take the time to find one that is fluent in English or has spent some time in your home country. Having an accountant who understands your background and your mentality is a big reassurance.

A *ragioniere commercialista* does not have a university degree, a *dottore commercialista* does. Both charge the same fees and can carry out the same work. However, there are two distinct associate bodies: the *Ordine dei Ragionieri Commercialisti* and the *Ordine dei Dottori Commercialisti*. The Italian government is now trying to unify the two.

Below you can find more details about each type of accountant.

Ragioniere e perito commerciale
www.ragionieiricommercialisti.it
In Italy, students who choose to attend the *Istituto di Ragioneria* (technical high school) study Economics and Accountancy along-side the more traditional academic subjects. When they leave school they have two choices: they can either go to university and study *Economia e Commercio* (Economics and Business) or they can start work in a firm of accountants and take the state accountancy exam after three years. If they pass, they join the *Ordine dei Ragionieri Commercialisti* (Institute of Certified Accountants). The

abbreviation of the title in Italy is *Rag. Ragionieri* are also *revisori contabili* (official auditors) listed by the Italian Home Office.

Dottore commercialista
www.cndc.it
A *Dottore Commercialista* will have studied Economics and Business Studies at university and worked as a trainee in an accountancy firm before taking the state exam. On passing, he/she joins *Ordine dei Dottori Commercialisti* (Institute of Chartered Accountants).

Consulente del lavoro

www.consulentidellavoro.it
The *consulente del lavoro* often works in partnership with a lawyer or accountant to provide a 360 degree service to clients. Hiring a *consulente del lavoro* is essential if your company is to employ staff. He or she is qualified to draw up contracts for new employees, prepare correspondence, prepare pay slips, calculate your pension contributions and those of your employees and calculate some taxes. Labour law is particularly severe in Italy and penalties for irregular social contribution payments are high.

Case study

Dr. Max Ingold is a Swiss-Canadian chiropractor. He moved to Bussolengo, a small town 10km from Verona, in May 2003 after being offered a job in a health centre. He also has a **Partita Iva** (VAT number) and works as a private practitioner.

Emma: Dr. Max, what has been your experience with Italian bureaucracy?

Dr. Max: As a Swiss-Canadian, (albeit I never lived in Switzerland), we are used to being more organised. We do things in a logical sequence and when we look for information we are generally directed to the correct person. Not so in Italy.

Emma: Can you elaborate?

Dr. Max: You may be speaking to the correct person that can give you the answers you need but they will pretend not to know what you need. They will make sure that you come back a few times before they give you the answers. This even occurs to the Italians and I am often told not to fret about it because it's the way things are.

Emma: What do you think is the hardest thing for foreigners to get to grips with?

Dr. Max: The wait-and-see attitude and the non-accountability of the government and people in general. As an example, I hired a commercialista that was recommended to me.

Emma: Go on ...

Dr. Max: Little did I know I needed to keep on top of all the laws, rules etc that are constantly changing in Italy. The accountant would say 'you need to pay these taxes'. You pay them and then ask if there is anything else to pay. 'No, you're all set'. Two weeks later they call you and say 'oops, we forgot. You also have this tax to pay. Because it's late, there is interest, too.' It is never anyone's fault.

Emma: That sounds just about right.

Dr. Max: Dishonesty seems to be the way of working things out. In Italy, the *caldaia* (boiler) for the house has to be inspected every year. Our neighbour in our 12 unit condominium charged us €50 the first year. The second year it's €110 if you want a receipt. The difference is because he has to attach a probe and do an extra 30-second test for emissions. When I press him for an answer and say that the price is ridiculous he then states that without a receipt he'll make it the same price as for all the other tenants, €70.

Emma: What about getting your qualifications translated. How easy was that?

Dr. Max: My qualifications are not recognised in Italy because chiropractic is not recognised. Initially prior to coming over from the USA, I had to have my chiropractic diploma, all courses taken and grades and a chiropractic licence from an American state/Canadian province translated into Italian and then apostiled by the Italian Consulate in New York. This needs to be done if one wants to practise in a Centro Convenzionato as the Ministry of Health wants to see that the person is actually competent. But for private practice none of this is necessary.

Emma: Would you say the system is user-friendly and set up to help self-employed/entrepreneurs, whether foreign or Italian?

*Dr. Max: Getting the **Partita Iva** was quite easy. Armed with my **permesso di soggiorno**, without which you can't do anything, and the **codice fiscale**, I had a **Partita IVA** assigned to me in a matter of minutes. This, I figure, is natural. When it comes to making sure the government is entitled to collecting taxes, paperwork flows easily.*

Emma: That's true. You've been in Italy a number of years now. How well would you say you are integrated into society and the Italian way of doing things?

Dr. Max: We've integrated fairly well. My advice is always get a second and third opinion and always question everything that is being told to you. Never accept the first answer as being factual.

PUBLIC OFFICES

In his book *Burocrazia fuori Legge* (*Bureaucracy outside of the law*), economic journalist, Marco Rogari, claimed that Italians are normally forced to queue for at least 45 minutes in a public office. In a year, that amounts to two working weeks lost in queuing and completing bureaucratic procedures. As if that wasn't enough, there are more than 35,000 laws governing public administration in Italy.

Familiarising yourself with government agencies and public offices is a must because you will find yourself in and out of them a lot as you prepare to set up your business in Italy. Offices open at funny hours and will shut just as you get to the counter, doors won't have signs on them, and *gli statali* (civil servants holding all ranks of office) will often deal with you while holding a phone conversation or speaking to their friends. You will also be sent from counter to counter and office to office before finding someone who can give you the right answer. What will exasperate you even more is discovering that the reason the *fila* (queue) is moving so slowly is because there is only one *sportello* (counter) open even though there is a group of four or five other employees laughing and joking in the corridor.

Before you start questioning your sanity and tearing your hair out, just remember that every other expat who has set up a business before you has gone through the process and survived. The experience at the *Questura* is probably the worst. There's a fair bit of postcode lottery going on. In the worst case scenario, you will start queuing at 7am and once the *Questura* opens at 8am, you will be left outside in a freezing courtyard while you wait for your number to be called.

What we cannot stress enough is that you need to be prepared. The old adage 'forewarned is forearmed' is particularly apt here.

Never enter a public office without knowing the specific name of the document you need and the reason why you need it. For some documents you will need a *marca da bollo*, a public tax stamp costing €14.62. These can be bought from the *tabaccaio* (tobacconist's). Have a couple of these tucked away in your wallet at all times. That way, you can avoid the hassle of queuing up for 30 minutes, getting to the front of the queue, finding out you don't have the stamp and starting the procedure all over again.

Figure 2.2 sums up the most important public offices you have to deal with when you set up a business in Italy.

Figure 2.2

Camera di Commercio	Chamber of Commerce
Registro delle Imprese	National Business Register
Agenzia delle Entrate	Tax authorities
Guardia di Finanza	Tax police
Questura	Italian police headquarters
Vigili del Fuoco	Firefighters
ASL	Local health authority
Consorzio industriale	Industrial consortium

Camera di Commercio

www.camcom.it

There are 103 branches of the Camera di Commercio located throughout Italy. Your first contact with the Camera is likely to be when you register your business in the *Registro delle Imprese* (National Business Register).This defines the existence of your business, its activity and records any activities which take place during the lifespan of the business. The types of businesses that need to be included in the *Registro delle Imprese* are those operating in the following sectors:

◆ production of goods and services;
◆ transportation of people or goods by land, sea or air;
◆ banking and insurance;
◆ any auxiliary companies operating in the above sectors;
◆ agriculture.

The *registro* is divided into two categories: *sezione ordinaria* (ordinary section) and *sezione speciale* (special section). The *sezione ordinaria* is for partnerships, corporations, cooperatives, consortiums, foreign companies with head offices or administrative offices in Italy, and individual entrepreneurs with large commercial ventures. The *sezione speciale*, meanwhile, is for self-employed people, agricultural entrepreneurs and artisans.

When you register, the Camera will assign a registration number to the business corresponding to its *Partita Iva* (VAT number). Through this register, banks, creditors and other interested parties can check your company's history and accounts.

If your business also requires certificates, authorisations or licences, the Camera will provide these.

In addition, the Camera works with ISTAT, the national statistic office, to provide official facts and figures and provides business support. Should you have a query that your accountant, *notaio* or *consulente di lavoro* are unable to solve then pay a visit to the Camera. In Italy, it is represented by the Union Camere, in the EU by Eurochambers.

Agenzia delle Entrate

www.agenziaentrate.it

The *Agenzia delle Entrate* is the tax office. It verifies tax returns and makes checks on company accounts, including those of sole traders. In Italy, these inspections are carried out by both the tax office and by the *Guardia di Finanza* (tax police), and no prior warning is given. The tax office has a local branch where you or your accountant can go whenever you have any queries. Today, thanks to an overhaul of the system, staff at the tax office are far more willing to help than they used to be. For example, they will provide you with your *Partita Iva* (VAT number), explain how to pay specific taxes or how to calculate them. In some circumstances, they will also do your accounting for you.

The *Agenzia delle Entrate* is normally open in the morning from 9am to 1pm, although it is sometimes open in the afternoon.

Guardia di Finanza

www.gdf.it

The *Guardia di Finanza* is a special police force which is run along military lines and is responsible for Italy's economic and financial matters. It is the country's oldest police force and regulated by the Ministry of Finance. Its functions include preventing, investigating and prosecuting tax evasion and financial offences. However, in reality, businesses do not have a lot to do with the *Guardia di Finanza* unless they have been investigated for tax evasion. In 2003, Parmalat was the largest Italian food company and the fourth largest in Europe, controlling 50 per cent of the Italian milk market. When the Parmalat scandal came to light in December 2003 after the company defaulted on a €50 million bond, the *Guardia di Finanza* was responsible for retrieving financial documents which later acted as evidence of the tax evasion and fraud. The *Guardia di Finanza* also control and carry out checks on *merce contraffatta* (counterfeited goods).

Questura

www.poliziadistato.it

Regardless of whether or not you have an EU passport, you will need to visit the *Questura* to obtain your *permesso di soggiorno* (permit to stay). If you also plan to take on non-EU employees, you will have to visit again for the *nulla osta* (authorisation). If your company activities are in any way related to precious jewels, betting, explosives, guns or other dangerous material, you will have to obtain a permit from the *Questura*. We don't want to scare you, but some traders in Italy who have business premises in dangerous areas carry a gun for safety reasons. If you want a gun for this reason, you will have to apply to the *Questura* for authorisation.

The *Questura* also has a public safety function and can make random inspections in shops or business premises to check safety legislation is being adhered to.

Vigili del Fuoco

www.vigilidelfuoco.it

Vigili del Fuoco play an important role in health and safety. As well as issuing and renewing fire prevention certificates, the fire service also gives advice on new projects for buildings, issues the certification for fire prevention and the correct installation of plants and machinery.

ASL

ASL (*Azienda Sanitaria Locale*) inspects workplaces to ensure they conform to Italian health and safety regulations. It also investigates accidents which happen in the workplace and protects employees who have an accident on your work premises or immediately outside of your premises.

If your company will be selling food or beverages or you have a canteen for workers or customers, you will require authorisation from *ASL*. Employees involved in the handling of food and beverages will also have to attend a medical on *ASL* premises.

Consorzio industriale

There are thousands of *consorzio industriale* throughout Italy. Each *consorzio* is based in a city's *zona industriale* (industrial area) and aims to increase the number of people employed in the area. As such, it helps SMEs (small- and medium-sized enterprises) buy and sell commercial property in the *zona industriale* at a good price. The *Consorzio* also supervises the construction of industrial factories. If you wish your business premises to be located in the *zona industriale*, you should contact the *Consorzio Industriale* for assistance.

> *Mario's Pearl of Wisdom*
>
> When the British Home Secretary, David Blunkett, was forced to resign in December 2004 after having fast-tracked the visa application of his ex-lover's nanny, my Italian friends didn't know what all the fuss was about. To them, it was a perfectly acceptable situation because all he was doing was a favour for someone. This is common practice in Italy so don't be afraid of using the same tactics. You might assume that this also gives you licence to take short cuts in other areas, but it .

▶

doesn't. However frustrating you find the red tape, there is no way of avoiding it. Help yourself by grabbing a pen and piece of paper and list all the authorities you will need to go to before your business is ready to trade. Find out what authorisations are dependent on authorisations from other institutions and make sure you get these first. This research can be done surfing the web or making a few phone calls.

As you can see, you will be dealing with a lot of authorities so take the time to find out where all the institutions are located, visit them and note down their opening hours and how helpful the staff are. It is also a good idea to get to know staff there as having a good working relationship can help immensely. But now that you know what each person does and the role of the Italian institutions, it is time to answer the question: *che diavolo vuoi fare* or what on earth do you want to do?

3

Finding the idea

Now that you know Italy's red tape really is as bad as you feared, *complimenti* for not giving up in exasperation before you have even begun. If you have the patience and the commitment to negotiate the tricky maze of Italian bureaucracy, you certainly have what it takes to join the Italian *imprenditori* (entrepreneurs).

With that in mind, it is time to do the legwork. In other words, it is time to stop talking about setting up your own business in Italy and time to do something about it.

We've already told you the story of how How to Italy came about. It doesn't matter whether or not you already have the business idea because the expatriate entrepreneurs we know in Italy have all arrived in different ways:

- British GP, Simon Curtis, moved to Italy with his wife Cathy and three children and thought he would have no problem walking into a job in the Italian national health service. When that didn't happen, he set up his own private practice.
- Brit, Dave Marsh, set up Tuscan Moto Tours after realising it was possible to make money from his passion for motorbikes and his love for northern Tuscany where he lives.
- American, Valerie Ryder, moved to Italy with her Italian husband and uses her previous experience as the European director

of finance and administration for a multinational to coach corporate women. She now has offices in Milan, Paris and Boston.

- American, Tracy Roberts, arrived in Rome in 1982 to teach English. Two years later, she realised she wanted a new challenge: The English Yellow Pages were born.
- Brit, Bronya Sykes, spotted a gap in the market and came up with the idea for Chatterbox, an English-language nursery in Cagliari.
- American, Claire Smith, was an accountant in Dallas before moving to Italy. Unable to find a job, she decided she would set up her own business. She turned her talent for interior design into a business and now makes a good living revamping the homes of wealthy Italians.

As you can see, none of these people were entrepreneurs in their prior lives. Some found something they were passionate about and decided to launch a business based around it (Dave and Claire). Others (Simon and Tracy) set up their businesses because they realised they couldn't get work or they wanted a more secure future. Valerie wanted to run her own business after years of the corporate world and Bronya spotted a gap in the market.

Don't make the mistake of thinking you have to come up with a unique idea that nobody in the history of either the world or Italy has ever thought of before because that is simply not true. Look at Bronya: she set up an English-language nursery school which has now grown into a *scuola elementare* because parents wanted an English-language school to send their children to once they became too old for the nursery. There are dozens of English-language nurseries and childcare centres throughout Italy but there weren't any in Cagliari. Bronya took someone else's idea and modified it for the city where she lived. She knew there would be a market because there were plenty of expatriate and Italian parents who wanted their children to be looked after in an English-language environment.

ADAPTING AN EXISTING IDEA TO THE ITALIAN MARKET

Trends in English-speaking countries often arrive in Italy and you can work this to your advantage. For those of you who don't live in Italy already, spend an afternoon just walking around your home town or city listing all shops and commercial activities around you. If you can't find a product or service you can introduce to Italy, we will buy you a cappuccino when you visit us in Sardinia.

BRAINSTORMING

We love brainstorming and what could be better than getting together with friends or family, opening a bottle of red *Barolo* or drinking frothy *cappuccinos*, and kickstarting the process of running your own business in Italy?

Questions to ask:

- What are your skills and experience? Can you translate this into a business?
- What do you love doing? What are your hobbies?
- Can you improve on a product/service you've already seen?
- Do you know of a gap in the market?
- Do you want to aim at the expatriate or Italian market?

If you're having problems coming up with ideas, here are a few to get you started:

Personal trainers

The *palestra* (gym) is a busy place in Italy and full of image-conscious Italians working out or posing in their funky attire. Although the use of personal trainers is not widespread, they are gradually gaining in popularity.

Children

With Italian homes being typically much smaller than American, Canadian and UK ones, they tend to be too cramped for birthday parties. Hosting art, craft and themed parties in halls and other venues is beginning to catch on.

Babies

Baby yoga and baby massage sessions have started in Milan, but are thin on the ground elsewhere.

Health

Italians are obsessed with good health. Italians talking about bodily functions is the same as Brits talking about the weather. Anything aiming to improve health is a guaranteed winner.

Well-being

Italian women are always immaculately turned out and girls start plucking their eyebrows in *scuola media*. Having an *estetista di fiducia* (personal beautician) is a must, but there are times when she can't fit you in and you have an important meeting the next day. Walk-in, no appointment nail/eyebrow bars would solve the problem. For a country which views spas as a health and well-being essential, Italy has surprisingly few day spas.

English-language services

English-language theatres, cinemas and bookshops are not just popular with the expatriate population, but also with Italians who have lived abroad and subsequently repatriated, as well as with language students at high school and university.

Businesses catering for English-speaking expatriate communities

There are lots of expatriates in Milan, Rome, Turin, Genoa, Naples and Venice who have been transferred to the cities by their companies. Many of these expatriates and their families do not speak Italian well and would appreciate dealing with English-speaking lawyers, builders, hairdressers, doctors, dentists and other health professionals.

Real estate

In the popular expat cities, along with expat cluster areas like Tuscany and Umbria, there is no shortage of estate agents selling to the foreign market. But there are quite a few areas off the beaten tourist track where you can still find houses for under €90,000.

Tourism

In 2004, Italy was the fifth most visited country in the world and tourism accounts for around 12 per cent of Italy's GDP, according to a February 2006 report by the Minister for Innovation and Technologies. But there are still lots of charming villages and towns that tourists have yet to discover, especially in the south and the islands.

Internet and E-commerce

In 2004, 28.87m people out of Italy's 59.115m population used the internet (data from www.internetworldstats.com). In other words, that amounts to 48.8 per cent, or less than half of the population. A lot of SMEs (small- and medium-sized enterprises) and schools still do not have corporate websites.

Virtual personal assistants

Bilingual virtual assistants who speak English and Italian are very hard to find, but with more and more sole trade companies setting up, having someone you pay as and when you need them to take phone calls and answer client emails when you are unavailable would be extremely useful. We know, we've been looking for someone.

AIMING AT AN EXPATRIATE OR ITALIAN MARKET?

Establishing exactly who makes up your target market is essential even at this stage. If you are planning to work from home and you will only be dealing with expatriates, then speaking fluent Italian won't be too much of a problem as it won't impact on the quality of the service you offer. But if you are planning to take advantage of a gap in the market and sell to Italians, then speaking the language is a must. Claire, the accountant-turned-interior designer could only speak basic Italian at the beginning and the disadvantages were obvious. She couldn't market her business because she didn't have sufficient language skills.

We also know of someone who owns a B&B and who has lost customers because when Italian clients phone up, he can't communicate with them. We're not saying you need to be fluent in Italian before setting up the business, but if you really can't speak the basics, it seems sensible to make language learning your first priority.

Case study

Dave Marsh runs Tuscan Moto Tours in Lunigiana, in northern Italy. He lives there with his wife, Sue, and their son, Giacomo.

Emma: So, Dave, what came first, moving to Italy or starting the business?

Dave: I had been made redundant and my wife had just had a fifth session of bowel surgery for her Crohn's disease. Also the year before, I had had open heart surgery to fix a large hole in my heart. We came to Italy for three months to consider what to do next in our lives. My wife drove from the UK and I followed on my motorbike.

Emma: So you had no plans at that stage to set up a business?

Dave: No, none whatsoever. Every day while Sue recuperated and worked on her book, I went out on my bike and fell in love with the mountain roads.

Emma: Sounds great.

Dave: It was.

Emma: At what point did you think 'Ah, I'm going to live here forever and run my own business'?

Dave: After being here for two months, Sue asked what I planned to do when we got back to the UK. I replied that all I really knew was that I no longer wanted to be a call centre manager.

▶

Emma: Right, so being in Italy helped you understand it was time to do something different?

Dave: Exactly. I have always wanted to find a way to earn a living from riding my bike and I wanted to race when I was younger but had no way of raising the necessary finance. Sue knew this.

Emma: So, that's when you came up with the idea?

Dave: No, in reality it was my wife's idea. She suggested that I set up a motorcycle touring business as I have a great deal of riding experience and if I loved these roads then so would others. She also said: 'That would be living your dreams.' I just picked up the idea and ran with it.

Emma: Sue's a genius. But how did you convince yourself it was a winning business idea?

Dave: When I worked as a financial advisor, we once had a motivational speech from a very successful businessman. He asked for a definition of success and I replied: 'Earning a living doing something you love.' His reply was: 'If you can find an idea for a business based on something you are passionate about, talk about a lot, are capable of getting others enthusiastic about and are knowledgeable about, you have the basis of success. The rest is down to hard work.' I've never forgotten those words.

DECIDING WHICH IDEA IS RIGHT FOR YOU

Setting up a business in Italy is going to be a challenge right from the start, so you need to believe in the idea 100 per cent. As you learnt in Chapter 2: Key figures and institutions, you will have a lot of red tape to overcome. You will also have to understand a lot of confusing tax laws which we explain in Chapters 15 and 16. Don't approach an idea only with the aim of making you rich because, unless you work '*in nero*', the high taxes the Italian government creams off you means you are not likely to become a millionaire very quickly.

So if you have spotted a gap in the Italian market but you aren't passionate about the idea, our advice is to leave it well alone. Passion really is everything, at least at the beginning. You'll be putting in long hours to get your start-up off the ground and so it stands to reason that you should be doing something you love. After all, you are probably moving or have already moved to Italy to enjoy the more relaxed lifestyle on offer. If you end up finding yourself tied to your desk doing a job you hate, what will you have gained?

Mario's Pearl of Wisdom

We Italians are `esterofili`. This Italian word means we love foreigners and all things which are foreign. That's a good reason why products or services that you choose to import from your own country have a high chance of succeeding. Remember that while you may have many of the same skills as Italians, you also have many others. The main advantage is your fluency in English. But don't undervalue the simple fact of living in another country. Having chopped and changed jobs far more often than most of your Italian counterparts, you're more flexible as a result. You can also bring a fresh insight to different problems and a new way of solving them.

So now you've got the idea, it's time to find out whether or not it's *vincente* (a winner).

4

Market research

When we came up with the idea for our consultancy aimed at foreigners wanting to move to Italy, we didn't know anything else. We didn't have a name for our potential company. We didn't know if anyone else had hit on the same concept and was already successfully selling their services. We didn't know how big our potential market was and we didn't know how much we could charge. In short, the question we couldn't answer was this: will this business be a success?

On the car journey on the way back from the beach (to recap, we came up with the idea of the consultancy service when we were at the beach on a warm September afternoon), we started coming up with names for the new company. As you can tell from the list below, we weren't particularly inspired:

- Living La Dolce Vita;
- Living and Working in Italy;
- Moving to Italy;
- Expat Italy;
- Figs on the Beach – we have no idea how that one came up, but suspect it had something to do with Emma's love of eating fresh figs on the beach.

We knew that all the names were, quite frankly, pants. They weren't catchy and they didn't encapsulate what we were planning to do. We ditched them, as you might expect, instantly.

When we got back home, Emma decided it was time to call on the creative genius of others: she pulled out all her back copies of *Elle*, *Vogue*, *Glamour*, *Marie Claire*, *Italy*, *Italian*, *Italia*, *Bell'Italia* and started trawling them for inspirational phrases. Needless to say, the names she did come up with as a result had already been taken (a quick Google search told us this).

'Geez,' she moaned to Mario, pacing up and down the patio. 'This is impossible. What we need is a name that lets people know how we can help them realise their dream of moving to Italy. A name that lets them know how we can help them settle into the country and find work'.

Looking back that was the moment we both knew we wanted the business to be called How to Italy. We called Emma's mum (our 24-hour business advisor) and several friends who confirmed the name was a winner. Mario rushed to the computer to see whether or not the domain had already been taken. The seconds it took for the result to come through felt like hours. When the word 'available' flashed up it was all we wanted. We registered the name immediately. It was now time for market research.

THE IMPORTANCE OF MARKET RESEARCH

Although Italy is the land of small businesses, the failure rate is high. But don't get disheartened. This is usually because someone has had an idea and run with it before investigating the market and deciding whether or not it was feasible. Spending hours, days, weeks or months researching the market, ploughing through streams of verbose Italian sentences that seem to make no sense whatsoever and coming up with one dead end after another is tiring, but don't be tempted to take the short cut. The more prepared you are, the higher your chances of success.

Carrying out *una ricerca di mercato* (market research) is essential. It is important to talk to as many people as possible, but don't expect all the information to be free. If you plan on talking to experts, they are likely to charge for their services. The upside is that you are getting an insight that you probably wouldn't have been able to find elsewhere.

ITALIAN PUBLICATIONS

Monthly magazines on Italy are a good way to check out your competition. Buy a copy of each magazine and read the adverts and the classifieds which are mostly placed by expatriates who have set up their own businesses in Italy. This will give you a clearer idea of what the competition is on both a national and regional basis. But don't just look at the adverts. If the companies have brochures, order them. If they have a website, surf it. Until you really know more about the product or service, how can you know whether or not they are real competition?

There are a number of English-language magazines which are published monthly and dedicated to Italy and the Italian lifestyle:

Italy
www.italymag.co.uk

Italia
www.italia-magazine.com

The Italian Magazine
www.italianmagazine.co.uk

ItalyItaly
www.italyitalymagazine.com

Italy Down Under
www.italydownunder.com.au

FACTS AND FIGURES ON ITALY

One of the first steps is to gather facts and figures about Italy so that you can build up an accurate picture of investment and opportunities in the country. Italians may be vague when it comes to telling you the best way to go about a particular procedure, but their official organisations excel at providing you with statistics when you need them.

The following organisations and websites are all good sources of information:

Italian newspapers and magazines

If you speak Italian, Italy's newspapers and magazines are a valuable resource. Try to read them on a regular basis. Not only will they give you a clear insight into the economic and financial situation of Italy and help you understand what is happening in each Italian region, they will also introduce you to the emerging trends in terms of new products and services. Italy has more than 200 different newspapers, along with a wide range of mainstream and more specialised magazines.

The *Corriere della Sera* (www.corriere.it) and the *La Repubblica* (*www.repubblica.it*) are probably the leading general newspapers and *Il Sole 24 Ore* (www.ilsole24ore.com) provides the best financial coverage. All three have weekly supplements on *lavoro* (work-related themes).

Italy has a wealth of weekly magazines. *Panorama* (www.panorama.it) and *Espresso* (www.espressonline.it) might put scantily-clad women on the front cover, but they are serious investigative magazines, dealing with both economic and political topics. Italy also has an Italian-language version of *Vanity Fair* (www.voguevanity.it). If you are looking to launch a foreign trend or product in Italy, then don't forget to read the Italian versions of *Glamour*, *Elle*, *Vogue*, *GQ*, *Conde Nast* etc.

If you are in Italy on a regular basis, you can pick up the magazines at the airport lounge before catching the plane back home. Otherwise, consider taking out an *abbonamento* (subscription) for a fixed period of time.

The Made in Italy official portal
www.italtrade.com
This is the portal for the *Istituto Nazionale per il Commercio Estero* (the Italian Institute for Foreign Trade) which is the Italian government agency entrusted with the promotion of trade, business opportunities and industrial co-operation between Italian and foreign companies. It lists Italian-themed trade fairs taking place

around the world and also provides a comprehensive list of trade fairs throughout Italy. It runs seminars on export management in English, French, Spanish and Italian and provides statistics on various industry sectors.

Istituto di Commercio Estero

www.ice.gov.it

The *ICE* (Italian Trade Commission in English) is a government-run organisation based in Rome. It has 16 offices in Italy and a further 104 worldwide which are spread throughout 80 different countries. As well as promoting trade between Italy and these countries, the *ICE* also organises trade fairs and international conferences. If you are planning on exporting goods from Italy to various countries, the *ICE* will prove a particularly valuable resource.

Confcommercio

www.confcommercio.it

The General Confederation of Trade, Tourism, Services and SMEs is the largest enterprise-representative in Italy, with 800,000 members from the trade, tourist, service and transportation sectors. It provides free financial and legal advice for its members and will be able to provide you with facts and figures of its key sectors.

The British Chamber of Commerce for Italy

www.britchamitaly.com

The Chamber produces two publications:

Focus on Italy, which is full of facts, figures and information on doing business in Italy, and the *Trade Directory and Members' Handbook* which is published bi-annually. It contains up-to-date information on a wide range of industries, commercial activities and professions involved in business between Great Britain and Italy.

The British Chamber of Commerce can also provide assistance with commercial enquiries and key business contacts.

The American Chamber of Commerce in Italy

www.amcham.it

The Chamber produces two publications; *Italian American Business*, which is a point of reference in all fields of trade between Italy and the US. It contains a wealth of information about the American market, including updates on laws, customs, statistics, fiscal and currency regulations and treaties. It also provides information on imports, exports and investments, along with more general topics linked to doing business between Italy and the USA.

The Annual Directory, which lists thousands of professionals and companies involved in trade between Italy and the US.

AmCham also provides information on Italy-US import/export volume and type, a list of trade fairs in the US and Italy and internet access to online data banks through its website.

The Italian Chamber of Commerce and Industry in Australia

www.icciaus.com.au

The Italian Chamber of Commerce (ICCI) produces two publications. The quarterly magazine *Voi Tutti* covers contemporary Italian lifestyle and has features on food, wine, design, culture, interviews, fashion, cars, travel, trade, commerce and social events.

The Directory of Italian Trade Shows and Exhibitions includes more than 170 trade shows and exhibitions held in Italy and sorts them by date and industry, along with websites and full contact details of organisers.

The ICCI in Australia also arranges pre-arranged business trips and appointments to assist manufacturers, exporters or industry figures meet new contacts in Italy. The Chamber will organise the entire trip on your behalf.

The Italian Chamber of Commerce in Canada
www.iccbc.com
The Italian Chamber of Commerce in Canada (ICCBC) produces *Connexus*, a quarterly magazine exploring the business and investment opportunities that exist between Italy and Canada.

The ICCBC can also carry out market entry research and provide market background information such as size, supply and demand trends, import/export statistics, competitors and channels of distribution in Italy.

English Yellow Pages
www.englishyellowpages.it
This annual telephone directory lists organisations, businesses, services and professionals that speak English. It can be bought in Florence, Milan, Naples and Rome.

Case study

*Aimie Louie is the co-director of **Easy Milano**, an expats classified ads magazine in Milan. Originally from New York she moved to Milan, via Paris, in 1999. The first issue came out in February 2000.*

Emma: Aimie, let's get straight to the question that everyone wants to know. Did you come to Milan knowing that you were going to set up a business?

Aimie: Absolutely not. I was living in Paris, studying art.

Emma: So what happened?

Aimie: In Paris there is **Fusac**, a classified ads magazine for expats that everyone reads and you just can't do without it. When we got to Milan, we were surprised to find there was nothing like it.

Emma: So what happened next?

Aimie: We did some research and we found that there were similar magazines in Florence and Rome that had been going for years, yet in Milan there was no native English-speaking community. I cannot imagine what expats did before there was **Easy Milano**.

Emma: You said you did some research. What form did that take?

Aimie: We just wanted to make life easier for people. I found out what clubs and associations there were for expats and started talking to people in Milan to find out their reactions. At the beginning we went to clubs and bars to promote it. I then talked about our plans to get people to advertise and see if they would be willing to be a distribution point.

Emma: Lots of work involved then.

Aimie: Absolutely. At the beginning we were working all the time. I'd walk into a bar and say 'Hi, my name's Aimie. We have this magazine for expats. Would you be willing to stock it?'. We were doing PR ourselves and promoting the magazine by going to all the events where expats

▶

would be and going to the cinema to hand out the magazine while people were queuing up. We didn't actually get to see the movie. We went home to sleep.

Emma: So what's the feedback been from the Italians in Milan. Are they happy with your idea?

Aimie: You know, it's been a really mixed reaction. Even now a lot of Italians don't get it. They've seen foreigners but they think we are going home. They don't actually get that we live in Milano by choice and are not refugees.

Emma: Yep, I know that situation. But what about other reactions?

Aimie: People who own the bars and restaurants love it. I've got them to do Halloween and Thanksgiving. I have to instruct them on everything. They try to make gourmet pumpkin pie and cranberry sauce, and I'm like, 'no, forget fresh stuff. We want tins of artificial stuff. I know it's gross but we won't eat it otherwise'.

Emma: And do they listen?

Aimie: Sure, after all, it means mid-week they get a whole restaurant full of Americans. It's good business for them.

Trade fairs

Trade fairs dedicated to Italy are an excellent way of finding out information about your potential market and your rivals. Go along and play the part of a chatty, inquisitive customer looking to find out more about the products on offer. Flattery goes a long way, particularly if it makes the stand of the person you are talking to look busy.

Each year, the UK hosts two major trade fairs dedicated to Italy:

Viva Italia Show

www.vivaitaliashow.com

The Viva Italia Show showcases the best of Italy, including new products, trends and destinations. It also stages property seminars, language, cookery and art lessons, fashion shows and hosts travel and tourism forums.

La Dolce Vita

www.ladolcevitaevent.co.uk

The event features a mini wine festival, a cookery theatre and cooking school, a piazza-style environment with Italian bars, restaurants and music and property features.

BOX OF INSPIRATION

Once you start finding out all the information, you are going to need somewhere to store it all. Emma's recommendation is to create a box of inspiration in which you put every bit of information that could be potentially useful in the setting up of your new business. When you come across interesting articles on the internet, don't just save them in your favourite links or on your hard drive, but print them out and put them in your box. Do the same when you come across an informative or inspirational piece in a magazine. When you find information in a book, photocopy the pages and put it in the box and when you get ideas from having talked to someone, jot down the conversation on a piece of paper and put that in the box, too. For example, if you intend to export Italian olives to your home country, your box of inspiration would be full of articles relating to olives, the different types of olives and the places they grow in Italy, export rules and regulations, the health benefits of olives, the success of companies already selling olives etc. In short, if you are not already an *esperto* (expert) on the product or service your business will be selling, you need to become one.

As soon as you start to zoom in on your idea, you will be amazed at how many opportunities come your way and how often you notice information that could be of potential interest to you. You will begin passively researching your idea even in your sleep! The point is this, you need to become an expert on your topic at Mastermind-level before your business is up and running otherwise your customers will be losing out.

THE IMPORTANCE OF THE TRIP TO ITALY

You might already be living in Italy or you might already have a second home there. Nevertheless, it is a good idea to spend a working 'holiday' in the area to take your market research to the next stage. Don't underestimate the importance of this trip and don't treat it as a relaxing break because it is not going to be one. You are on a mission to find out as much about your business and your location as possible. Planned properly, you will be able to check out your competitors, find potential suppliers and even start thinking about the best location for your company. Contact a few local estate agents and visit offices and business premises that are available for rent. It will give you a good idea at an early stage of what costs are like and what you will get for your money. This means that when it comes to writing the business plan, your figures will be more accurate.

The Pagine Gialle (www.paginegialle.it) are the Italian equivalent of the Yellow Pages and the online version is particularly comprehensive, containing links to company websites. We find it an invaluable resource and couldn't do without it.

Mario's Pearl of Wisdom

If your new business idea requires you to know about the area you will be setting up your business in, make sure you know the ins and outs before launching your start-up. Even if you are still living **all'estero** (abroad) at the moment, plan a recce trip to discover your options. Yes, it may cost you money now, but wouldn't you rather that than placing everything on a dream, moving (which is very stressful and expensive) and finding out it doesn't work? Starting a business in Italy obviously carries risks so surely it makes sense to minimise the ones you can.

Remember to take lots of photos during your trip as your memory might play tricks on you when you get back. These will serve as a useful visual reminder of what you saw and proves that with every step you take, your new business concept is gaining life.

5

The business plan

Now that you have done your market research, congratulations on getting this far. It is time to turn all that data and information you have been gathering into a real business based in Italy.

In your haste to get ahead and join Silvio Berlusconi and his fellow *imprenditori*, you might be tempted to skip *il business plan* in order to get straight on with getting your show on the road. But not having a business plan is a no-no.

The importance of a comprehensive, thoughtful business plan cannot be overemphasised. It will force you to detail the expenses your start-up will incur, the projected sales and monthly expenses and the volume of business you will need to generate in order to to meet your obligations. It is the CV of your business and much hinges on it: outside funding, the management of your operation and finances and the promotion and marketing of your business. Without it, how can you achieve your goals and objectives?

If you are the creative sort (like Emma), having to deal with facts and figures can be a gruesome task that leaves you saying *che paura!* (how scary!), but you need to get over this and tackle it nonetheless. You will feel much better once you have done it as you will end up with a clear idea about your business, the industry you are getting into and the potential strengths and weaknesses of your venture. In some cases, it will also prove that the idea in its current form will not make any money and that you need to rethink the project.

This happened to Emma. Back in 2004 when Emma was still a teacher, she was asked by an Italian friend to become a partner in a tourism start-up. The concept of the venture sounded great in theory and Emma was tempted to become a *socio* (partner). However, when it came down to the facts and figures, Emma's friend seemed reluctant to produce the business plan so Emma prepared one herself. Emma's friend already had another tourism business and it soon became clear that one of the reasons she was so keen to have Emma on board was so that the monthly rental for her plush city centre offices would now be shared between two people. Had Emma not written the business plan, she could have ended up as a partner in a failing business and accountable for half the losses.

By writing the business plan, you can see if the idea you have in your mind is realistic, applicable and valid. In other words, the idea is not just an idea, but can become something more. Don't worry about making the business plan complicated. What is important is that your ideas, enthusiasm and commitment are evident in the document you produce. In Italy, there are lots of companies offering to write your business plan for a fee, but we would be pretty wary of them if we were you. Often, the people who end up writing this important document don't spend much time with you to find out what is so special about your idea. To be honest, if they don't 'get' it, do you really want them playing a vital role in the ultimate success of your new business?

DIFFERENT TYPES OF BUSINESS PLANS

There are two types of business plans: personal ones to help you shape your business and public ones that will be seen by potential outside investors and your bank manager. In the case of the latter you will need to go into more detail. In addition to stating how your business is going to make money, you also need to include profiles of you and your *soci* (business partners) if you have any; a *riassunto del business* (business summary); industry overview; your niche in the market; marketing plan (including target market and advertising and promotion plan); stage of development and production process; and risk management (what you will do if your employees quit, you run out of cash or there is not a high demand for your offering on the market). This might seem long-winded and unnecessary, but it proves to financiers that your business plan is as strong as your dream. They are more likely to back you if you have done your homework.

Where you are writing a personal plan for your eyes only, you do not have to make it quite as comprehensive – especially if you have no start-up costs and no business partners or employees.

HOW TO GET GOING

Writing a personal business plan is pretty easy. To kick-start the process, ask yourself the following questions:

1. What does this company do and what sector does it operate in?
2. How many people do you need for your company?
3. Where do you want to set up the company?
4. Why will this idea of business be successful? Will it pay?
5. Who are your competitors and why are you better than them?

6. How important is speaking Italian to the success of your business. What is your level of Italian now? What steps will you take to improve your Italian?

7. How much money do you need?

These questions might seem really simple but, honestly, at this stage you do not need to know much more than that. Once you start writing the answers, your business plan will begin to take shape. Make sure what you write is clear to understand, but don't make the mistake of thinking you cannot go back and change what you have written. Of course you can, or, even better, you must go back and amend it. Don't worry about making the plan perfect either. That doesn't matter. What matters far more is being able to convert your business plan into a successful business in Italy.

As for our business plan for How to Italy, we edited it at least eight times before being happy with it. We prefer to think of it as a living document that we can continually go back to to check on our progress and to see how our objectives and plans have changed since we came up with the idea in September 2005.

AN EXAMPLE OF A BUSINESS PLAN

Let's suppose Sally has taught English for the past six years, gradually working her way up the school hierarchy and eventually becoming director of studies. She loves teaching, but knows that she is not going to get any further up the career ladder unless she takes the plunge and sets up her own school. She has a feeling that Terni, where she lives, is not yet saturated by language schools and that there is still room in the market for her own venture. Her dream is to open a private English language school in the centre and offer services different to those of her competitors.

Sally makes a start on the business plan by briefly answering the questions we mentioned previously. She also adds in a couple of other details:

1. *Type of business to set up*: language school.
2. *Activity*: teaching English using advanced methods.
3. *Employees*: just two teachers at the beginning.
4. *Location*: Terni, the main town in Umbria.
5. *Why it will pay*: in Italy there is an increasing number of people who want to learn English. Also, I can work with schools that often need teaching assistants.
6. *Who are my competitors*: there are few language schools located in the centre of Terni and the price of the lessons, in my opinion, is too expensive.
7. *How will the service be better*: I will provide better prices with a high standard of lessons and I'll be successful.

The brief answers to the above questions have provided Sally with a general overview of the situation. But in order to write the business plan, she needs to go into more detail:

1. *What kind of school do you want to set up?* It is crucial to decide this from the outset. Italy, just like any other country, has schools catering for very young learners, adult students and mature students. You can also choose to teach standard English, business English, English for tourism and so on. Again, you will need to be clear who your target market is. You might decide to concentrate on teaching young learners from the age

of 11 to 18 because you like the interaction and the fun lessons you can plan. Just by asking these questions, we are getting a clearer idea about the business and its aims.

2. *What does 'using advanced methods' mean?* It means there will be a lot of multimedia interaction and that all students will be supported by laptops with interactive programs designed by the teacher. The students can also work from home using the school website. In addition, the school has a partnership with various language schools in England so that students can go on to consolidate their language skills in a full-immersion, authentic English environment. In Italy, not a lot of schools are equipped with advanced technology. From a marketing point of view, this means that your school will be able to compete with the established schools in the town because it will offer something different.

3. *How many employees will you have?* I have two friends who are qualified, very good teachers and who are interested in working for the school, one full-time, one part-time. I know that at the very beginning I will not be able to give them a good salary, but we agreed that the hourly fee will at least match that of the competitor schools.

4. *Where will the school be situated?* I have seen a flat to rent in the south-west of Terni which I like because it has a large car park in front of it. The flat is big enough to have three classes running at any one time and small enough not to look empty when not many students are around. In Italy, the main towns are full of English schools, but in smaller towns there is still room for growth.

5. *Will it pay?* Yes, I think so because we are offering new courses. We can also offer self-study courses for students looking for a cheaper and more flexible option. Many state schools

also require teaching assistants and I have good contacts with the state schools so I am sure I will be able to develop a partnership with them.

6. *Competitors?* The population of Terni is about 120,000. The established schools have up to 12 students in one class.

7. *How will the service be better?* I can offer smaller, more personal courses at a better price along with the use of interactive lessons. Students will have an incentive to use my school because of the cheaper lessons and the variety of learning methods.

Is the project viable?

The information Sally has jotted down so far has only hinted at her intentions. What it has not yet shown us is whether or not the project is viable – this is because we still don't have a clear picture of the precise product offering – the number of courses, the duration and level of each course and the supplementary activities (conversation groups, self-study, English-language library) – or the pricing structure and potential revenue. There is no mention of the services offered by rival schools and their exact prices. We know of a couple of language schools that have failed because the teachers were so enthusiastic about setting up their own business they didn't spend sufficient time on the business plan.

Sally has got this far and is still intent on setting up her business. Her next task is to get to grips with an Excel spreadsheet (much easier than using a calculator and scribbling figures on a piece of paper) and start making some financial calculations. At this stage, remember that she is only playing around with different numbers to find out what her options are. She will also need to allow for a margin of error. When you come to calculate your potential income, make sure you also include the worst-case scenario. It is far better not to be over-optimistic and allow for the fact that you might have very few clients at the beginning that believe your business is going to outshine your rivals from the very first day.

Let's imagine that Sally thinks that the request of learning English in Terni is higher than it actually is, and that she mistakenly estimates that there will be double the number of students that actually end up enrolling in her language school. In this case, she has made a wrong assumption and her profit and loss account needs to be revised, because what Sally thought of as being a profit is probably a loss.

Projected forecast

Now let's move on to the next step and write down some figures. The first thing to do is to decide what the potential sales of your business are likely to be. In Sally's case, her sales are the courses she successfully sells to students and the income from teaching assistance in local *scuole pubbliche* (state schools).

Next, we have to estimate the annual income of our business. As Sally plans on opening a language school, she will have to estimate how many students will attend each English course (she plans on running beginner, pre-intermediate, intermediate, upper intermediate and advanced courses, as well as individual lessons) and how much she will charge for them. Sally's experience as a teacher tells her that she has to offer courses at various times because, for example, not all of her beginner students will be able to make the same lessons. Consequently, Sally has decided to run two courses per week at the lower levels and one course per week at the higher levels.

Given that Sally also plans to derive an important segment of the income from teaching assistance in local schools, she has to estimate the number of hours of teaching assistance that the school will provide during the academic year. Figure 5.1 below shows the income for teaching assistance during the year, the cost of paying teachers (€20 per hour) and the net income once the costs have been deducted.

Figure 5.1

Income from teaching assistence			
	Hourly rate	No. of hours	Total
Income for teaching assistants	€40.00	180	€7,200.00
Cost of teachers	€20.00	180	€3,600.00
Profit before taxation from teaching assistance			**€3,600.00**

Figure 5.2 below shows the different classes that the school will offer:

Figure 5.2

Beg. A
Beg. B
Pre-int A
Pre-int B
Int. A
Int. B
Upper int.
Advanced
Individual

Sally plans to run courses which run for a total of 60 hours and she plans to offer a 60-hour course in each semester. Her next task is to estimate how many students she expects to attend in the first term (from October to December) based on the fact that she does not want more than six students in each class.

In Figure 5.3 we can see how this would look in the spreadsheet:

Figure 5.3

No. of students	October	November	December
Beg. A	5	6	6
Beg. B	5	3	3
Pre-int A	5	5	5
Pre-int B	4	4	4
Int. A	4	4	4
Int. B	2	2	2
Upper int.	2	2	2
Advanced	3	3	3
Individual	2	2	1

Obviously, Figure 5.3 only shows us the calculations for the first term. However, in order to know whether or not running the school is a viable prospect, Sally also needs to know the figures for the rest of the year. She has started with October and ended with May when the school closes for the summer break. The numbers vary because Sally has assumed that some students will drop out and others will join the course. This is a good technique to adopt because it means you are allowing for ups and downs in your business.

Figure 5.4 shows us what Sally's spreadsheet will look like in the following two terms.

Figure 5.4

No. of students	January	February	March
Beg. A	6	6	6
Beg. B	4	4	4
Pre-int A	5	5	5
Pre-int B	5	5	5
Int. A	3	3	3
Int. B	2	2	2
Upper int.	2	2	2
Advanced	3	3	3
Individual	0	2	1

No. of students	March	April	May
Beg. A	6	6	6
Beg. B	4	4	4
Pre-int A	5	5	5
Pre-int B	5	5	5
Int. A	3	3	3
Int. B	2	2	2
Upper int.	2	2	2
Advanced	3	3	3
Individual	2	2	2

Sally has added March in both the second and third terms because she plans to finish the courses of the second term in mid-March. As soon as they have finished, the courses of the third term will start.

Because students will join and leave the course, it is difficult for Sally to make an accurate calculation. Instead, she decides to make the calculations based on the average number of students.

In Figure 5.5 we can see the average number of students for each course in each term, along with the overall average for each term.

Again, it is good to adopt this method for your own business plan as it will help you get a clearer picture of your business.

Figure 5.5

No. of students	October	November	December	Average
Beg. A	5	6	6	5.7
Beg. B	5	3	3	3.7
Pre-int A	5	5	5	5.0
Pre-int B	4	4	4	4.0
Int. A	4	4	4	4.0
Int. B	2	2	2	2.0
Upper int.	2	2	2	2.0
Advanced	3	3	3	3.0
Individual	2	2	1	1.7

No. of students	January	February	March	Average
Beg. A	6	6	6	6.0
Beg. B	4	4	4	4.0
Pre-int A	5	5	5	5.0
Pre-int B	5	5	5	5.0
Int. A	3	3	3	3.0
Int. B	2	2	2	2.0
Upper int.	2	2	2	2.0
Advanced	3	3	3	3.0
Individual	0	2	1	1.0

No. of students	March	April	May	Average
Beg. A	6	6	6	6.0
Beg. B	4	4	4	4.0
Pre-int A	5	5	5	5.0
Pre-int B	5	5	5	5.0
Int. A	3	3	3	3.0
Int. B	2	2	2	2.0
Upper int.	2	2	2	2.0
Advanced	3	3	3	3.0
Individual	2	2	2	2.0

Next, Sally needs to calculate what each student will pay for the 60-hour course. After looking up the rates of rival schools, she decides the school will charge each student €580 for a standard 60-hour course. Individual lessons, on the other hand, are more expensive and Sally has calculated these at a rate of €1,500 for a 60-hour course. Note that in the spreadsheet, some figures have been rounded up or down to avoid using decimals in the calculations.

In Figure 5.6, you can see the course prices and the total income per course:

Figure 5.6

No. of Students	October	November	December	Average	Course Price	Income
Beg. A	5	6	6	5.7	€580.00	€3,286.67
Beg. B	5	3	3	3.7	€580.00	€2,126.67
Pre-int A	5	5	5	5.0	€580.00	€2,900.00
Pre-int B	4	4	4	4.0	€580.00	€2,320.00
Int. A	4	4	4	4.0	€580.00	€2,320.00
Int. B	2	2	2	2.0	€580.00	€1,160.00
Upper int.	2	2	2	2.0	€580.00	€1,160.00
Advanced	3	3	3	3.0	€580.00	€1,740.00
Individual	2	2	1	1.7	€1,500.00	€2,500.00
						€19,513.34

No. of Students	January	February	March	Average	Course Price	Income
Beg. A	6	6	6	6.0	€580.00	€3,480.00
Beg. B	4	4	4	4.0	€580.00	€2,320.00
Pre-int A	5	5	5	5.0	€580.00	€2,900.00
Pre-int B	5	5	5	5.0	€580.00	€2,900.00
Int. A	3	3	3	3.0	€580.00	€1,740.00
Int. B	2	2	2	2.0	€580.00	€1,160.00
Upper int.	2	2	2	2.0	€ 580.00	€1,160.00
Advanced	3	3	3	3.0	€580.00	€1,740.00
Individual	0	2	1	1.0	€1,500.00	€1,500.00
						€18,900.00

▶

Figure 5.6 *continued*

No. of Students	March	April	May	Average	Course Price	Income
Beg. A	6	6	6	6.0	€580.00	€3,480.00
Beg. B	4	4	4	4.0	€580.00	€2,320.00
Pre-int A	5	5	5	5.0	€580.00	€2,900.00
Pre-int B	5	5	5	5.0	€580.00	€2,900.00
Int. A	3	3	3	3.0	€ 580.00	€1,740.00
Int. B	2	2	2	2.0	€580.00	€1,160.00
Upper int.	2	2	2	2.0	€580.00	€1,160.00
Advanced	3	3	3	3.0	€580.00	€1,740.00
Individual	2	2	2	2.0	€1,500.00	€3,000.00
						€20,400.00

As you can see, Sally has calculated the total income of each term. The total income for the school year, plus the annual total for each course, is shown in Figure 5.7 below.

Figure 5.7
Course type and annual total income per course

Beg. A	€10,246.67
Beg. B	€6,766.67
Pre-int A	€8,700.00
Pre-int B	€8,120.00
Int. A	€5,800.00
Int. B	€3,480.00
Upper int.	€3,480.00
Advanced	€5,220.00
Individual	€7,000.00
Total income	**€58,813.34**

Direct costs

Having come this far, Sally has gained a good idea of the school's assumed income in its first year of business. What she needs to calculate now are the direct costs, i.e. the costs related to these sales. These costs include the teachers' salaries which we can easily calculate. We know that the teachers are to be paid €20 per hour, that they will be teaching each course for 60 hours and that there are nine courses to teach in each term. That means that Sally has to cover the costs of 1,620 teaching hours (9 courses × 3 terms × 60 hours).

Figure 5.8 illustrates how much Sally's school will have to pay in terms of teachers' salaries in the first year.

Figure 5.8

No. of hours	1st term	2nd term	3rd term	Total no. hours	Cost of teaching hour	Total cost of teaching hours
Beg. A	60	60	60	180	€20.00	€3,600.00
Beg. B	60	60	60	180	€20.00	€3,600.00
Pre-int A	60	60	60	180	€20.00	€3,600.00
Pre-int B	60	60	60	180	€20.00	€3,600.00
Int. A	60	60	60	180	€20.00	€3,600.00
Int. B	60	60	60	180	€20.00	€3,600.00
Upper int.	60	60	60	180	€20.00	€3,600.00
Advanced	60	60	60	180	€20.00	€3,600.00
Individual	60	60	60	180	€20.00	€3,600.00
				1,620		€32,400.00

Gross profit

This is the total sales minus the direct costs. In Sally's case, the income from courses (A) minus the costs of teachers' salaries (B) (see page 68). At this stage, it is a good idea to calculate the percentages involved as this will give you a clearer picture of where you are spending the most on costs and earning the most in income.

In Figure 5.9, you can see how Sally expects the income of her school to be distributed in Year One. At this stage, it seems that Beginners make up the main source of income. The gross profit accounts for 45 per cent of the total income.

Figure 5.9

Income from students (A)		
	Total	**Percentage**
Beg. A	€10,246.67	17%
Beg. B	€6,766.67	11%
Pre-int A	€8,700.00	15%
Pre-int B	€8,120.00	14%
Int. A	€5,800.00	10%
Int. B	€3,480.00	6%
Upper int.	€3,480.00	6%
Advanced	€5,220.00	9%
Individual	€7,000.00	12%
Total income	**€58,813.34**	**100%**

Direct costs vary proportionally according to sales. Graphically, this concept can be summarised as shown in Figure 5.10. The area between the two lines is the gross profit.

Figure 5.10 Relationship between sales and direct costs

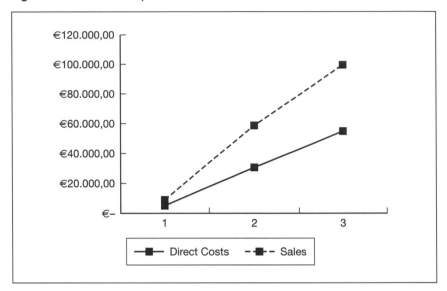

Note that in Figure 5.10 (above) we have assumed that the direct cost varies proportionally to the income, but in Sally's case this is not completely true on the grounds that she always has the option of adding additional students to her classes and so the cost of teachers' salaries doesn't change. It will only change if she decides to add additional courses because she will need to pay the teachers to teach them.

Fixed costs

Fixed costs are those that remain constant regardless of the increase or decrease in sales. Rent and insurance are two examples. Figure 5.11 is the spreadsheet entry for the fixed costs of the language school over a 12-month period (even though the school will only be open from October through to May, rent and insurance need to be paid all year round). The percentages shown are percentages of the income.

Figure 5.11

Fixed costs	Monthly rate	No. of months	Total	Percentage
Rent	€700.00	12	€8,400.00	14%
Insurance	€80.00	12	€960.00	2%
			€9,360.00	**16%**

Overheads

These are all indirect costs that vary depending on sales, but they are not proportional. The overheads Sally anticipates her school will have are shown in Figure 5.12 below. You can see how these convert into percentages of the total outgoings of the total income. Again, working out the percentage is a good idea as it allows you to see where you can make savings.

Figure 5.12

Overheads	Monthly rate	No. of months	Total	Percentage
Telephone	€120.00	12	€1,440.00	2%
Electricity	€80.00	12	€960.00	2%
Gas for heating	€50.00	12	€600.00	1%
Stationery	€40.00	12	€480.00	1%
Bank charges	€50.00	12	€600.00	1%
Accountant	€100.00	12	€1,200.00	2%
Miscellaneous			€1,000.00	2%
			€6,280.00	**11%**

Now that Sally has done all the calculations she needs, she can put them all together to see how profitable her language school will be. Figure 5.13 shows that the total profit before taxation is €14,373.34.

Figure 5.13

Income from students (A)			Total	Percentage
Beg. A			€10,246.67	17%
Beg. B			€6,766.67	11%
Pre-int A			€8,700.00	15%
Pre-int B			€8,120.00	14%
Int. A			€5,800.00	10%
Int. B			€3,480.00	6%
Upper int.			€3,480.00	6%
Advanced			€5,220.00	9%
Individual			€7,000.00	12%
Total income			**€58,813.34**	**100%**
Direct Costs (B)				
	Rate	**Hours**	**Total**	
Teacher	€20.00	1,620	€32,400.00	55%
Gross Profit (A–B)			**€26,413.33**	**45%**
Fixed costs	**Monthly rate**	**No. of months**	**Total**	
Rent	€700.00	12	€8,400.00	14%
Insurance	€80.00	12	€960.00	2%
Total Fixed Costs			**€9,360.00**	**16%**
Overheads	**Monthly rate**	**No. of months**	**Total**	
Telephone	€120.00	12	€1,440.00	2%
Electricity	€80.00	12	€960.00	2%
Gas for heating	€50.00	12	€600.00	1%
Stationery	€40.00	12	€480.00	1%
Bank Charges	€50.00	12	€600.00	1%
Accountant	€100.00	12	€1,200.00	2%
Miscellaneous			€1,000.00	2%
Total overheads			**€6,280.00**	**11%**
Profit before taxation from student income			**€10,773.34**	**18%**

▶

Figure 5.13 *continued*

Income from teaching assistance			
	Hourly rate	**No. of hours**	**Total**
Income from teaching assistance	€40.00	180	€7,200.00
Cost of teachers	€20.00	180	€3,600.00
Profit before taxation from teaching assitance			**€3,600.00**
Total profit before taxation			**€14,373.34**

However, Sally still has to pay taxes on this amount. Figure 5.14 shows us that once she has payed her taxes to the *Agenzia delle Entrate*, she can only expect to take home €8,983.34 in her first year.

Figure 5.14

Total profit before taxation	**€14,373.34**
(minus) Taxes (37.25%)	**€5,390.00**
Net profit	**€8,983.34**

Rethinking the figures

Unfortunately, Sally's language school is not viable at this stage because the school simply will not bring in enough money to make it worth her while. But had she not written her business plan, she would not have known this and would have plunged into a business unwittingly destined for failure.

However, don't make the mistake of thinking that it is all doom and gloom. Sally already has a good basis for her business plan. If you are in the same position as her and realise that, as things stand, your venture is not going to make you enough to live on, Mario recommends starting from your net profit and working backwards. So, if you want to take home €25,000 in your first year, you need to start playing around with your initial calculations to find out what you need to do to achieve this income.

In Sally's case, she needs to rethink the number of students in each class and find out how many more she would need in order to start making her business viable. As she increases the number of students in each class, she can see the net profit increase.

Sally knows she either has to increase the number of students on her courses (for instance with a strong advertising campaign), or the hours of teaching assistance in schools in and around Terni.

But what you need to remember is that there is a cut-off limit to these variables. After all, Sally cannot teach 50 students in one class because there simply is not room for them all and the quality of teaching would be abysmal. Similarly, she cannot increase the number of courses because then she has to increase the amount she has to pay in teachers' wages. If Sally decides to increase the hours of teaching assistance in local schools, will she have enough teachers to cover the lessons?

In the end, Sally decides to increase the number of students enrolled in each course without adding new courses. Her new calculations are shown in Figure 5.15.

In Figure 5.16, you can see the impact that this has had on the profit and loss account. The total profit before taxation is now €42,900 which is much higher than before.

Figure 5.15

No. of Students	October	November	December	Average	Course Price	Income
Beg. A	6	6	6	6.0	€580.00	€3,480.00
Beg. B	6	6	6	6.0	€580.00	€3,480.00
Pre-int A	6	6	6	6.0	€580.00	€3,480.00
Pre-int B	6	6	6	6.0	€580.00	€3,480.00
Int. A	5	5	5	5.0	€580.00	€2,900.00
Int. B	4	4	4	4.0	€580.00	€2,320.00
Upper int.	4	4	4	4.0	€580.00	€2,320.00
Advanced	4	4	4	4.0	€580.00	€2,320.00
Individual	2	3	3	2.7	€1,500.00	€4,000.00
						€27,780.00

No. of Students	January	February	March	Average	Course Price	Income
Beg. A	6	6	6	6.0	€580.00	€3,480.00
Beg. B	6	6	6	6.0	€580.00	€3,480.00
Pre-int A	6	6	6	6.0	€580.00	€3,480.00
Pre-int B	6	6	6	6.0	€580.00	€3,480.00
Int. A	5	5	5	5.0	€580.00	€2,900.00
Int. B	4	4	4	4.0	€580.00	€2,320.00
Upper int.	4	4	4	4.0	€580.00	€2,320.00
Advanced	4	4	4	4.0	€580.00	€2,320.00
Individual	4	4	4	4.0	€1,500.00	€6,000.00
						€29,780.00

No. of Students	March	April	May	Average	Course Price	Income
Beg. A	6	6	6	6.0	€580.00	€3,480.00
Beg. B	6	6	6	6.0	€580.00	€3,480.00
Pre-int A	6	6	6	6.0	€580.00	€3,480.00
Pre-int B	6	6	6	6.0	€580.00	€3,480.00
Int. A	5	5	5	5.0	€580.00	€2,900.00
Int. B	4	4	4	4.0	€580.00	€2,320.00
Upper int.	4	4	4	4.0	€580.00	€2,320.00
Advanced	4	4	4	4.0	€580.00	€2,320.00
Individual	4	4	4	4.0	€1,500.00	€6,000.00
						€29,780.00

Figure 5.16

Income from students (A)			Total	Percentage
Beg. A			€10,440.00	12%
Beg. B			€10,440.00	12%
Pre-int A			€10,440.00	12%
Pre-int B			€10,440.00	12%
Int. A			€8,700.00	10%
Int. B			€6,960.00	8%
Upper int.			€6,960.00	8%
Advanced			€6,960.00	8%
Individual			€16,000.00	18%
Total income			**€87,340.00**	**100%**
Direct Costs (B)				
	Hourly Rate	**No. of hours**	**Total**	
Teacher	€20.00	1,620	**€32,400.00**	37%
Gross Profit (A–B)			**€54,940.00**	**63%**
Fixed costs	**Monthly rate**	**No. of months**	**Total**	
Rent	€700.00	12	€8,400.00	10%
Insurance	€80.00	12	€960.00	1%
Total fixed costs			**€9,360.00**	**11%**
Overheads	**Monthly rate**	**No. of months**	**Total**	
Telephone	€120.00	12	€1,440.00	2%
Electricity	€80.00	12	€960.00	1%
Gas for heating	€50.00	12	€600.00	1%
Stationery	€40.00	12	€480.00	1%
Bank charges	€50.00	12	€600.00	1%
Accountant	€100.00	12	€1,200.00	1%
Miscellaneous			€1,000.00	1%
Total overheads			**€6,280.00**	**8%**
Profit before taxation				
from student income			**€39,300.00**	**45%**

▶

Figure 5.16 *continued*

Income from teaching assistance			
	Hourly rate	**No. of hours**	**Total**
Income from teaching assistance	€40.00	180	€7,200.00
Cost of teachers	€20.00	180	€3,600.00
Profit before taxation from teaching assistance			**€3,600.00**
Total profit before taxation			**€42,900.00**

Sally now needs to calculate her net income based on these new figures. At the moment she is working with a taxation rate of 37.25 per cent. See Chapter 15 on taxes for more detail.

Figure 5.17 shows that the school is now, in theory, much more profitable as Sally will take home €26,919.75.

Figure 5.17

Total profit before taxation	**€42,900.00**
(minus) Taxes (37.25%)	**€15,980.25**
Net profit	**€26,919.75**

Sally has already done her market research so she knows how many people live in Terni, how many people there are between the ages of 15 and 40 (her target market), how many high schools there are offering after-school language courses and how many private language schools there are. There are only three other language schools in Terni and their prices are shown in Figure 5.18 overleaf.

Figure 5.18

English schools	Course price
Language in Action	€600
The International Centre	€590
How to English	€610
Sally's school – still needs a name	€580

Sally is now sure that she can compete in the market especially because she intends on offering interactive lessons.

As we have said before, your business plan should be a conservative estimate of your business. In reality, you should plan to increase your income and decrease your outgoings in order to hike up the profit.

Cash Flow Statement

As part of your business plan, it is a good idea to include a cash flow statement, which reports the movement of cash in your business. This statement tracks your receipts and payments on a month-by-month basis and allows you to see your cash flow which is the difference between the two. If you have too many outgoings and not enough money coming in, a cash outflow occurs. To cover this, you will either need to temporarily invest some of your own money into the business to cover this difference or ask the bank for a loan.

Let's go back to Sally's school. In her business plan, Sally assumed that all the students would pay all of the course costs upfront. In reality, though, some students will not be able to pay the entire cost in one go and others will pay later than expected.

Before opening for business, Sally also has to buy the didactic materials and the laptops for interactive use. Figure 5.19 shows Sally's list of investments:

Figure 5.19

Investments	
Laptops	€9,600
Teaching books	€400
Dictionaries	€400
Total investments	**€10,400**

Remember that an investment is not a cost because it lasts more than one year. That is why the cost of each year related to the investments is called *depreciation* and it is the result of the economic life of the item. In the case of laptops, for example, the economic life is probably three years, after which they will be outdated and need to be replaced.

Figure 5.20 is a copy of Sally's cash flow statement for her school. If you look at the row total receipts, you can see that the school only receives money in October, January and March – the start dates of the English courses. The school doesn't have other income.

In Figure 5.20 under the row 'total receipts', there is the row payments. As you can see, the 'payments' vary each month. This is because some payments are paid on a quarterly and twice-yearly basis. For example, insurance payments are made only twice a year and the *commercialista* (accountant) is often paid on a quarterly basis.

The investments are all made in October because they are necessary for the running of the school. However, no other investments are foreseen for the first year of business.

The final row of Figure 5.20 shows us the cash flow or, in other words, the amount of cash that Sally's school has available each month.

Figure 5.20

	Oct	Nov	Dec	Jan	Feb	Mar	Apr	May
BALANCE (€)	–	3,389	–1,615	–7,309	6,587	1,343	15,809	10,565
Payment by students (€)	19,513			18,900		20,400		
TOTAL RECEIPTS (€)	19,513	–	–	18,900	–	20,400	–	–
PAYMENTS (€)								
Teachers	4,050	4,050	4,050	4,050	4,050	4,050	4,050	4,050
Rent	700	700	700	700	700	700	700	700
Insurance	480					480		
Telephone	240		240		240		240	
Electricity	80	80	80	80	80	80	80	80
Gas for heating	50	50	50	50	50	50	50	50
Stationery	40	40	40	40	40	40	40	40
Bank charges			150			150		
Accountant			300			300		
Miscellaneous	84	84	84	84	84	84	84	84
INVESTMENTS (€)								
Laptops	9,600							
Teaching books	400							
Dictionaries	400							
TOTAL PAYMENTS + INVESTMENTS (€)	16,124	5,004	5,694	5,004	5,244	5,934	5,244	5,004
CASH FLOW (€)	3,389	–1,615	–7,309	6,587	1,343	15,809	10,565	5,561

Having calculated the cash flow, we can see that in some months (November and December) the cash flow is negative, which means that the school does not have enough money to cover the expenses. But there is no need to panic because although there is a shortfall in November and December, it is only temporary. Come January when the new students pay their course fees, there will be enough money once more. Indeed, if you have a look in the last column, you can see that in May the school will have €5,561 in the bank which is positive.

To solve the cash outflow in November and December, Sally will need to invest some money in the business. She has €5,000 savings and decides to use this to alleviate the problem. Figure 5.21 shows the effect that this investment has on the cash flow.

Figure 5.21

	Oct	Nov	Dec	Jan	Feb	Mar	Apr	May
BALANCE (€)	–	8,389	3,385	2,309	11,587	6,343	20,809	15,565
Personal money (€)	5,000							
Payment by students (€)	19,513			18,900		20,400		
TOTAL RECEIPTS	24,513	–	–	18,900	–	20,400	–	–
PAYMENTS								
Teachers	4,050	4,050	4,050	4,050	4,050	4,050	4,050	4,050
Rent	700	700	700	700	700	700	700	700
Insurance	480					480		
Telephone	240		240		240		240	
Electricity	80	80	80	80	80	80	80	80
Gas for heating	50	50	50	50	50	50	50	50
Stationery	40	40	40	40	40	40	40	40
Bank charges			150			150		

▶

Figure 5.21 *continued*

	Oct	Nov	Dec	Jan	Feb	Mar	Apr	May
Accountant			300			300		
Miscellaneous	84	84	84	84	84	84	84	84
INVESTMENTS								
Laptops	9,600							
Teaching books	400							
Dictionaries	400							
TOTAL PAYMENTS +								
INVESTMENTS (€)	16,124	5,004	5,694	5,004	5,244	5,934	5,244	5,004
CASH FLOW	8,389	3,385	–2,309	11,587	6,343	20,809	15,565	10,561

Clearly, the situation has improved as there is no longer any out-flow in December. However, there is still an outflow of €2,309 in December, but Sally has no more savings to fall back on. She cannot rely on friends and family and so decides to ask the bank manager for a small *prestito* (loan) to cover the shortfall.

Of course she will not ask for €2,309 (the total outflow for December), but €5,000. That way, she will have some cash left over should anything go unexpectedly wrong.

Figure 5.22 is the reworked cash flow stament using Sally's €5,000 savings and the €5,000 bank loan which she will give back in March.

Figure 5.22

	Oct	Nov	Dec	Jan	Feb	Mar	Apr	May
BALANCE (€)	–	13,389	8,385	2,691	16,587	11,343	20,809	15,565
Personal money (€)	5,000							
Bank loan (€)	5,000					–5,000		
Payment by students (€)	19,513			18,900		20,400		
TOTAL RECEIPTS	**29,513**	**–**	**–**	**18,900**	**–**	**15,400**	**–**	**–**
PAYMENTS								
Teachers	4,050	4,050	4,050	4,050	4,050	4,050	4,050	4,050
Rent	700	700	700	700	700	700	700	700
Insurance	480					480		
Telephone	240		240		240		240	
Electricity	80	80	80	80	80	80	80	80
Gas for heating	50	50	50	50	50	50	50	50
Stationery	40	40	40	40	40	40	40	40
Bank charges			150			150		
Accountant			300			300		
Miscellaneous	84	84	84	84	84	84	84	84
INVESTMENTS								
Laptops	9,600							
Teaching books	400							
Dictionaries	400							
TOTAL PAYMENTS + INVESTMENTS	**16,124**	**5,004**	**5,694**	**5,004**	**5,244**	**5,934**	**5,244**	**5,004**
CASH FLOW	**13,389**	**8,385**	**2,691**	**16,587**	**11,343**	**20,809**	**15,565**	**10,561**

With the additional temporary income from Sally's savings and the loan, we can see that the problem has now been resolved.

Obviously, this is a very simple example of cash flow and we have only calculated it for the first year of business. Your own cash flow statement will probably be less complicated if you are self-employed and more complicated if you have to hire employees and your initial investment is much higher.

Now you have done your business plan, you know whether or not you have a viable product. But don't throw your business plan away just yet. Keep it handy as you will need to refer to it constantly as your project takes shape. When you are surrounded by paperwork and confusion, grab yourself a *cappuccino*, a glass of red wine or your favourite *gelato* (ice cream) and remind yourself of your dream, the reason you are putting in all of this effort, and just how far you have come.

Mario's Pearl of Wisdom

When I was 22 and at university in Italy. I remember attending a lecture about setting up a business. The lecturer talked about business plans and the importance of asking yourself about the viability of each stage of the business. After she had finished talking, a mature student put up his hand and told her she had missed out one important point. The lecturer encouraged him to speak. 'I agree with what you've said'. he said. 'But you haven't mentioned that you need to know the right person to get rent at a decent price, you need to know the right person who can start marketing your company to your clients and you need to know the right people in order not to make enemies'. It sounds stereotypical, but it still holds true today. Don't underestimate the importance of getting to know as many people as possible before your company starts trading and also the fact that you might have to pay out key money to get what you need done.

Case study

Morgan Cox was born in London, but brought up in Menorca, Spain. He lives in Legnano, a town just outside of Milan, with his partner Elena and his two daughters Valeria and Sofia. He runs Teacher Training.it.

Emma: Morgan, in a nutshell what exactly is Teacher Training.it all about?

Morgan: As the name suggests, we train people to teach English as a foreign language. Our main product/service is the University of Cambridge CELTA. It really is the first step for anyone considering a move into English Language Teaching. We also offer post-CELTA seminars and personalised training courses for schools in the Lombardia region. We will soon be extending our range of courses into more specialised areas, such as teaching young learners, teaching Business English, teaching 1-2-1, and the more advanced Cambridge DELTA. We also offer specialised English courses for individuals and groups. These are delivered by highly qualified and experienced teachers only, that is to say teachers with the DELTA and more than ten years' experience. A premium service at a premium price.

Emma: What experience do you have?

Morgan: I started teaching in January 1992 after doing my CELTA. I worked for a couple of schools before doing my DELTA (a more advanced qualification) at the British Council in Milan. I was then offered a job there and stayed for six years. This is where I trained to become a CELTA and DELTA tutor. I became head of teacher training, which I did for about three years. During that time I also started an MBA with the Open University and recently finished it. The British Council is a great place for professional development.

Emma: But most teachers go on to set up their own private language schools. What made you decide to specialise in teacher training?

Morgan: It seemed a logical progression from my previous experience. I had been training people on CELTA courses for more than five years when I decided to go it alone. There are very few people with the experience, qualifications and reputation to run these courses and it seemed a shame to let my resources and capabilities go to waste. Besides, training prospective and existing teachers is, in many ways, more rewarding than teaching English. I'm glad I made the decision to set up on my own.

Emma: Let's talk about the business plan. Did you have one?

Morgan: Of course I did!

Emma: So let's hear about it. How long did doing the market research and writing the business plan take you?

Morgan: In my opinion, market research is absolutely crucial. I'm sure we can all think of examples of products or services which went belly up because nobody had bothered to find out whether there was a demand for it. I spent absolutely ages doing market research, and I still do because the market is never static, is it? Real and perceived needs change all the time.

Emma: What would your advice be to expats?

Morgan: What I would say, having lived as an expat most of my life, is that any expat has a potential advantage in the knowledge and experience they might have built up from living in different cultures and contexts. Innovation seems to be a key concept at the moment for gaining strategic advantage over one's competitors, so being exposed to – or better still, seeking exposure to – models and ideas from different cultures in an increasingly global marketplace strikes me as pretty important. Having said that, it's not enough to be original because if the model/idea doesn't appeal or apply to the local context, then you're heading for failure. So, be original and daring, but don't overlook market research and a thorough business plan that you revise over time.

(6)

Raising finance

Now that you have written your business plan, you have a good idea of the costs involved in starting up your business in Italy. When we started How to Italy, we made the conscious decision not to inject loads of cash at the beginning and to grow organically. With that in mind, we split our business goals into several phases and decided to concentrate on one phase before moving onto the next.

Nevertheless, if you are planning on opening a restaurant, setting up a B&B or running a shop, there's a good chance that you will need to invest a lot of money in the start-up. But if you don't have the money what do you do?

Give up is the wrong answer. There are various sources of finance in Italy so make sure you spend some time thinking about what are the best options for your business.

BANK LOANS

If you intend to be resident in Italy, you will find it hard to obtain a bank loan from your country of origin. However, Italian banks have recently discovered the lucrative market of business banking and are now offering SMEs and sole traders a range of specialist banking services. Unicredit Banca (www.unicreditbanca.it) offers new business clients *il Kit Start-Up* (the name says it all) and makes up to €10,000 finance available on presentation of your business plan and other documents. Similarly, the Banca di Roma has launched *Nuove Imprese* (New Businesses) aimed at start-ups or at companies which have been trading for 12 months or less. The terms and conditions of their financing depends on where about in Italy (north, centre, south or the islands) the company is registered, but in general will loan up to 70 per cent of the investment plan on the condition that you and your business partners invest at least 30 per cent of your own money.

Be aware that some banks specify that you need to have been resident for a specific number of years before agreeing to giving you a loan. This is especially true if you are a *professionista* (professional) or have a *ditta individuale* (sole trade-company). We cover this in more detail in the chapters relating to choosing your company structure.

Up until recently, customers used to have a very personal relationship with their bank manager which meant that long-standing clients used to get much more favourable terms than new ones. That also meant that short cuts could be taken when arranging bank loans. But with the introduction of Europe-wide Basel II, banking practices have been standardised under the Basel Committee on Banking Supervision. Italian banks can no longer hand out more favourable loans to friends and associates, but have to adhere to the sound risk credit assessment and valuation for loans. If you do yet know anyone in Italy then this will undoubtedly work in your favour.

Difference between bank branches in the north and south

There is still a huge discrepancy in the services provided in northern Italy and southern Italy. On the whole, and clearly there are exceptions, banks in the country's richer northern regions (Piedmont, Lombardy, Valle D'Aosta, Trentino-Alto Adige, Veneto, Friuili-Venezia Giulia, Liguria and Emilia – the northern section of Emilia Romagna) are far more adept at considering bank loans than those in the south and the islands (Campania, Puglia, Basilicata, Calabria, Sicily and Sardinia) where bank clerks may or may not have dealt with a business plan before and do not have the experience to evaluate their risk. Do not underestimate this if you apply for a loan. When Emma went into a branch of her Italian bank in Sardinia and the bank clerk, who had been serving her for six months, found out she was English, the following conversation ensued:

Bank clerk: You're English?

Emma: Yes, I am.

Bank clerk (checking Emma out and looking her up and down, disappointedly): Oh, but you look like one of us.

We don't know whether the clerk was expecting Emma to have horns or pink skin, but what we do know is that we wouldn't want such a person vetting our loan application. If you do still decide to apply for a loan, make sure your business plan is translated into Italian and if possible get an Italian business partner on board. It will make life much easier.

When applying for a loan, don't just head to the bank that's nearest. Go to all of them, meet the *funzionario* (bank manager) and ask to talk about possible bank loans. Some branches of some banks will need authorisation from the head office before giving out a loan while others are autonomous. Don't necessarily go for the bank that offers you the best deal, but think about the bank that makes you feel most comfortable. That way, you'll have more room for leverage in the future should you need to renegotiate the terms for whatever reason.

The main Italian banks which offer loans to small businesses are:

San Paolo
www.sanpaolo.it

Unicredit
www.unicreditbanca.it

Banca di Roma
www.bancaroma.it

Banco di Sardegna
www.bancosardegna.it

Banca Intesa
www.bancaintesa.it

Banca Nazionale del Lavoro
www.bnl.it

Monte dei Paschi di Siena
www.mps.it

Gruppo Banca Carige
www.gruppocarige.it

Banco di Sicilia
www.bancodisicilia.it

Banca Generali
www.bancagenerali.it

Banca Fideuram
www.bancafideuram.it

Banca Mcdiolanum
www.bancamediolanum.it

Fineco
www.fineco.it

BUSINESS ANGELS

A business angel might be the financial help you need to get your start-up off the ground. After all, if Roberto Soru hadn't had the benefit of one, then Tiscali, the Italian telephony and internet giant, might never have got past the business plan stage. Though Tiscali is a success story, there are few investors that want to plough their money into the start-up of someone *sconosciuto* or unknown to them. Nevertheless, IBAN, the Italian Business Angels Network, (www.iban.it) brings together start-ups and growing businesses with potential investors. If you are aiming your business at your home country, you might also want to think about contacting a business angel there. www.advantagebusinessangels.com is UK-based, as is the Business Angels Network (www.vcr1978.com) which has a database of investors throughout Europe. The *Angel Investor News* is published monthly by the Academy Group and distributed to more than 20,000 private investors, venture capitalists and entrepreneurs in 98 different countries. Its website www.angelinvestornews.com lists the profiles of a number of business angels. The Tribe of Angels (www.tribeofangels.com) is a Jewish group of industry leaders working mainly in the US and Israel. www.angelinvestmentnetwork.ca is the Canadian web-based portal and matching service of angel investors seeking investments and entrepreneurs seeking capital. www.businessangels.com.au is in Australia and provides a central register for business angels and businesses or start-ups to find each other.

Before approaching a business angel, look at your business from their point of view. Make sure you know what your precise plans for your business are, what the new funds will be used for and how much revenue and profit you stand to make not just for the first year, but for each year over a five-year period. After all, how can you expect a potential financer to believe in your project if you cannot talk confidently about what you plan to do and how you plan to do it?

INVESTMENT INCENTIVES

The standard funding on offer is a *fondo perduto* (one-off grant) and a *prestito d'onore* (a low-interest loan) to be paid back over a set number of years. Start-ups and SMEs with a turnover of less than €30,000 are entitled to apply for loans. The maximum amount that can be borrowed is €2 million.

EU FUNDING

Until 2006, there were lots of EU incentive programmes which allocated millions of euros to Objective One status areas – that is, those with a pro capita gross domestic product (GDP) lower than 75 per cent of the EU average. These regions were Campania, Puglia, Basilicata, Calabria, Sicilia and Sardinia, along with a few northern provinces. Incentive opportunities for these poor and underdeveloped areas covered research and technological innovation, training, development of local entrepreneurship and business creation.

The main EU aid programmes between 2000 and 2006 were the following:

- the European Regional Development Fund – the ERDF is aimed at addressing the regional imbalances within the EU;
- the European Social Fund – the Social Fund is aimed at improving social inclusion and the participation of women in the labour market;
- the European Agricutural Fund – the EAF aims to improve rural development and agricultural structure.

The next wave of funding will be from 2007 to 2013. At the time of writing, however, Italian regions were still not sure what percentage – if any – of allocated funding they would receive. You can find information about the different types of European funding available, along with details of how to apply, at: www.welcomeurope.com.

NATIONAL FUNDING

The Italian government also provides financial incentives for start-ups and growing businesses that encourage the following:

- creation of new and existing production plants (Law 488/1992);
- investments for the re-launch of production areas (Law 181/89);
- local development (Location Agreement);
- creation of special business types (Decree 185/00);
- female entrepreneurship (Law 215/92);
- research and technological innovation (Law 140/1997);
- agro-industry development (Law 266/97);
- new investments and new employment (Law 388/00, art. 7, 8).

Application procedure

The allocated funds are not in a pot of gold that can be dipped into throughout the year as and when applications are made. Each region has its own timescales and deadlines for each of the financial incentives on offer. In order to be in with a chance of funding, you will need to adhere to the strict timescales for making the request. When doing so, make sure your documents are filled in exactly as required, no matter how irrelevant the information may seem. If you leave anything out (and we mean anything), the application you slaved over will probably end up in the reject pile, unless you know someone who knows someone who can get it put in the right pile straight away.

Timing

You need to be aware that there is often a long delay between the funding application going through and the award being made. In some cases the delay becomes so long, that the award times itself out so you end up getting no money at all. In August 1998, the then *sottosegretario* (vice chancellor) Giorgio Macciotta discovered 36 *mila milliardi di lire* (approximately €18 billion) that should have already been distributed to southern Italy in the form of state incentives had still not been paid out.

As you can see, it is best not to rely too heavily on the promise of financial incentives from the Italian government, whether national or regional. There is often a lot of *raccomandazione* (the Italian equivalent of nepotism) going on and, unless you happen to know someone in the office that will be evaluating your business plan and application, you probably won't get a look in.

Information

To find out about the financial incentives in your area, contact your local *regione* for more details. The websites of each region are listed below:

- www.regione.abruzzo.it
- www.basilicatanet.it
- www.regione.calabria.it
- www.regione.campania.it
- www.regione.emilia-romagna.it
- www.regione.fvg.it (Friuili Venezia Giulia)
- www.regione.lazio.it
- www.regione.liguria.it
- www.regione.lombardia.it
- www.regione.marche.it
- www.regione.molise.it
- www.regione.piemonte.it

- www.regione.puglia.it
- www.regione.sardegna.it
- www.regione.sicilia.it
- www.regione.toscana.it
- www.regione.taa.it (Trentino-Alto Adige)
- www.regione.umbria.it
- www.regione.vda.it (Valle D'Aosta)
- www.regione.veneto.it

BIC ITALIA

www.bic-italia.net

Bic stands for Business Innovation Centre. There is a Business Innovation Centre in each Italian region and these are run in association with the Italian government. They are support organisations for innovative entrepreneurs and SMEs. Again, they list details of financial incentives and deadlines. The advantage of going through Bic is that many of them also have English-language sites and are used to dealing with foreigners. On Bic Italia's home page, you will find a list of all the Bics in Italy along with their contact details.

Once you have decided which route to opt for, you need to work on your sales pitch to win over the financers that you wish to impress. Italians are natural showmen and women so you won't go wrong adopting their natural sense of exuberance. When you come to making your pitch, make sure your business plan has been professionally translated into Italian and that you or someone on your team can talk about it in fluent Italian. What could be worse than having your request for finance turned down purely because there was a gap in communication and you hadn't been

able to successfully transmit your personality and your enthusiasm for the task ahead?

Mario's Pearl of Wisdom

One of the more obvious ways of raising finance is selling your
property back home and injecting the cash into your start-up. If you
don't have a property to sell, then you may also be able to remortgage
your Italian home (if you have one) and use the money from that. Lots
of successful businesses in Italy grow organically. They start small in
one area and when they have made enough profit, expand into the next
area. This is definitely something you should consider if you don't have
the funds to start big. One of my former clients started out as a small
building firm and now imports and exports all over the world.

Case study

We met Morgan Cox when he told us about his business plan. He is the
director of TeacherTraining.it, a teacher training organisation which he
runs in Milan.

Emma: What was the hardest part in the stage from coming up with
the idea to opening the school?

Morgan: Taking the plunge. It's very difficult to make the mental
decision to leave paid employment in order to pursue a dream. Dreams
don't pay the bills!

Emma: You can say that again. So how did you go about it?

Morgan: For the past three years, I have taken a very cautious
approach by simply renting space to deliver my courses. This has meant
never having a major financial burden on the one hand, but not being
fully in control of my own destiny on the other hand. This is my next
challenge, getting my own premises.

▶

Emma: If you've never had a major financial burden, how did you finance your project?

Morgan: I didn't get any outside financing. I think I have a very old-fashioned view of money and financing. I have never borrowed more than a few thousand euros because the thought of debt makes me feel uneasy. So it's probably taken me ten times longer to get where I am today than it could have, but at least I have no debts.

Emma: What are your views on the financial incentives that are available in Italy for new businesses? Were you tempted to apply at any point for funding?

Morgan: I have never really taken these options into consideration. Apart from being put off by the amount of bureaucracy they would no doubt involve, the very idea of owing large amounts of money for extended periods of time sit very uneasily with me. I know financing can be useful, but I'm a very small business and have a family to support.

Emma: Did you ever apply for Italian bank loans?

Morgan: No, pretty much for the same reasons I've already mentioned.

Emma: How has your school grown since opening its doors for the first time?

Morgan: It's been growing slowly but steadily but I'm happy about that because if we had grown too quickly, it would have been very difficult to maintain and develop the quality of our courses. I have always believed very strongly in quality above all else. I'm certain that people of all backgrounds appreciate quality when they experience it. Continual investment and development of the quality in our courses is the added value that I believe makes our present and past customers recommend us.

(7)

Company structures

At this point, you have found your idea, done your market research and know that your business has the potential to be a winner. If you have asked anyone for money, you have successfully convinced them, too. The next step is getting down to the nitty gritty and deciding what company structure to choose. Once you've done that, you will be able to register your business at the *Camera di Commercio* (Chamber of Commerce) and get your *Partita Iva* (VAT number). After that, you will be a true *imprenditore*.

As you've probably gathered by now, doing anything in Italy is a complicated business. Naturally, the same holds true when it comes to choosing the company structure. Mario has drawn up a flow chart to help make this process simpler for you. Make sure you spend enough time considering what is best not only for your company in its start-up phase, but what is best for it as it grows. A lot of expatriates decide to go into business with fellow expats who end up leaving the company for various reasons. They often form partnerships because they are the most economical option. But if you and your *socio* (business partner) decide down the line that being in a partnership isn't advantageous or you want to go it alone, you'll find yourself coughing up a few more thousand euros to get through the red tape, along with the costs of the *notaio*, you will also have to pay to transform your company from one structure to another and the costs of registering this new *società* (company) with the *Camera di Commercio*.

DIFFERENT COMPANY STRUCTURES AT A GLANCE

In Italy, you can choose between working as a *professionista* or *lavoratore autonomo* (professional self-employed person), operating a *ditta individuale* (sole trader), operating a *società di capitale* (corporation) or forming a *società di persone* (partnership). The main difference between them is that sole proprietors and partnerships are liable for the company debt whereas associates are protected against company liabilities if they have set up a *società di capitale*.

There are two possible partnerships in Italy:

Società in nome collettivo (Snc)	General partnership
Società di accomandita semplice (Sas)	Limited partnership

There are three possible corporations in Italy:

Società a responsabilità limitata (Srl)	Limited liability company
Società per Azioni (Spa)	Joint stock corporation
Società in accomandita per azioni (Sapa)	Partnership limited by shares

There are also cooperatives which can be set up with a minimum of nine members. There are two possible types of cooperatives:

Cooperative a responsabilità limitata	Limited liabilities cooperative
Cooperative a responsabilità illimitata	Unlimited liabilities cooperative

Non-profit companies are known as *ONLUS* in Italy.

At first glance, it seems much easier to just set up a partnership, cspccially if you arc friends with your business partner. At the beginning, you are so enthusiastic about the new business, you know you will never fall out, so the partnership is an economical way to get started. But Mario has this word of warning: back in 2005, he became the consultant for a travel agency in Umbria. The travel agency was a partnership between two Italian friends who had known each other for a long time. Mario was called in to carry out a company audit and discovered that one of the associates had stolen tens of thousands of euros from the company and, up until the audit, had successfully hidden the losses. The twist was that the associate who had stolen the money was now asking for the company to plead bankruptcy. The other partner was unwilling to do this because he knew his *socio* was responsible for the missing money and wanted to carry out an investigation. However, because he was in a partnership and not a corporation, he had no comeback and had no choice but to pay his share of the losses from his own *patrimonio* (personal incomc).

HOW TO DECIDE THE TYPE OF COMPANY?

Don't worry if you haven't got a clear idea about what type of business you want to set up. We realise it is confusing when you are not sure how the system operates in Italy. But this flow chart (Figure 7.1) should clear up your confusion and help you explore the different options open to you.

From the flow chart, you can see that the first question to ask yourself is whether you want to run the business yourself or with other people. In Italy, people who work as *lavoratori autonomi* are normally lawyers, accountants, health professionals and consultants to name just a few.

Figure 7.1 How to choose the right company

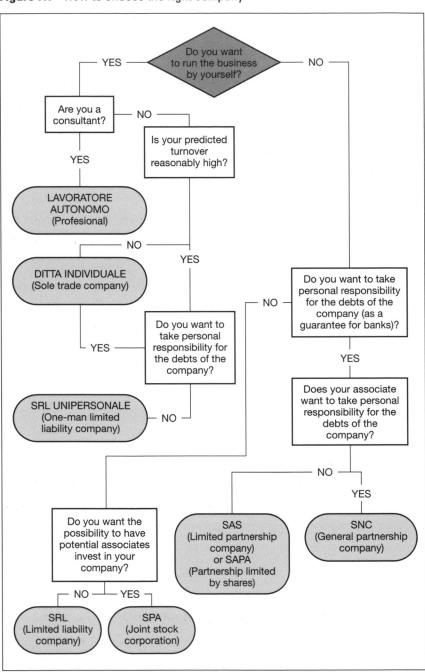

RESPONSIBILITY FOR DEBT

The next question to ask is how much personal responsibility you want for your debts. If your share capital is limited to 3 per cent, you won't want to be fully responsible for the debts of the company whereas, if you have 90 per cent of the share capital, you probably want to be the company's director. But acting as director means running the business, thus being aware of the economic situation of the company. In other words, by agreeing to run the company, you accept that you are fully responsible for the debts of the company.

If you have a *socio* (business partner), you need to sit down together and find out whether or not he or she wants to be an active partner in the business and willing to take responsibility for the company's debt should you have any. If your partner is willing to assume responsibility then you might want to take joint responsibility for running the company. In this scenario, the *Snc* is ideal. If your business partner wants less responsibility, then you can open an *Sas*, which was created especially to resolve this problem. This company allows for two different types of partners: one who is the *socio accomandatario* (administrator) and takes full responsibility for the debts of the company and another who is the *socio accomandante* and who only risks the amount he or she invests in the company.

SUMMARY

Below is a bare bones summary of the each possible company structure to make it easy for you to take in the main points at a glance. After you have looked at each table, turn to the relevant chapter for more in-depth information on what procedures you need to follow to get your business up and running.

Figure 7.2 *Lavoratore autonomo* (self-employed)

Pros	Cons	Comment
◆ This is for self-employed workers who are either registered in the *albo* (professional association) or in the Camera di Commercio.	◆ Full responsibility for the liabilities of the company	◆ You can start in a short time and don't need a *notaio* (notary) to set up the business (cheaper)
◆ You can still take on staff	◆ Not many costs are deductible	◆ You need a *Partita Iva* and the registration in the Camera di Commercio or in the *albo*
◆ Quick decisions can be taken (no formalities)		
◆ Banks can give you credit on the basis that you are a professional		

Figure 7.3 *Ditta individuale* (sole trade company)

Pros	Cons	Comment
◆ Lower costs to set up than a partnership	◆ Full responsibility for the liabilities of the company	◆ You can start in a short time and don't need a *notaio* to set up the business (cheaper)
◆ Easy to do your own accounting so cost of *commercialista* (accountant) reduced because there is less work to do		◆ You need a *Partita Iva* and the registration in the Camera di Commercio or in the professional body
◆ In some cases, the *Agenzie delle Entrate* (tax office) will keep your books for you		
◆ Quick decisions can be taken (no formalities)		
◆ Banks can give you credit on the basis of your savings		

Figure 7.4 *Società di persone* (partnership), *Snc* (unlimited partnership), *Sas* (limited partnership)

Pros	Cons	Comment
◆ The so-called *accomandanti* in *Sas* are not fully responsible for the liabilities of the company	◆ All associates in *Snc* are fully responsible for the liabilities of the company	◆ You need an accountant and a notary to set up the business
◆ Banks can give you credit on the basis of the associates' patrimony	◆ The so-called *accomandatari* in *Sas* are fully responsible for the liabilities of the company	◆ In *Snc* the associates can be administrators. In Sas only the *accomandatari* can be administrators.
◆ Associates can decide any amount of share capital to invest in the company when setting up the business	◆ The profit of *Sas* and *Snc* is considered income (and then taxed on associates) even if not withdrawn ◆ Higher costs than a *ditta individuale*	

Figure 7.5 *Società a responsabilità limitata* (corporation), *Srl* (limited liability company)

Pros	Cons	Comment
◆ The associates are not personally responsible for the liabilities of the company	◆ Due to some formalities, quick decisions can not be always taken	◆ You certainly need an accountant and a notary to set up the business
◆ The *Srl* can be set up with only one associate	◆ It can be compulsory to designate auditors (when the share capital is higher than €120,000) who must check the accounts (and have to be paid)	◆ You need a *Partita Iva* and the registration in the *Camera di Commercio*
	◆ The books of the company (board of directors, shareholders' meetings, auditors) have to be taken	◆ The *Srl* can not issue bonds
	◆ Fiscal law requirements more complicated than sole trade business	◆ A *Srl* can not be set up if the share capital is less than €10,000

Figure 7.6 *Società per Azioni SpA* (joint stock corporation)

Pros	Cons	Comment
◆ The shareholders are not personally responsible for the liabilities of the company	◆ Due to some formalities, quick decisions can not be always taken	◆ You certainly need an accountant and a notary to set up the business
◆ A *SpA* can issue bonds	◆ It is compulsory to designate auditors who must check the accounts (and have to be paid)	◆ You need a *Partita Iva* and the registration in the *Camera di Commercio*
	◆ The books of the company (board of directors, shareholders' meetings, auditors) have been taken	◆ The share capital is divided in shares which can have different rights
	◆ Fiscal law requirements more complicated than sole trade business	◆ A Spa can not be set up if the share capital is less than €120,000

In the next chapters, we explain the ins and outs of each of these company structures and what you need to do to register them. So, if you are still a bit confused about which one is right for you, don't be. Even though you may know which structure is right for you, we recommend you read about the company structures in the order we have presented them as it will give you an overall view of the situation in Italy.

Mario's Pearl of Wisdom

You've already done a lot of the hard work, but choosing your company structure is probably one of your most difficult tasks. Company structure is written into Italian law, but the problem is that laws are being modified all the time in my country, so it's not always clear what the situation is and what you need to do. The problem with this is that we have another rule in Italy: *Ignorantia legis non excusat*, or, in plain English, ignorance of the law is no excuse. When you are ready to register your business, check with an **avvocato** (lawyer) or **notaio** that no major changes have been made to the Italian law. After major laws have been brought in, the laws will be published in an Italian-language booklet and sold in Italian bookshops. It's worth buying a copy and wading through it.

8

Lavoratore autonomo

In Italian, the term *lavoratore autonomo* literally means that you work in a professional capacity, but that you are not an employee of a company.

The phrase *lavoratore autonomo* is also used to specify your company structure in the *Registro delle Imprese* (National Business Registry). A *lavoratore autonomo* is normally known as a *professionista* (professional) and is someone who provides services to companies or individuals based on their own knowledge and their education and training. For example, lawyers, accountants, consultants and health professionals (doctors, dentists, chiropractors, reflexologists etc.) all fall into this category. If Emma was running How to Italy by herself, she would work as a *lavoratore autonomo*, issuing invoices in her name for each consultation she did. Mario, as a *commercialista* (accountant), temporary manager and a management consultant, is also a *lavoratore autonomo* in the work he does outside of How to Italy. Sally, who wants to set up the language school, would be a *lavoratore autonomo* if she was working as a freelance English teacher, and/or doing translation work. But because she has a language school, she is no longer a freelance teacher, but does what is known in Italian as *commercializzare i servizi* (selling services) on an organised basis. In this case, she needs to open a *ditta individuale* (sole trade company), but we will look at that in the next chapter.

DOCUMENTS NEEDED TO SET UP YOUR BUSINESS

Setting up as a self-employed person is straightforward. You will need your *passaporto* or *carta d'identità* (id card), your *visto* (visa) from the Italian Embassy in your own country if needed, your *permesso di soggiorno* (permit of stay) from the *Questura* (police headquarters), your *residenza* (residency) from the *comune* (town) where you live and your *codice fiscale* (tax code) from the *Agenzia delle Entrate* (tax office).

Take originals and photocopies of all of these documents, along with your *carta d'identità* or passport to the Agenzia delle Entrate located in the main town of the *provincia* you live in and ask to open a *Partita Iva* (VAT number).

You will have to fill in a detailed form entitled the *Dichiarazione di Inizio Attività (AA9/7)* which is your declaration to start a business. The *Agenzia delle Entrate* no longer stocks hard copies of this form so the onus is on you to download it from the organisation's website (www.agenziaentrate.it). Click on '*modulistica*' and then '*altri modelli*'.

Figure 8.1 shows Quadro A which is the first section of the form you need to fill in. You need to insert your full name and your *codice fiscale* (tax code). The tax officer will fill in the rest.

Figure 8.1

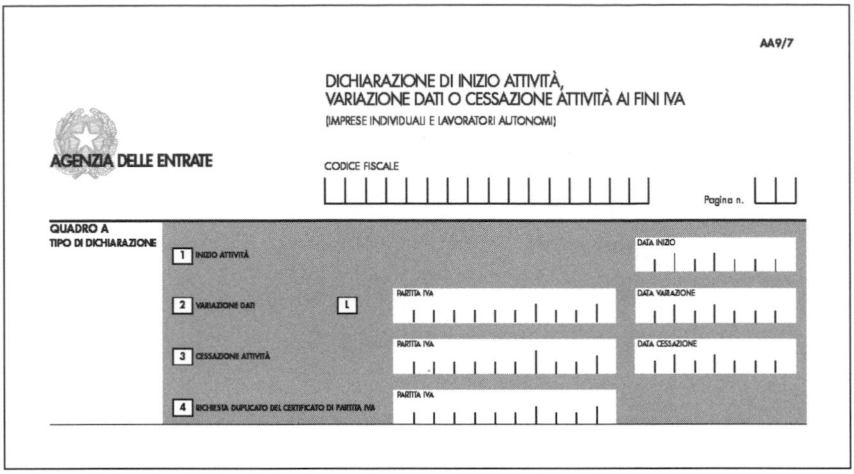

Industry codes

Each industry area and sub-section of that industry area has a specific code which you need to indicate in the section 'Codice
Attività of Quadro B' as seen in Figure 8.2 opposite. There are literally hundreds of codes so we can't list them all here. The full
listings can be found on the *Agenzie delle Entrate* website on the
following page: http://www1.agenziaentrate.it/documentazione/
atecofin/ricerca/ateco.php. If you have trouble filling in the form,
try to make a list of the codes that you think could be relevant and
show these to the officer at the *Agenzie delle Entrate* when you
apply for the *Partita Iva*. Tax officers are normally very helpful.
If you prove that you have made an effort to find the information,
they will help you with the rest.

You also need to indicate the *volume d'affari presunto* (the pre-
dicted annual turnover) of your company and the company

address. Where this is in a *palazzo* (apartment block), your address must be precise down to the stair number and the flat number. This should be indicated in your rental or property deeds.

Figure 8.2

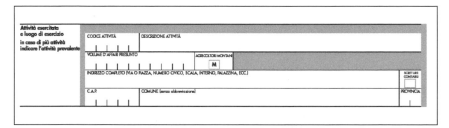

In Quadro C (Figure 8.3), you need to fill out your *codice fiscale*, name and surname, date of birth and country of birth and your address.

Figure 8.3

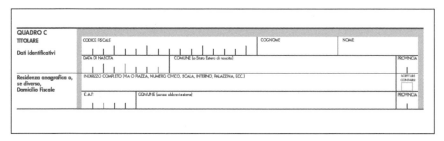

In Quadro F (Figure 8.4), you need to insert your *codice fiscale* again, your name and the postal address where the tax registers are kept. You also need to tick Box A as you are setting up a new business.

Figure 8.4

QUADRO F
SOGGETTI DEPOSITARI E LUOGHI DI CONSERVAZIONE DELLE SCRITTURE CONTABILI

TIPO COMUNICAZIONE A C
CODICE FISCALE
INDIRIZZO COMPLETO (VIA O PIAZZA, NUMERO CIVICO, SCALA, INTERNO, PALAZZINA, ECC.)
C.A.P. COMUNE (senza abbreviazioni) PROVINCIA

TIPO COMUNICAZIONE A C
CODICE FISCALE
INDIRIZZO COMPLETO (VIA O PIAZZA, NUMERO CIVICO, SCALA, INTERNO, PALAZZINA, ECC.)
C.A.P. COMUNE (senza abbreviazioni) PROVINCIA

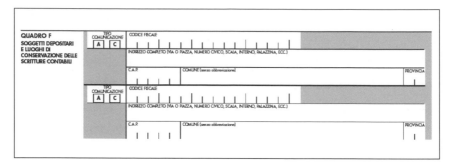

Having filled out the form, you will need to indicate which Quadri you have filled in (i.e. A, B, C and F), add the date, your *codice fiscale* (yes, you really do need it for everything in Italy) and your signature. Figure 8.5 shows this part of the form.

Figure 8.5

QUADRI COMPILATI E FIRMA DELLA DICHIARAZIONE

Il sottoscritto dichiara di aver compilato i seguenti quadri A B C D E F G H (barrare) Totale Pagine

DATA CODICE FISCALE

I dati richiesti nella dichiarazione devono essere indicati obbligatoriamente per non incorrere in sanzioni di carattere amministrativo e, in alcuni casi, di carattere penale. Secondo la legge n. 675 del 1996 (legge sulla privacy), tutti i dati dichiarati sono dati di natura privata. L'amministrazione si impegna a trattarli nel pieno rispetto delle norme. Le informazioni che riguardano il titolare, i responsabili e le modalità di trattamento dei dati, nonché i diritti esercitabili sui dati stessi sono consultabili all'interno delle istruzioni per la compilazione del modello.

FIRMA DEL DICHIARANTE

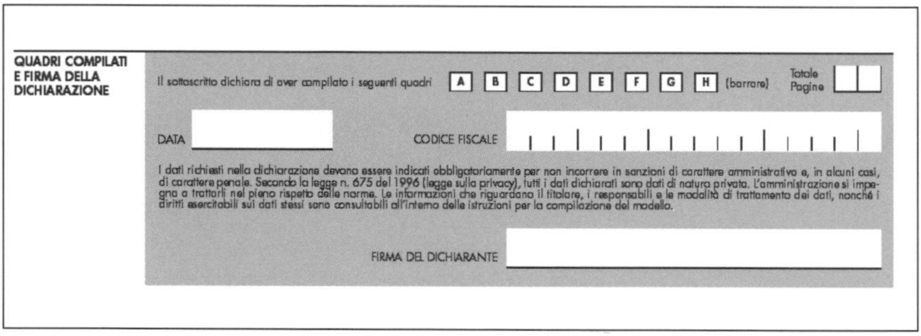

Once the tax officer has checked and authorised your form, you will immediately be issued with a *Partita Iva*. You do not have to pay for this.

PROFESSIONAL ASSOCIATION

As a *professionista*, who you pay the *cassa previdenziale* (social security contributions) to depends on your profession. If you are a professional, you make them to your *albo* (professional association) which you are legally obliged to join. Joining fees are steep: expect to pay approximately €500 as a one-off joining fee and around €400 in annual membership. The following is a list of professions with their own professional bodies:

accountant (*commercialista*);
auditor (*revisore*);
lawyer (*avvocato*);
pharmacist (*farmacista*);
biologist (*biologo*);
journalist (*giornalista*);
tourist guide (*accompagnatore turistico*);
architect (*architetto*);
orthodontist (*odontoiatra*);
dietician (*tecnologo alimentare*);
doctor (*medico*);
health worker (*assistente sanitario*);
obstetrician (*ostetrico*);
radiologist (*tecnico di radiologia medica*);
veterinary surgeon (*medico veterinario*).

These professional associations are regional rather than national which means, annoyingly, there are no national websites. To find out the website of the professional association in your area, type '*ordine* + the Italian name for your profession + the name of the Italian *regione*' into a search engine. The professional body for tourist guides is registered at the Regione's *Assessorato per il turismo* (tourist office).

Before joining these professional associations, you will have to have your qualifications (including courses taken and grades achieved) officially translated and apostiled by the Italian consultate or embassy in your country. You will also have to apply for *riconoscimento* (legal recognition) of your training course and qualification. Even if you are an EU citizen, expect long delays.

Each professional association has different requirements, so check with your local branch what you need to do. By registering with the professional association, you should not need to register with the *Camera di Commercio*. However, your professional association will be able to guide you on this.

CAMERA DI COMMERCIO

If your profession has no professional association, then you will have to submit a declaration of your new business to the *Camera di Commercio*. You will need a *marca da bollo* (tax stamp) for €14.62 from the *tabaccaio* (tobacconists). Depending on your profession, the Camera may or may not keep the the register of your professional association. If it does, it will deduct your pension contributions. Other, newer professions or those that are not recognised by the Italian government (eg, chiropractors) do not pay social security contributions to a professional association, but will pay *Gestione Separata INPS* (see next paragraph). Where the government does not recognise your profession, you will still need your qualifications officially translated, but you do not need to apply for *riconoscimento*.

GESTIONE SEPARATA INPS

If your profession does not have a professional body, then you must make payments of *Gestione separata INPS* (separated social security payments). As of January 1, 2006 the general rate was 18.20 per cent for an income of up to €39,297. Where the income is higher than €39,297, the rate is 19.20 per cent. The rate is 15 per cent for pensioners.

If you are a full-time teacher but also teach outside of your main job, then the rate to pay to the *Gestione separata* is 10 per cent. If you are retired, then it is 15 per cent. Let's suppose you are a business consultant and charge €1,000 for a two-day project. Using the F24 model, you will have to pay €182 in *Gestione Separata INPS*. If you have been given project work with the '*lavoro a progetto*' contract, your *INPS* payment is 18.20 per cent or 19.20 per cent, depending on how much you have earned in the tax year. However, you are only liable for one third of this tax as the remaining two thirds must be paid by the company hiring you. When this is the case, payment of *Gestione separata INPS* is made monthly. If you do not have such a contract, it is paid with all your other taxes.

INPS
www.inps.it
Where you aren't a member of a professional association, you will need to pay compulsory pension contributions to *INPS* (*instituto nazionale previdenzia sociale* – National Institute of Social Previdence).

An example of the amount to be paid to the INPS for the '*Artigiani*' (year 2005) is shown in Figure 8.6.

Figure 8.6

Profit of the year	Percentage for the owner and relatives who are 21 years old or older	Percentage for owner's relatives younger than 21 years old
From €13.133.00 up to €38.641.00	17.20%	14.20%
beyond €38.641.00 up to €64.402.00	18.20%	15.20%

Payment must be made by 16 February, 16 May, 16 August, and 16 November, using the F24 model.

Mario's Pearl of Wisdom

*If you haven't run your own business in the last three years, then you can take advantage of the special Government incentive which is aimed at encouraging people like you to open a **Partita Iva**. Known as the new activities' regime (L. 388/2000), it simplifies all your tax fulfilments and, at the same time, reduces your taxation to a rate of 10 per cent. This special tax band is only available if the gross income for the tax year (January 31 to December 31) is less than €30.987.41. But don't worry if you go over. If you don't earn more than €46.481 gross (i.e. 50 per cent more than €30.987.41), you are still taxed with a rate of 10 per cent, but the following year you are taxed with the ordinary rate. If this option interests you, ask the Agenzia delle Entrate or a **commercialista** for further information.*

Having a *commercialista* isn't strictly necessary when you are a *lavoratore autonomo*, but we recommend you use one anyway. Filling in tax returns is a heavy going task for anyone at the best of times and the headaches this can cause multiply when you are not all that familiar with what you need to declare and when. If you really are reluctant with use one, then at least consider it for the first couple of years while you are finding your feet and getting used to the way everything works.

$$\boxed{9}$$

Ditta individuale

In setting up a *ditta individuale* (sole trade business), you will go through similar steps as the *lavoratore autonomo* (self-employed worker).

You will need to take the originals and photocopies of all the necessary documents to the *Agenzia delle Entrate* (tax office) and ask for your *Partita Iva* (VAT number) as before.

You will fill out the form as before, but this time in Quadro A, you need to write your name or your business name. If you do not have a company name, then simply write your full name. If, however, you wish to trade with a business name, write the name of the business and then '*di*' plus your own name. For example, Sally Smith who wants to open the language school has decided to trade as a *ditta individuale*. She could either choose to trade as Sally Smith or English Today di Sally Smith.

If you are not resident in Italy and have a business already operating abroad, you must indicate the address of the registered office, the country, the country it is registered in and the *numero identificazione iva stato estero* (EU VAT identification number).

CAMERA DI COMMERCIO

As a *ditta individuale*, your trade does not have a professional association which you must join. Instead, you must register with the *Camera di Commercio* (Chamber of Commerce). The next step is to submit a declaration to the Camera di Commercio of your business, along with the proposed start date. To do this, you will need a *marca da bollo* (tax stamp) for €14.62 from the *tabaccaio* (tobacconists). You must specify whether you are an *artigiano* (tradesperson) or a *commerciante* (trader). If you are an *artigiano*, you can only employ members of your own family. In Italy, taxidrivers, carpenters, metal workers and delivery people are all considered *artigiani.*

The form you will need to fill in is known as the *Iscrizione di imprenditore individuale nel registro delle imprese.* In Figure 9.1 you can see the form used by the *Camera di Commercio* in Milan. Fill in the section Il sottoscritto (the undersigned), with your name and surname. In the section '*In qualità di (titolare)*' you need to write your role within the company which is likely to be *titolare* (owner). In the space for '*all'Ufficio del Registro Imprese di*' you need to write the town you will be registered in. In this case, Milan.

Figure 9.1

INDICARE N° TEL. | / DI CHI PRESENTA IL MODELLO ALLO SPORTELLO: STUDIO, ASSOCIAZIONE, ECC.

CAMERA DI COMMERCIO, INDUSTRIA, ARTIGIANATO E AGRICOLTURA DI

I1

REGISTRO DELLE IMPRESE 1998

MARCA DA BOLLO

ISCRIZIONE DI
IMPRENDITORE INDIVIDUALE
NEL REGISTRO DELLE IMPRESE

C.C.I.A.A. di Milano - CedCamera

A) ESTREMI DI ISCRIZIONE NEL REGISTRO DELLE IMPRESE

Numero R.E.A.	Data di protocollo	Numero di protocollo	Data iscrizione	Numero Registro Imprese
	___/___/___		___/___/___	

Il sottoscritto: ______________________ in qualità di (titolare, etc.): ______________________

di impresa individuale, presenta all'Ufficio del Registro Imprese di: ______________________

Figure 9.2 shows you where you need to declare what type of business you are registering in the companies' register. Section A is for sole trader, section B is for tradespeople only working with their families and sections C and D are for those in agriculture. Tick the one applicable to you.

Figure 9.2

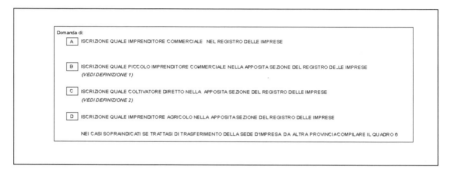

Figure 9.3 shows the *dati anagrafici dell'imprendiore*, where you will need to insert your *codice fiscale* (tax code), your brand new *Partita Iva*, surname, name, date of birth, nationality and sex.

Figure 9.3

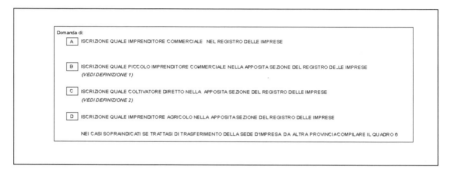

Finally, in Figure 9.4, there is the section relating to your new *ditta* (business). You need to indicate the *comune* (town), *frazione* (district), address, telephone and fax numbers, web url and email addresses.

Figure 9.4

☐ 4 / DITTA

☐ 5 / SEDE DELL'IMPRESA

Comune ______ Frazione o Località ______
Via, viale, piazza ecc. ______ Nr. civico ______ Cap ______
Presso (o altre indicazioni) (2) ______
Telefono ______ / ______ Telefax ______ / ______
Internet ______ e.mail ______

The form you fill in next depends on whether you are an *artigiano*, *commerciante* or *agricoltore* (farmer). The staff at the *Camera di Commercio* will be able to help you select the right form. However, to give you an idea of what the documents look like, we have included the registration form for tradespeople. See Figure 9.5 overleaf.

The following (Figure 9.6) is an example of the form of the Chamber of Commerce of Milan which you must use to be registered as a sales representative:

Figure 9.5

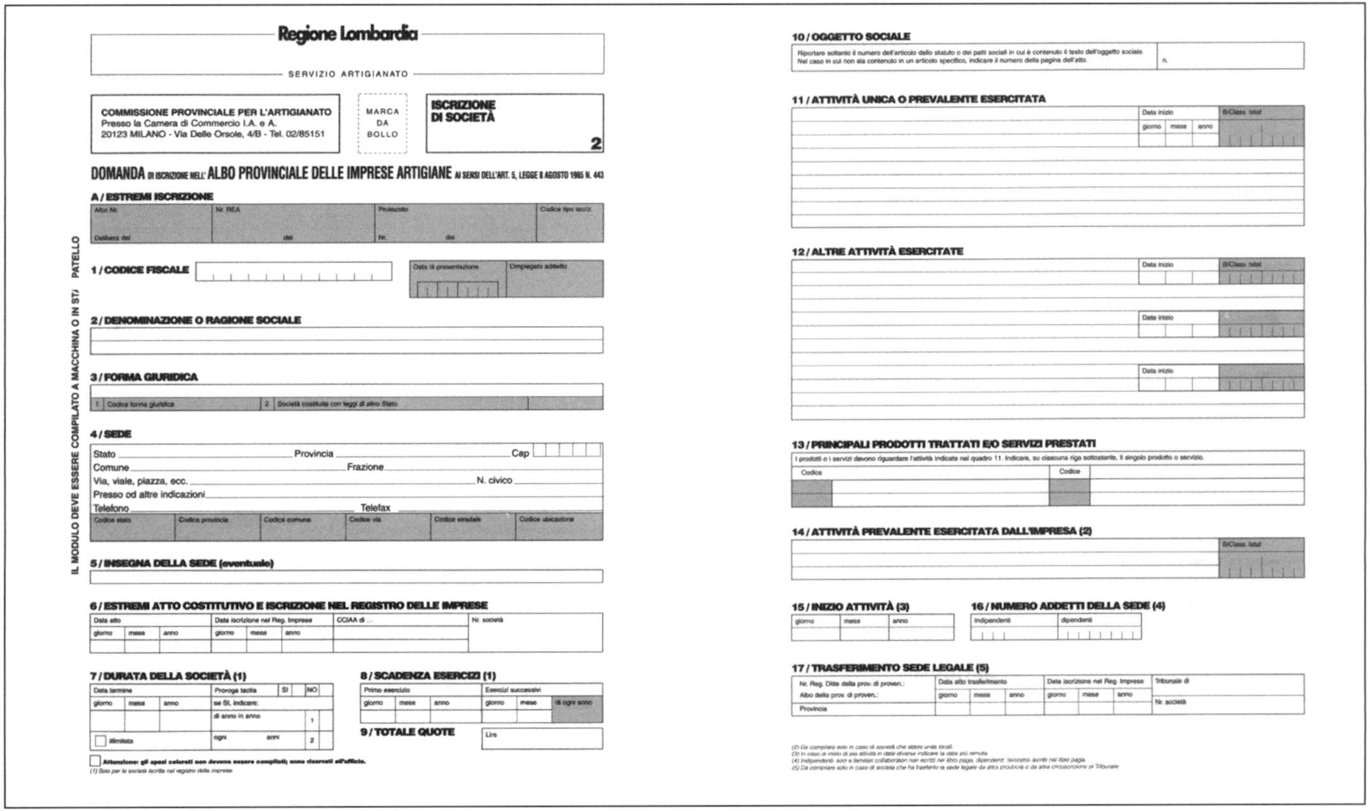

Regione Lombardia

SERVIZIO ARTIGIANATO

COMMISSIONE PROVINCIALE PER L'ARTIGIANATO
Presso la Camera di Commercio I.A. e A.
20123 MILANO - Via Delle Orsole, 4/B - Tel. 02/85151

MARCA DA BOLLO

ISCRIZIONE DI SOCIETÀ 2

DOMANDA DI ISCRIZIONE NELL' ALBO PROVINCIALE DELLE IMPRESE ARTIGIANE AI SENSI DELL'ART. 5, LEGGE 8 AGOSTO 1985 N. 443

IL MODULO DEVE ESSERE COMPILATO A MACCHINA O IN STAMPATELLO

A / ESTREMI ISCRIZIONE

Albo Nr.	Nr. REA	Protocollo	Codice tipo iscriz.
Delibera del	del	Nr. del	

1 / CODICE FISCALE

Data di presentazione	L'impiegato addetto

2 / DENOMINAZIONE O RAGIONE SOCIALE

3 / FORMA GIURIDICA

1 Codice forma giuridica | 2 Società costituita con leggi di altro Stato

4 / SEDE

Stato ____ Provincia ____ Cap
Comune ____ Frazione ____
Via, viale, piazza, ecc. ____ N. civico ____
Presso od altre indicazioni ____
Telefono ____ Telefax ____

Codice stato	Codice provincia	Codice comune	Codice via	Codice stradale	Codice ubicazione

5 / INSEGNA DELLA SEDE (eventuale)

6 / ESTREMI ATTO COSTITUTIVO E ISCRIZIONE NEL REGISTRO DELLE IMPRESE

Data atto			Data iscrizione nel Reg. Imprese			CCIAA di ...	Nr. società
giorno	mese	anno	giorno	mese	anno		

7 / DURATA DELLA SOCIETÀ (1)

Data termine			Proroga tacita	SI	NO
giorno	mese	anno	se SI, indicare:		
			di anno in anno	1	
illimitata			ogni anni	2	

8 / SCADENZA ESERCIZI (1)

Primo esercizio			Esercizi successivi		
giorno	mese	anno	giorno	mese	di ogni anno

9 / TOTALE QUOTE

Lire

Attenzione: gli spazi colorati non devono essere compilati, sono riservati all'ufficio.

(1) Solo per le società iscritte nel registro delle imprese

10 / OGGETTO SOCIALE

Riportare soltanto il numero dell'articolo dello statuto o dei patti sociali in cui è contenuto il testo dell'oggetto sociale. Nel caso in cui non sia contenuto in un articolo specifico, indicare il numero della pagina dell'atto. n.

11 / ATTIVITÀ UNICA O PREVALENTE ESERCITATA

Data inizio			B/Class. Istat
giorno	mese	anno	

12 / ALTRE ATTIVITÀ ESERCITATE

Data inizio | B/Class. Istat

Data inizio

Data inizio

13 / PRINCIPALI PRODOTTI TRATTATI E/O SERVIZI PRESTATI

I prodotti o i servizi devono riguardare l'attività indicata nel quadro 11. Indicare, su ciascuna riga sottostante, il singolo prodotto o servizio.

Codice		Codice	

14 / ATTIVITÀ PREVALENTE ESERCITATA DALL'IMPRESA (2)

B/Class. Istat

15 / INIZIO ATTIVITÀ (3)

giorno	mese	anno

16 / NUMERO ADDETTI DELLA SEDE (4)

indipendenti	dipendenti

17 / TRASFERIMENTO SEDE LEGALE (5)

Nr. Reg. Ditte della prov. di proven.: / Albo della prov. di proven.: / Provincia	Data atto trasferimento (giorno, mese, anno)	Data iscrizione nel Reg. Imprese (giorno, mese, anno)	Tribunale di / Nr. società

(2) Da compilare solo in caso di società che abbia unità locali.
(3) In caso di inizio di più attività in date diverse indicare la data più remota.
(4) Indipendenti: soci e familiari collaboratori non iscritti nel libro paga; dipendenti: lavoratori iscritti nel libro paga.
(5) Da compilare solo in caso di società che ha trasferito la sede legale da altra provincia o da altra circoscrizione di Tribunale

Figure 9.6

CAMERA DI COMMERCIO
INDUSTRIA ARTIGIANATO
E AGRICOLTURA DI MILANO

MARCA
DA
BOLLO

MODELLO 2 ✱ Numero di protocollo 13 / _____

**ALLA
CAMERA DI COMMERCIO
INDUSTRIA ARTIGIANATA E AGRICOLTURA
DI MILANO**

*RUOLO AGENTI E RAPPRESENTANTI DI COMMERCIO
- LEGGE 3 Maggio 1985 n. 204 -
CODICE ALBO 13*

(barrare l'ipotesi interessata)

☐ PERSONA FISICA   (QUADRI A - C)
☐ SOCIETÀ   (QUADRI B - C)

☐ ISCRIZIONE
☐ ISCRIZIONE PER TRASFERIMENTO DA ALTRA PROVINCIA

DATA	ANNOTAZIONI RISERVATE ALL'UFFICIO	FIRMA del FUNZIONARIO

QUADRO A - PERSONA FISICA

(COMPILARE QUESTO QUADRO SOLO IN CASO DI PERSONA FISICA)

IL SOTTOSCRITTO _____
nato il ___ / ___ / ___ a _____ Prov. _____
residente a _____ Prov. _____
in via /piazza _____ n. _____ C.A.P. _____
Tel. ___ / _____ codice fiscale _____

CHIEDE

(BARRARE L'IPOTESI CHE INTERESSA)

☐ di essere iscritto nel Ruolo degli Agenti e Rappresentanti di commercio tenuto dalla Camera di Commercio di Milano.

☐ l'iscrizione al **Ruolo degli Agenti e Rappresentanti Commercio** tenuto dalla Camera di Commercio di Milano, **ESSENDO** già iscritto nel corrispondente ruolo della Camera di Commercio di _____ al n. _____ dal ___ / ___ / ___
ed avendo trasferito la propria residenza o domicilio professionale nella provincia di MILANO.
(In questo caso non compilare il quadro relativo al requisito professionale ed allegare esclusivamente l'attestazione di versamento di EURO 123,11 sul c/c postale n. 8003)

**A tale scopo, consapevole delle responsabilità penali
cui può andare incontro in caso di false dichiarazioni,
in base all'articolo 76 del D.P.R. 445/2000**

DICHIARA

ai sensi degli articoli 46 e 47 del D.P.R. 445/2000

1. DI ESSERE CITTADINO _____ (nota 1)
2. DI ESSERE IN POSSESSO DEI DIRITTI CIVILI.
3. DI AVERE ELETTO IL PROPRIO DOMICILIO PROFESSIONALE NEL COMUNE DI _____ n. _____
_____) via _____
(compilare solo se diverso dalla residenza)

4. DI AVER ASSOLTO AGLI OBBLIGHI SCOLASTICI (vedi nota 2) avendo conseguito:
☐ LICENZA DI SCUOLA ELEMENTARE
☐ LICENZA DI SCUOLA MEDIA INFERIORE
presso Scuola _____
con sede in _____) nell'anno scolastico 19 ___ (___ / ___)
Via/Piazza _____ n. _____

5. DI NON SVOLGERE ATTIVITA' DI MEDIAZIONE PER LA QUALE E' PRESCRITTA L'ISCRIZIONE NEL RELATIVO RUOLO.
6. DI NON SVOLGERE ATTIVITA' IN QUALITA' DI DIPENDENTE DA PERSONE, ASSOCIAZIONI OD ENTI PUBBLICI O PRIVATI (AD ECCEZIONE DEL DIPENDENTE PUBBLICO IN REGIME DI PART-TIME NON SUPERIORE AL 50%), (nota 3)
7. DI ESSERE IN POSSESSO DEL SEGUENTE REQUISITO PROFESSIONALE

☞ CONTINUARE COMPILAZIONE NEL QUADRO C (A PAG. 5)

Membership fees cost €168 plus €31 to cover administrative costs. The actual amount varies in accordance with the type of work you do. The membership fees are paid at the post office. These instructions are shown in Figure 9.7.

Figure 9.7

ALLEGATI

❏ *Attestazione di versamento della Tassa sulle concessioni Governative di EURO 168,00 effettuato sul c/c postale n. 8003 intestato a: AGENZIA DELLE ENTRATE CENTRO OPERATIVO - PESCARA*
❏ **Versamento di EURO 31,00 per diritti di segreteria** *effettuato:*
•   *direttamente agli sportelli della Camera di Commercio (contanti, bancomat);*
•   *sul c/c postale n. **982207** intestato alla Camera di Commercio di Milano, indicando la causale "Iscrizione al Ruolo Agenti e Rappresentanti di Commercio" (allegare in questo caso l'ATTESTAZIONE del VERSAMENTO).*

Mario's Pearl of Wisdom

*Before deciding whether or not to become a **ditta individuale** read Chapter 11: Srl, because you also have the option of becoming a limited sole trade company. Before doing this, you need to work out what is best for the interests of the company, both now and in the long term. If you do not need to get into debt to finance the company and are planning to grow organically then the normal **ditta individuale** is a great solution as you do not have to worry about taking on too much debt and how to pay it back.*

10

Società di persone

Most people who decide to set up a *società di persone* (partnership) in Italy do so because in the short term it is the cheaper option. If you are strapped for cash and don't want to ask for finance, it seems ideal because you do not have to invest any money into the company initially.

But while the thought of setting up a business with a friend or relative sounds nice and cosy, the reality is that things can go wrong, especially when you're in Italy and not your own country.

ADVANTAGE OF SAS OVER SNC

We know we keep stressing the disadvantages of an *Snc* (unlimited partnership) but that is because we know so many expats and Italians who have had bad experiences and who have vowed never to set up an *Snc* again.

Just to reiterate the point, we have an American friend Anna who went into business with her Italian cousin to set up a company exporting Sardinian ceramics. They set up an *Snc* (*società in nome collettivo*) and agreed that Francesca would be responsible for the day-to-day running of the business, while Anna would invest an initial €10,000 in the firm in order to get the show on the road while she was waiting for her visa to come through. She would limit her involvement to just checking in from time to time.

Every time Anna saw Francesca and she asked how the business was going, she always got the same answer: '*Va tutto bene*'

'(Everything is great). I love running the company'. After a year, however, of always getting the same response, Anna decided to look at the accounts herself to find out the true story. Far from being '*tutto bene*' as Francesca had claimed, the company was thousands of euros in debt. But Francesca was not in a position to pay them. Anna was forced to sell her Audi to pay the debts that Francesca had accrued through not running the company as she should have.

But you should have seen her face when Mario told her she could have avoided this awkward scenario had the cousins decided to set up an *Sas* (*società di accomandata semplice*) (limited partnership) rather than the *Snc*. In the *Sas*, Anna would have been a *socio accomandante* or special partner rather than a general partner and therefore liable only for the money she originally put into the company rather than assuming responsibility for the entire debt of the company should her business partner not be able to pay her share.

DIFFERENCE BETWEEN SNC AND SAS

In the *Snc*, all the partners are fully responsible for the debts of the company and are, at the same time, administrators. In contrast, in the Sas there are two types of associates: *accomandatari* (general partners) and *accomandanti* (special partners). The former are the administrators of the partnership and are fully liable for its debts, while the latter cannot be administrators and are only liable to the extent of their capital contribution.

To clarify this point: let's suppose you set up an *Snc* with a business partner. In the company memorandum you declare you own 10 per cent of the company and your partner owns 90 per cent. Now let's fast forward two years down the line. You find out the company has liabilities for €50,000 and your associate can not pay 90 per cent as agreed. The creditors will expect you to pay the entire amount. Whilst the 'internal' agreement of the partnership decides on how profit is distributed, it does not protect you against the claim of creditors.

If you have a business partner who would like to be involved indirectly, then the *Sas* is the best option. From the liability point of view, the *Sas* lies in the middle between a *Snc* (unlimited liability) and an *Srl* (limited liability company).

HOW TO SET UP AN SNC OR AN SAS

Setting up a *società di persone* is straightforward, but more complicated than setting up a *ditta individuale* (sole trade business), because you have to take into account the wishes of your business partners.

The *Snc* or *Sas* can be set up only by a *notaio* (notary). He or she will draw up the memorandum which regulates the relationship between the associates and between the company and third parties. Fees vary depending on the size of the company and the part of the company, but expect to pay somewhere in the region of €1,500.

Your *commercialista* (accountant) will fix an appointment with the *notaio* to draw up the official company deeds. At the meeting, you will have to sign the *statuto* (article of association) which is the list of rules that your partnership must follow. This *statuto* is then attached to the *atto costitutivo* (company memorandum).

In order to draft the memorandum, the *notaio* will need to know the following:

1. name of the partnership (e.g. if How to Italy were an Snc or Sas, the full name of the company would be How to Italy snc or How to Italy sas);
2. name, surname, place and date of birth (town and country if born outside of Italy, the *comune* if born in Italy), nationality and town of residence of all business partners;
3. type of company you are setting up (Snc or Sas);
4. names of the business partners who will act as directors of the company and can act on its behalf;
5. address of the *sede legale* (registered office);
6. the assets granted, the value agreed and the method used to estimate them. If you or your business partner want your professionalism to be recognised as an asset, the *notaio* will need to know the monetary value you attach to the recognition of your skills. For example, you may decide that your consulting experience is an asset valued at €20,000 per year;
7. rules to follow in order to establish profit and loss;
8. how long the partnership will be trading for. This cannot be indefinite and is normally a 25-year period.

REQUESTING THE *PARTITA IVA*

As soon as the notary has set up the company and you have signed both the *statuto* and the *atto costitutivo*, you can apply for the *Partita Iva* (VAT number). Your *commercialista* (you should have one by now, if you haven't, find one quickly) will then register your company with the *Agenzia delle Entrate* (tax office). If you don't have a *commercialista* or they are not willing to go to the Agenzia delle Entrate on your behalf (if this is the case, it may be time to find a new one), you will need to fill out the form *AA7/7: Domanda di Attribuzione del numero di codice fiscale e dichiarazione di inizio attività, variazione dati o cessazione attitvità ai fini iva*. This is similar to the form a sole trader needs to fill out, but is expressly for companies made up of two or more business partners. Figure 10.1 shows you what form AA7/7 looks like.

Figure 10.1

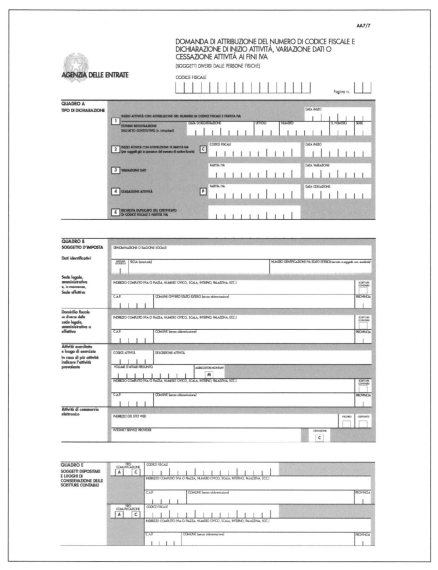

REGISTERING WITH THE CAMERA DI COMMERCIO

Once the company has been assigned its *Partita Iva*, the administrators of the partnership must sign the *Registro delle Imprese* (National Business Register) within 30 days. In reality, this is normally signed by the *notaio* on your behalf. The cost of the registering is approximately €300.

If your *notaio* does not sign the business register for whatever reason, Figure 10.2 shows you what the document you require looks like.

Figure 10.2

INDICARE N° TEL. ______ / ______ DI CHI PRESENTA IL MODELLO ALLO SPORTELLO: STUDIO, ASSOCIAZIONE, ECC.

CAMERA DI COMMERCIO, INDUSTRIA, ARTIGIANATO E AGRICOLTURA DI

S1

REGISTRO DELLE IMPRESE *1998*

MARCA DA BOLLO

ISCRIZIONE DI SOCIETÀ, CONSORZIO, G.E.I.E. ENTE PUBBLICO ECONOMICO NEL REGISTRO DELLE IMPRESE

A / ESTREMI DI ISCRIZIONE NEL REGISTRO DELLE IMPRESE

Numero R.E.A.	Data di protocollo	Numero di protocollo	Data iscrizione	Nr. Registro Imprese
	___ / ___ / ___		___ / ___ / ___	

Il sottoscritto ______ in qualità di ______

presenta all'ufficio del Registro delle Imprese di ______

domanda di iscrizione nel registro dei fatti previsti dalle norme vigenti e deposita:

☐ ATTO COSTITUTIVO DI SOCIETÀ COMMERCIALE, CONSORZIO, G.E.I.E. O ENTE

☐ ATTO COSTITUTIVO DI SOCIETÀ SEMPLICE: FORMA SCRITTA ☐ FORMA VERBALE (1) ☐

☐ ATTO DI TRASFERIMENTO DI SEDE LEGALE DALLA PROVINCIA DI: ______

REGISTRO IMPRESE NR. ______

B / ESTREMI DELL'ATTO

Data dell'atto	Numero Repertorio	Notaio Rogante / Autenticante	Codice Fiscale del Notaio
___ / ___ / ___			

☐ 1 / CODICE FISCALE

☐ 2 / PARTITA IVA (se diversa dal codice fiscale)

☐ 3 / DENOMINAZIONE O RAGIONE SOCIALE

☐ 4 / FORMA GIURIDICA

☐ 5 / SEDE LEGALE

Stato (2) ______ Comune ______

Frazione o Località ______ Cap ______

Via, viale, piazza ecc. ______ Nr. civico ______

Presso (o altre indicazioni) (3) ______

Telefono ______ / ______ Telefax ______ / ______

Internet ______ e.mail: ______

La sede degli uffici direttivi, amministrativi e gestionali dell'impresa è ubicata a questo indirizzo? SI ☐ NO ☐ (se NO, si allega mod. UL) (4)

☐ 6 / DURATA

Data termine ___ / ___ / ___ ☐ Illimitata | Proroga tacita ☐ indeterminata (art. 2273 c.c.) ☐ ogni ___ anni

(1) In tal caso nella casella 'data atto' indicare la data di costituzione.
(2) Indicare nel solo caso di società estera con sede secondaria in Italia (art. 2506 Codice Civile).
(3) L'indicazione è obbligatoria se la sede è presso uno studio professionale, associazione, ecc.
(4) Salvo il caso in cui la sede amministrativa sia ubicata in altra provincia, in tal caso il modello UL deve essere presentato in quella provincia.

This form must be sent back via email to the *Camera di Commercio* (Chambcr of Commercc) in the town where your business is   registered.

Mario's Pearl *of* Wisdom

Before setting up an **Snc** or **SAS** ask yourself if this really is the route you want to go down, or you are only doing so to save money. If your company needs finance or a bank loan and you need to be trading for several years before you expect to make any profit, then you may be better off with a limited liability company. If your ***commercialista*** (accountant) is any good, they will be on top of all the different options and can advise you on the best structure for you. Listen to what they have to say as they have your best interests at heart. They want you to be a success as much as you do because it means that you will go on being their client for longer!

11

Srl

If you decide to set set up an *Srl* (limited liability company), then you are on much safer ground as you have limited liability if your business venture in Italy doesn't go as well as expected. You are protected against liabilities except against the quota capital that you and your business partners put into the business to set it up. Under Italian law, an *Srl* requires a minimum quota of €10,000. However the actual initial investment required is only 25 per cent of the agreed initial capital. In other words, if you want to set up an *Srl* with the minimum initial capital of €10,000, you only need to deposit €2,500 in the company bank account.

This initial capital must already be in the bank account before the *notaio* (notary) draws up the company memorandum. It will only be given back once your new company has been registered in the *Registro delle Imprese* (National Business Register).

In order to set up the business, the *atto costitutivo* (article of incoporation) and the *statuto* (article of association) is needed. For the Article of Association, the *notaio* will require the following information:

- name, surname, place and date of birth, residence and nationality of all business partners;
- company name which has to indicate at the end: Srl (How to Italy would be How to Italy Srl);

- address of the registered office;
- a list of the companies activities (now and in the future);
- details of the share capital proposed and paid, not less than €10,000 (initial investment);
- assets given by every associate and the value estimated;
- the single fraction of the capital belonging to every associate;
- the rules concerning the company, indicating those specifically related to the administration;
- the name of the people who are in charge of the administration and those who are in charge of the control of the accountancy;
- the cost of setting up the company, even approximately;
- how the company plans on trading. As with the *Snc* (general partnership), this is normally fixed for a date in the future.

Under the law, Legislative Decree n. 6/2003, the law has been changed in order to simplify the formal acts required for businesses. One of the main changes is that an *Srl* no longer needs to call a meeting of the business partners in order to accept the decisions made by the director.

When the capital of the company is more than €120,000, it must be subject to regular audits. The auditors must not be related to the administrators of your company or the employees and must be university professors in economics or law or registered in one of the professional associations governing accountants or lawyers. You can designate between three and five auditors.

The cost of the notary is approximately €2,500 and registering with the *Camera di Commercio* (Chamber of Commerce) will cost around €650. This must be done within thirty days of the *statuto* and *atto costitutitivo* being signed.

ONE-MAN LIMITED LIABILITY COMPANY (*SRL* OR *SPA UNIPERSONALE*)

As a sole trader, you also have the chance to run an *Srl* or *Spa* (joint stock corporation). Under the Legislative Decree n. 6/1993, this allows you to have the same advantages as business partners in a limited liability company and gives you the possibility to distinguish your personal wealth from that of the company, thus limiting your liability. However, before you opt for this company structure, be aware that when Italian banks decide whether or not to give a loan to a *ditta individuale* they take into account the sole trader's wealth. In the *Srl* or *Spa unipersonale* there is not this guarantee. As a result, the total minimum capital must be paid as a deposit, rather than the 25 per cent that a normal *Srl* would have to pay. If this is not done, the sole trader is fully responsible for all company liabilities.

Under Italian legislation, every official document (letters, invoices, emails etc) must state that the company is *unipersonale* (sole company). In this case, How to Italy would be How to Italy Srl Unipersonale or How to Italy SpA Unipersonale.

Mario's Pearl of Wisdom

*We won't mince our words. Setting up an **Srl** is definitely the best way to protect your own assets should the company run up massive losses and you are forced to dissolve (**liquidare**) it. But there is a flip side to every coin or, as we say in Italy, **ci sono due faccie ad ogni medaglia**. With the introduction of Basel II, banks are much more stringent when it comes to evaluating the risk of lending money to a company. What does that mean in practical terms? It means that the bank will not give an **Srl** money unless it has a guarantee. So, it is important to keep in mind that if you are unwilling to risk your own money, don't expect that others do so on your behalf.*

Case study

Lin and Graham Lane moved to Umbria in 2001. They had bought a house in the region six months previously. When they decided to emigrate, they told their family and sold their house within 24 hours. They now run La Porta Verde, a successful company helping expats find their ideal property in the region.

Emma: Why did you move to Italy?

Graham: You want a list? The food, wine, coffee, ice cream, clothes, architecture, history, culture, scenery, weather and even the sports cars. Everything Italy does, it does so well. The only downside is the bureaucracy and having to deal with Italian driving. However, the high level of bureaucracy does mean that there are fewer problems with buying a house here as everything is checked and double checked so much. And the driving? Well, you get used to it!

Emma: That's definitely true. Were you aware of all the different company structures when you were setting up La Porta Verde?

Graham: Yes, they are broadly similar to the UK with **Snc**, **Srl** and **Spa**. Initially, we set up as a Dutch company registered in Holland and operating in Italy. But when we split with our Dutch partner, we became an Italian company.

Emma: Were you an **Srl** right from the start?

Graham: No, first we registered with the Chamber of Commerce as an Snc and then changed to an **Srl** a few months ago.

Emma: Why was that? Most people seem to go for the cheaper option of an Snc. What made you change your minds?

Graham: La Porta Verde has proved very successful. Becoming an Srl is just one step in the growth of the company for which we have great ambitions. It is better to be an **Srl** for tax reasons and also for credibility within the industry. Every company has to be registered with the Chamber of Commerce, too and must fall into one of many pre set categories.

Emma: Who did you get advice from?

*Graham: Our notary and our **commercialista**, Andrea Antonioni, who also writes the news column for **Italy** magazine.*

Emma: And how did you find him?

*Graham: We were introduced to our commercialista at a dinner party and, as he spoke English and also understood the tax laws in Britain, he seemed ideal. He has given us an enormous amount of help over the years. Getting our **Partita IVA** and registering with the **Camera di Commercio** through him was a breeze.*

Emma: So what advice would you give to other expats looking to set up a company in Italy?

*Graham: One, learn as much Italian as you can before you come here. Two, read good books on moving to Italy. Three, even as an individual get a good **commercialista** because the tax laws are so complicated here. Four, you are starting a new phase in your life by moving to Italy. Treat it as an adventure and expect the odd thing not to go your way*

(12)

Spa

Setting up an *Spa* (joint stock corporation) is more complicated than the company structures we have looked at but, given the investment involved, you are likely to already have considerable experience of running a business.

SHARE CAPITAL

To set up an *Spa*, the initial share capital must be at least €120,000. The shares are not all the same. They can be *nominative* (owned by name) or *al portatore* (owned by a holder) and must indicate the following:

♦ the name of the company and the registered office;
♦ the date of the memorandum and the date of the registration and the national business register where the company is registered;
♦ the nominal value or, if shares have no nominal value, the total number of shares issued and the amount of the share capital;
♦ the amount of the partial payments on shares;
♦ rights and specific obligations;
♦ (eventually) limitations in transferring shares (i.e. pre-emptive rights).

ARTICLE OF ASSOCIATION

When the *notaio* (notary) is drawing up the *statuto* (article of association), the following information must be included:

- surname, name (or name of the company), the date and the place of birth (or the date of foundation, the address (or the registered office), the nationality of the associates and the promoters, the numbers of shares related to each associate;
- the name of the company and in what town the registered office is (and possible branches);
- the activity which represents the aim of the company;
- the amount of share capital proposed and paid;
- the number of shares and their nominal value, their characteristics and the way they have been issued and the means of transaction;
- the assets given by every associate and the value estimated;
- the rules concerning how the profit has to be divided;
- the benefits possibly agreed to the promoters or foundation associates;
- the number of administrators and their powers. The *statuto* should state who can act on behalf of the company;
- the number of auditors;
- the nomination of the first administrators and auditors and, if decided, the person (or the company) responsible for the accounting control;
- an approximation of the total amount of the total costs for setting up the company (to be paid by the company itself);
- the duration of the company or, if the company has been set up for an undefined period of time, by when the company can leave the company (in any case not less than one year).

The article of association must also detail a list of the rules which explain how the company is organised and works.

SHAREHOLDERS

To set up the company all the shareholders must *sotto scrivere il capitale* (sign for the entire share capital). What this means is that all are legally obliged to pay for their part of the share capital.

As per the *Srl* (limited liability company), shareholders must deposit 25 per cent of the share capital in the bank and official proof must be shown to the *notaio* before the company is set up.

Within 30 days, the *notaio* must present the memorandum, together with the article of association, to the *Registro delle Imprese* (National Business Registry). As soon as the company is registered, it becomes a *personalità giuridica* or corporation. For every act made before this time, those who put in place the acts (i.e. the future partners), are personally liable.

An *Spa* can also be set up using a public method, although this is more complicated and involves asking the public to buy shares at a certain price. This is extremely rare for start-ups because the public cannot check the history of the company before deciding whether or not to make an investment.

INTERNAL ORGANISATION

The *Spa* has the following *organi sociali* (internal boards)

* *Assemblea ordinaria* and *Assemblea straordinaria* (the General Meeting and Extraordinary Meeting);

- *Consiglio di Amministrazione* (the Board of Directors);
- *Collegio Sindacale* (the Auditors).

The General Meeting's main tasks are to approve the balance sheet and designate the administrators and their relative compensation. The Extraordinary Meeting decides on issuing bonds, changing the memorandum, and designates the liquidators when the company has to be dissolved.

In order to stabilise the property of the shares and avoid any possible surprises when the general meeting is held, shareholders vote or when they decide to sell/buy shares, the Italian law established the *patto parasociale*. This is a list of rules that shareholders must agree to when voting or buying and selling shares. These rules are valid for five years and must then be declared. At the start of every general meeting, these *patti parasciali* must be declared.

The Board of Directors run the company.

The auditors control that the law and procedures are respected inside the company. They also, in some cases, can replace the administrators when they do not provide for some fulfilments (for example, calling the General Meeting). With the new Legislative Decree n. 6/2003 it is required that specific auditors must be designated with the aim of controlling the accounting (*Revisori contabili*). This new law has also introduced two new organisations, the so-called *Sistema Dualistico* and the *Sistema Monistico*.

The first one modifies the traditional organisation of the *Spa* with the introduction of two news bodies: the *Consiglio di Gestione* (which roughly has the same role and responsibilities as the Board of Directors) and the *Consiglio di Sorveglianza* (which replaces, in some aspects, the General Meeting).

In the *Sistema Monistico* the administration of the company and the control of it is delegated to a Board of Directors. The Board designates, internally, a body for the control of the company (composed also by auditors).

Mario's Pearl of Wisdom

Not many people start out with the idea of creating an **Spa**. Normally, they start out small, perhaps a **ditta individuale** or an **Srl**. As the business gets bigger and more successful, a lot of **imprenditori** think about opening up the business to outside investors. It is at that point that they go to a **notaio** to change the old company into its new **Spa** structure. My own personal advice would be to stay small until you feel confident with the way business is done in Italy. At that point, go for it and grow the business all you like.

13

Banking

Your business is nearly up and running. Now it is time for you to set up a bank account so that clients have somewhere to pay the money they owe you.

Italy is the birthplace of modern banking. The first institution resembling a modern bank was opened in Venice in 1135. By 1250, there were more than 80 banks and branches in the city alone. The prominent Medici family, which ruled Florence and later Italy, even had bank branches as far as away as Paris.

BANKS IN ITALY

There are three types of banks in Italy: commercial banks, cooperative banks (*banche popolari cooperative*) and cooperative credit banks (*banche di credito cooperative*). Italian banks used to be very archaic with hundreds of different banks. When Emma was a student in Bologna in 1997, she remembers having a real problem accessing her money because the *filiali* (branches) of the banks were often limited to a single province or region. Thus, when she went to visit friends in Bergamo, she had to take out enough money in advance because the *Bancomat* (cashpoint) in Bergamo wouldn't accept her cash card.

Fast-forward five years and the situation has changed enormously. There have been a number of acquisitions and mergers meaning the smaller independent banks have been swallowed up by or have merged with the giants such as Unicredit Banca, Banca Intesa and San Paolo. Consequently, the *Bancomat* has become standardised and you can withdraw cash wherever you go in Italy. It is pot luck as to whether you get cheerful, helpful bank staff or miserable ones who don't see why they should serve you before they go for their *pausa caffè* (coffee break) in the local bar. But make the most of your foreign accent when you speak Italian as it helps break the ice. Emma knows all about model boats thanks to one bank worker, has had coffee bought for her by another who wanted to make the most of practising her very bad English for five minutes, and with another who always talks about the beautiful English castles. What this means is that when the bank computer is down, she can leave a form with the bank staff detailing the list of transactions she needs carried out and get back to the office without wasting time. When Emma goes back the following week, she can skip the queues and pick up the receipts.

BANK OPENING HOURS

Banks are open from Monday to Friday, though a few banks in the larger cities are also open on Saturday mornings. They open at around 8.30am and close around 1.30pm. They open again at 2.30pm or 3pm for an hour or an hour-and-a-half.

BANK CHARGES

To say bank charges in Italy are high is an understatement. Unless you have online banking, you are charged every time you pay by cheque, every time you cash a cheque, every time you make a bank transfer and every time you receive one. Some banks will also charge you for paying with your debit card, while others will charge you if you exceed a certain number of debit card payments per month. In addition to these charges, you will pay to have your monthly statement sent to you and you will also pay a monthly running fee to the bank. Some banks have now introduced fixed all-inclusive fees at around €35 per month. Think about how much you expect to be using the bank on a monthly basis as this will impact on which bank and option you decide to go for. It is still standard practice to charge you for closing your bank account and transferring to a rival. However, one bank has now abolished its charges for transferring your account to a different bank, so it should only be a matter of time before the others follow suit.

CHOOSING YOUR BANK ACCOUNT

When you open your *conto corrente bancario* (bank account), you will need to specify you want a business account. Even though this isn't necessary if you are a *lavoratore autonomo* (self-employed worker) or have a *ditta individuale* (sole trade business), Mario strongly recommends that you open one anyway. This way, if the *Guardia di Finanza* (tax police) or the *Agenzia delle Entrate* (tax office) wants to check your account for whatever reason, you have separated your business outgoings from your personal outgoings. By law, you are required to keep your tax records for five years. Having bank account statements that match your tax records means you can easily prove your tax situation is what you say it is.

Branches of major Italian banks located in the big cities are obviously going to be better equipped to deal with the needs of expatriates than their smaller branch offices in southern Italy and the islands. Remember, though, that you are not limited to using an Italian bank. A number of foreign banks have set up in Italy and staff are normally better equipped to deal with the needs of foreign clients. But just as the smaller independent banks were bought by the major Italian banks, some foreign banks have suffered the same fate. Abbey National Bank of Italy, which was acquired by Unicredit on 31 December 2003, was one of these.

Italian banks are carefully scrutinised by Banca d'Italia, the Italian Central Bank. It safeguards the system's financial stability and promotes its efficiency. Patti Chari was set up in October 2003 to help bring transparency to Italian banking and to improve relations between banking and the business sector. All the major banks adhere to Patti Chiari. On its website www.pattichiari.it the section '*c/c a confronto*' contains an online tool to help you find the most suitable business account for your needs.

OPENING A BUSINESS BANK ACCOUNT

To open a business bank account, you will need to take the following documents to a branch office:

- passport/ID Card;
- *codice fiscale* (tax code);
- *Partita Iva* (VAT number);
- letter from the *comune* showing proof of *residenza* (if you are a sole trader and/or are *lavoratore autonomo*);
- *certificato camerale or certificato di iscrizione all'albo* (document from the *Camera di Commercio* (Chamber of Commerce) or the Italian professional association of which you are now a member).

BANK STATEMENT

The *estratto conto* (bank statement) normally gets sent to you every three months, although you can receive it monthly for an extra fee. Of course, if you have a *conto corrente online* (internet banking) then you can check your account as often as you like for free.

PAYMENT BY CHEQUE AND CLEARANCE TIMES

At the top of the cheque, you will see a space followed by the word '*li*' followed by another space. Write the town in the first gap and the date in the second gap. For example, *Milano li 28/06/06*. British '7's often resemble the Italian number 1, so make sure you cross the downstroke of the 7 to avoid confusion. When writing the number in words, do not use capitals and do not leave spaces. For example, €145 would be written as *centoquarantacinqueeuro* and not *cento quaranta cinque euro*.

If your customers are small firms, don't expect to be paid with bank transfers. You will usually be given a cheque. You will not be able to pay the cheque in unless you have signed it on the back under the word *girate* (endorsed). Check whether or not words *non-trasferibile* are written on the front of the cheque. If not, you might want to add them because open cheques can be endorsed by a third person who can then pay them into their own bank account.

Once cheques have been paid in, the money will be credited to your account instantly, but you will not be able to withdraw that money until the cheque has cleared. This can take anywhere from two to nine working days depending on whether it is drawn on the same bank or a different bank. These days are known as *giorni banca* in Italian.

BOUNCED CHEQUES

Make sure you always have enough money in your bank account or overdraft because *assegni a vuoto* (bounced cheques) are illegal in Italy and you can be prosecuted.

DEBIT AND CREDIT CARDS

On opening your bank account, you can decide what type of card you want: an ATM (*Bancomat*), debit or credit card (*carta di debito/carta di credito*). You can choose whether to have a separate debit and credit card or one that doubles up as both. This is known as a *Carta Sì*. A credit card will cost you anywhere between €35 and €110 per year depending on the bank and the type of card you choose.

You can withdraw up to €500 per day from a *Bancomat*. If you are dealing with micro firms in Italy, you may find yourself using cash a lot as they are unlikely to accept your debit and credit cards.

OVERDRAFTS

When you open your bank account, ask the bank manager for a *conto scoperto* (overdraft) as these aren't given automatically. This will allow you to be covered if you find your clients haven't paid you on time and you are reliant on that income to pay your tax bill.

In Italy, the *scoperto di conto corrente* is always agreed for a *tempo indeterminato* (non-fixed period of time). Before you start thinking that this is one positive aspect of the Italian banking system, be aware that the bank can ask you to repay the overdraft at any time. You will have *quindici giorni* (a fortnight) in which to do so.

BILL OF EXCHANGE

If your business is growing, your agreed business overdraft may not be enough to cover your financial needs. If your clients pay with a *cambiale* (Bill of Exchange – a written order by one person to pay another a specific sum on a specific date sometime in the future), you can ask your bank for a *sconto di portafoglio*. In this case, the bank will loan you the amount of money you will receive from your clients as specified in the Bill of Exchange. Of course, for this privilege you will have to pay interest to the bank. Each bank has their own rate, so ask your bank manager about this.

INVOICE ANTICIPATION

If your customers pay by bank transfer, the bank will loan you money on production of the invoices you have issued and for which you are awaiting payment. This contract is called the *anticipo su fatture* (invoice anticipation) and works in a similar way to the *sconto di portafoglio*. However, because the bank does not have a guarantee that your clients will pay, it will only lend you part of the money – normally around 80 per cent of the total. It is often tricky to obtain and will often depend on your relationship with the bank and your past success with getting invoices paid.

Another common way to receive money in advance is factoring. With this operation, a company gives its commercial credits to a bank (factor) which receives the payment from the debtor.

ASKING FOR A LOAN

All banks which are part of the Patti Chiari evaluate your request by taking into account several different factors:

- *Your company and the sector it operates in.* The bank will want to see evidence of your current financial situation, market forecasts for your industrial sector, information on your products/services, your position in the market and your competitors.
- *The reasons for the loan.* The bank will want to know your company's financial needs.
- *Your company's capacity to pay back the loan.* An in-depth analysis by the bank will allow it to see whether or not you have the right economic and financial conditions to succeed in the project requiring finance and your likelihood of paying back the loan without defaulting.
- *The capital invested by you and/or your business partners.* The bank will take into account the amount of money you and/or your business partners have invested in your company as a sign of how much you believe in your proposal.

Opening your bank account really isn't difficult at all, but do remember to take all your personal and business documents with you. We also suggest that you make a copy of your business plan and take that along, too, so that the bank manager has a better idea of what your business is about. It will help prove that you are serious about your business – which, you are, of course.

Mario's Pearl of Wisdom

Expats who live in the same Italian town as you are a valuable resource, so make the most of them. Ask them if they would mind telling you who they bank with and the level of customer service they receive as you are always better off opening your account at a bank already used to dealing with foreigners and their requests on a day-to-day basis. The bank staff are far more likely to understand any obstacles you face and will know ways to overcome these. If you live in a small Italian town which doesn't have any expats, then make sure you ask the bank manager whether the branch has dealt with expats in the past. Explain your concerns. If the bank manager takes the time to listen to you and doesn't mind your haltering Italian, you're onto a winner. If not, it's time to move on to the next bank to see what they say.

14

Setting up the office

If you haven't already done so, the next challenge is deciding where in Italy you will be operating from and whether you will need business premises or are able to work from home.

If you have fallen in love with a gorgeous little Italian village during your summer holiday and have decided to turn your summer holiday into all-year-round reality, or you are moving to the home town of your Italian partner, think twice, think thrice and think some more.

Of course, there are some people like Dave Marsh who lives in the mountains of Lunigiana in northern Tuscany. He vowed never to leave after a holiday in the area and, as you read in Chapter 3: Finding the idea, has now set up Tuscan Moto Tours there. Other people haven't been so lucky though. We know of one British expat who moved to her husband's village in southern Italy and subsequently set up a corporate relocation company. The problem was that she often had to get to meetings in Rome and Naples, but it took her more than 40 minutes to reach the nearest train station. And Simon Curtis, who set up the medical centre for expats in Tuscany, originally moved to Le Marche, but realised he wasn't going to find clients there.

Ask yourself the following questions:

- What is public transport like?
- Will I find clients in the area I want to live in?
- How important is it for me to have expats or Italian professionals around me to network, both formally and informally, with?
- Does broadband internet access reach the Italian town or village I wish to live in?

PUBLIC TRANSPORT

The standard of *i mezzi pubblici* (public transport) in Italy depends on where you live in the country and varies widely between the north and south, the major cities and the provinces. If you do end up living in a rural area and you expect to do a fair bit of travelling, having your own car are essential.

BUSES, TRAMS AND THE METRO

Even though there is no national bus company, Italy boasts more buses than any other European country. Services in the provinces can be a nightmare, but within cities are surprisingly efficient and cheap.

Rail travel

The FS, or Ferrovia dello Stato, is the state railway. Trains run frequently and prices depend on whether you catch *locale*, *diretto*, *espresso*, *intercity*, *Eurocity* or *Eurostar trains*. The former stop in every station and are the cheapest trains while the latter are high-speed trains stopping at only the major stations. The ES, which is the equivalent of France's TGV, runs between Milan and Rome and only stops in Bologna and Florence.

The FS has now put its train timetable online at www.trenitalia.it. If your business requires you to travel a lot in Italy and you are flexible as to where you will move, it is worth playing around with the Trenitalia site, typing in potential towns and destinations to find out the train frequency. Take it from us, train travel in Sardinia is particularly bad. It takes four hours to get from north to south and coastal towns (bar Alghero, Cagliari and Olbia) aren't served by train.

AIR TRAVEL

If you will be travelling back and forwards between Italy and other European or international destinations, then make sure you are also located near an airport. The main ones are shown below.

Main Italian airports

Airport	City (Km)	Telephone number
Fertilia	Alghero (13)	070 6010
Falconara	Ancona (18)	071 2075892
Palese	Bari (12)	080 5243263
Orio al Serio	Bergamo (5)	035 224425
G. Marconi	Bologna (6)	051 212333
Papola Casale	Brindisi (6)	0831 529091
Elmas	Cagliari (7)	070 60108
Fontanarossa	Catania (7)	095 252333
Levaldigi	Cuneo (21)	0172 374374
Peretola	Florence (4)	055 27888
Cristoforo Colombo	Genoa (7)	010 54938
S. Eufemia	Lamezia Terme (40)	0968 53166
Lampedusa	Lampedusa (1)	0922 970299
Linate	Milan (10)	02 26851
Malpensa 2000	Milan (46)	02 74852200
Capodichino	Naples (7)	081 5425333

▶

Airport	City (Km)	Telephone number
Costa Smeralda	Olbia (6)	0789 52600
Punta Raisi	Palermo (32)	091 6019333
Pantelleria	Pantelleria (4)	0923 911078
Natale Palli-	Parma (3)	0521 230063
Baganzola Parma		
S. Egidio	Perugia (5)	075 61646
Pasquale Liberi	Pescara (6)	085 4213022
Gallileo Gallilei	Pisa (2)	050 501570
Tito Minniti	Reggio Calabria (5)	0965 331444
Miramare	Rimini (6.5)	0544 33156
Leonardo Da Vinci	Rome (35)	06 65645
(Fiumicino)		
Ciampino	Rome (25)	06 65641
Città di Torino	Turin (18)	011 57698
Birigi-Aereostazione Sen.	Trapani (16)	0923 873636
Vincenzo Florio		
Loc. S. Giuseppe	Treviso (4)	041 5216333
Ronchi dei Legionari	Trieste (31.5)	040 631485
Marco Polo Tessera	Venice (13)	041 5216333
Villafranca Veronese	Verona (12)	045 8035700

FINDING THE IDEAL BUSINESS PREMISES

Most property in Italy is rented out through word-of-mouth to avoid paying the *provvigione* (estate agents' fees) and, unless you are familiar with the area and have a wide circle of contacts, you might encounter problems finding out what property is available.

When buying or renting through an *agenzia immobiliare* (estate agent), you will have to pay a *provvigione* (commission). Estate agents normally ask for 10 per cent of the annual rent and four per cent of the purchase price. Most estate agents are local, but there are some nationwide chains. These include Gabetti (www.gabetti.it), Grimaldi (www.grimaldi.net), Professione Casa (www.professionecasa.it), Solo Affitti (www.soloaffitti.it), Tecnocasa (www.tecnocasa.it), Tempocasa (www.tempocasa.com) and Toscano (www.gruppotoscano.it). The stereotypical view Italians have of foreigners is that they are all rich. While this is clearly not the case, Italian property owners believe they can justifiably hike up the prices when renting or selling to expatriates. To avoid this, make sure you are accompanied on potential viewing trips with an Italian who knows what you are looking for and who can negotiate with the estate agent or property owner on your behalf. There are lots of relocation agencies in Italy which deal specifically with expatriate relocation and charge around €500 per day. You may be on a tight budget, but if you do not speak good Italian or are unfamiliar with the process of Italian real estate market and its protocol, it is an initial outlay you should consider making. Relocation consultants are highly experienced in negotiating with estate agents and will have good relationships with them.

Rental contracts

The terms and conditions of a *contratto di locazione* (rental contract) varies depending on whether it is a domestic or company lease. A domestic lease runs for a four-year period and a business lease for six years, unless you are renting it as a hotel structure whereby it becomes nine years. As a rule of thumb, these will not have opt out clauses so make sure you negotiate one. Check the small print carefully, and if your command of Italian is not good enough to understand the contract, don't wing it. Have it translated professionally to ensure you know what you are putting your signature to or ask a relocation agency to negotiate the lease on your behalf. Landlords are often reluctant to *registrare* (register) the contract in order to avoid paying taxes. Before having the contract drawn up, double check that the landlord or estate agent will be registering it otherwise you will be unable to write off this expense. We hate to say it, but some Italian landlords (as with any nationality, of course) are unscrupulous and are just waiting to catch you out.

Home office verses business premises

Setting up the office is, thankfully, pretty straightforward as the process you go through is much the same as any other country. Because Mario has a 'roll-up-the-shirt-sleeves-and-get-stuck-in' approach, he often works with clients at their company premises. As for Emma, she tends to conduct most of the How to Italy consultations by phone or email, so for us it was a waste of money renting office space. We much prefer working from home with a commute of 15 seconds (yes, we've timed it) from the bedroom to the office.

On the occasions that Emma does meet clients face-to-face, she chooses the slick T-Hotel in Cagliari aimed at business people. Alternatively, if clients are up for it, she arranges to see them in a beach café overlooking the sea.

Of course, if you plan on hiring employees from the outset or your new business adventure is a restaurant, school or something requiring space, you will obviously need to source premises.

Renting premises

There are few office blocks in Italy. Most offices are housed in a standard *appartamento* in a *palazzo*. Literally meaning 'palace' it is the Italian term for a block of flats. As such, your office will also resemble an apartment. The bathroom will, literally, have a bath or shower in it. However, the cost of renting a flat for *uso commerciale* will be a lot higher compared to renting a similar property for living in. Before signing on the dotted line, here are some things to check:

- *Noise levels*: Italians are like other southern Europeans and do everything with gusto. In an apartment block, walls are thin so expect to share everything with your neighbours. When Emma taught English, her lessons were punctuated by the television of the family above. And she knew when she was missing something funny, because she and her students could hear the family's raucous laughter.
- *Ease of parking*: Italians may be health fanatics but they don't like walking so make sure your premises are easily accessible by public transport or have free parking spaces near by. We know of one Italian company that went belly up because customers were reluctant to leave their car more than 100 metres from the office.

Home office

Working from home does seem to offer some good tax breaks – but only if you fall into certain categories. If you are a *lavoratore autonomo* and don't have a *studio* (office) in the same *comune* (town) you can write off quite a few of your expenses. All office equipment is 100 per cent deductible while telephone, electricity, gas and water bills are 50 per cent deductible because they are shared between business and home use. If you are not a home owner, your rent qualifies as a 50 per cent deduction, no matter what size your office. Those who have mortgages are not quite so lucky as there is no tax relief.

If you have a *ditta individuale* and, for whatever reason, you work from home, your rental contract will need to be in your business name. Calculate the number of *metri quadri* (square metres) your home office takes up and deduct it on a pro rata scale from the rent. Housing expenses can also be deducted at the same pro rata scale although, to avoid any disputes with the authorities, we advise you to install a separate *contatore* (meter) for the *luce* (electricity). You will also need to install two telephone lines – a business line (with business rates) and a private line with domestic rates.

Renting an office/business premises

As this is your official office or business premises, 100 per cent of the costs are deductible. When choosing your office location, remember that Italians place great importance on the '*bella figura*'. To Italians, the fact that you have a city centre office means you are successful at what you do and, therefore, you will automatically be treated with more respect (along with the office, your car should be a spotless Alfa Romeo, Audi, Mercedes or BMW).

Outsourced offices and meeting space

If you do not need a permanent office, consider using an out-sourced office. The advantage of such an arrangement is that you can upsize or downsize as and when you need to and do not have to take out insurance or worry about the health and safety implications. Outsourced offices also have *sale riunioni* (meeting rooms) for hire, so this is ideal if your home office or rented studio isn't suitable for meeting clients or colleagues in. Companies offering these services also provide *uffici virtuali* (virtual offices) with secretaries which are ideal if you do not have the budget to take on a secretary initially.

The demand for outsourced offices in Italy is slowly increasing. Below are the names of several companies providing these services throughout the country:

- Regus

  www.regus.it

  Part of the worldwide chain, Regus has nine designated business centres in Italy, five of which are in Milan and four in Rome. In addition to office space, meeting rooms and virtual offices, Regus also offers *mini cabine ufficio* (office cubicles) for professionals who only need a *scrivania* (workdesk).
- Business Center

  www.businesscenter.it

  Based in Padua, the Business Center offers a variety of services from office space through to virtual secretaries who will answer phone calls in your company name. The Business Center has English speaking staff.
- Pick Center

  www.pickcenter.com

  Pick Center has four business centres in Rome, both in the city centre and the outlying areas. The centres are open 24 hours and offer a complete range of services. The offices in the business centre share a reception area, waiting room and breakfast bar where visitors will be greeted by Pick Center staff.

◆ Michelangelo Business Center

www.mbcenter.it

The MB Center has centres in Modena and in Turate, located just off the A9 motorway between Milan and Como. In addition to the standard range of services, the MB Center also has showrooms for hire.

◆ The Italy Center

www.italycenter.it

The Italy Center is located in Naples and has single and double offices, meeting rooms, conference facilities and a call centre which you can use on both a short-term and long-term basis.

Connecting to utilities

Enel (www.enel.it) and Acea Spa (www.aceaspa.it) supply Italy's electricity, while connection to the waterboard is a local affair. In the north, the service is often efficient whereas in some small towns in southern Italy you have no way of reading your own water meter and you might not even receive a bill for five years. Gas will either be supplied via the mains or you might have to buy bottled gas. It depends where in the country you live. If you are not sure, ask the *agente immobiliare* through whom you found your property.

Case study

Sally Jones is a graphic designer and lived in rural Sardinia until February 2006 before moving back to the UK for family reasons. She had a home office in her four-bedroomed house she shared with her husband.

Emma: Wow, working from home in a house surrounded by thousand-year-old olive groves and sea views sounds like paradise. Was it?

Sally: Yes, it was. It was lovely being able to wake up and have breakfast on a sun drenched patio, to work under the shade of the olive trees during the intense summer heat and not to have to spend hours stuck in Newcastle traffic to get back home for dinner.

Emma: Ah, I was right. Definitely paradise.

Sally: Yes, you're right. In terms of scenery, I couldn't have wished for anything better. I used to visit my husband, then my boyfriend, and every time it was the perfect antidote to the stresses of New York. I knew I wanted to live here but ...

Emma: But?

Sally: But I was only viewing the place through the eyes of a tourist. I was so enamoured with the laidback lifestyle that I hadn't fully considered the implications of living here. I thought everything would carry on in the same idyllic way as before but I was wrong.

Emma: Why was that exactly?

Sally: Being in a remote area here just isn't the same as being in a remote area in the UK. In the UK, villages have a wealth of professionals and downshifters who have decided to opt for a better work-life balance. My brother lives in a small Dorset village. There is a national magazine editor, a publisher, an artist, a surveyor, an architect, a well-known photographer, a surgeon and a pilot among others.

Emma: I see.

▶

Sally: Here, it's a much different story. Sardinian villages are very traditional and very old-fashioned. Women tend to stay at home and look after the children and the men are labourers, carrying on the family trade. Working from home meant I was alone all day so there were days when I longed to share a quick after-work drink with another professional. Sadly, there just weren't any around.

Emma: Yes, I'm familiar with that myself and I know it's a similar story for other expats who don't live in the major towns or expat areas in Italy. So how did you combat this situation?

Sally: I joined a couple of internet networking associations and made sure I met up on a monthly basis. It certainly helped but people didn't really take my working from home seriously because it's not something Italians tend to do.

Emma: But isolation apart, what other problems did you have?

Sally: Not having broadband connection because we were considered too remote from the main exchange. That was a real pain because when I was surfing the net, clients couldn't phone me. With dial-up, it also meant I lost out on the benefits of Skype. It just wouldn't have been worth it without having the flat rate of broadband.

Emma: So if you were moving to Italy all over again with the intention of setting up a home business what would you do?

Sally: That's a no-brainer! I'd rent a place in an area I liked for a three to six month period with the aim of working to see how feasible my dream actually was. I'd also check broadband arrived in the town I was looking to live in as it's an essential for me.

TELEPHONE

The Italian telephone giant Telecom Italia was privatised in 1997 and this has led to a liberalisation of the market. Due to other companies muscling in on Telecom's former monopoly, price wars have broken out. In 2005 and 2006, different companies were constantly slashing their prices to make them more competitive.

In the early 1990s, the Italian phone infrastructure underwent extensive modernisation and there are now fibre-optic cables and high speed lines in most cities. Of course, as tends to happen everywhere, most rural areas have been left on old analogue exchanges.

There are six main phone companies in Italy: Telecom Italia, Fastweb, Infostrada, Tele2, Tiscali and Energit as shown below. Make sure you check whether or not the phone company you are interested in provides ADSL (broadband) and phone services in your area as the coverage varies between them.

Given that a price war is now happening, we have not included pricing details as these are constantly changing.

- Telecom Italia
  www.187.it (private users) www.191.it (business users)
- Fastweb
  www.fastweb.it
- Tele2
  www.tele2.it
- Infostrada
  http://www.infostrada.it

- Tiscali
  www.tiscali.it
- Energit
  www.energit.it

Wi-fi

Italians were wary of the internet when it first invaded the country, but they are gradually getting used to it. Even so, the country still lags behind other European states in the take up of internet *senza fili* (wireless). Northern Italy has fairly good coverage, but it is abysmally poor in the south and the islands. www.jiwire.com gives you a list of all the public WI-FI access points in Italy.

Mobile phones

The four main mobile phone operators in Italy are Tim (the mobile phone subsidiary of Telecom Italia)(www.tim.it), Vodafone (www.vodafone.it), Tre (www.tre.it) and Wind (www.wind.it). Tre specialises in UMTS and video phones, Wind usually has the cheapest deals but Tim and Vodafone undoubtedly offer the best coverage throughout Italy.

Choosing your mobile phone company and choosing tariffs
We haven't included any information here on tariff plans as these are constantly changing as Tim and Vodafone try to outdo one another. Each company often offers huge incentives (up to €500 of free calls) if you swap companies and doing this can be advantageous. If you find a phone and offer you like with one of the companies, sign up to the other one and then accept the financial incentive to swap. It's a cheap trick but it works.

Voice over Internet Protocol (VoIP)

In recent years, a number of firms offering low-cost telephony via the internet have emerged which means you can run your new company from Italy, but still have a London, New York, Sydney or Toronto (or anywhere else you choose) telephone number. The cost is a fraction of a traditional phone line. These calls are directed to a special IP phone, phone adaptor for use with normal phones or a piece of VoIP software for any computer connected to any broadband internet connection anywhere in the world. The result is that you can offer the reassurance and convenience of a local presence at a very reasonable cost without even being in that country.

Sam Morgan runs WiredEyes, an Anglo-Italian internet consultancy firm in Cagliari. Fed up with the high cost of living in London, he moved to Sardinia in 2004, but his customers can still contact him on a London number. He says: modification 'using VoIP allows us to have a prestigious UK 0207 (central London) number as well as a Milan, Rome and even a local Cagliari number all routed over the internet to our premises here in Cagliari. One of the great things is that if we move, our numbers simply move with us. If we go to visit the UK we simply take our IP phone and plug it into any broadband internet connection and instantly our calls are received where we are. Most of our numbers are either free, which means no line rental, or very cheap (£1 per month). We pay less than a third of what we used to for calls to normal phones and mobiles, and it is free to many other VoIP phone lines, so the cost saving can be excellent.' Most VoIP providers give you voicemail and voicemail email alerts, caller ID, call hold and music on hold, 3-way calling and call divert. With some VoIP providers you also get fax over IP, virtual PBXs and web calling which you wouldn't otherwise be able to afford on a tight start-up budget.

- VoIPFone
  www.voipfone.co.uk
- Skypho
  www.skypho.net
- Skype
  www.skype.com
- Free Conference Call
  http://freeconferencecall.com/gizmo

PRIVACY LAWS

The Italian Data Protection Act, which came into force on 30 June 2003, stipulates how company documents relating to personal data, criminal records and sensitive matters must be kept and dealt with. Under the 2003 Act, each company and self-employed person must have a *documento programmatico della sicurezza* (security document). This document should specify that all *informazioni sensibili* (sensitive information) is kept in a locked drawer or cupboard and that it can only be accessed by those authorised to do so, and that each computer user should have a password to avoid other people accessing their files.

As the *titolare* (owner of the business), you need to ensure this document is available at all times in the workplace. If checks are made, you will be asked to prove that what is stated in the document is also practised. The company should have a designated *responsabile del trattamento dati* (the person in charge of data protection) and a *responsabile della manutenzione strumenti elettronici* (the person in charge of maintaining all electrical systems in the workplace) to protect against computer viruses and to ensure that backups are made on a regular basis. The *incaricati al trattamento* are employees you have appointed to follow the procedures related to the data protection. At all times, you must keep the employee informed of what you are using their personal information for.

Mario's Pearl of Wisdom

When you have chosen who you want to provide your telephony, mobile and internet services (and you don't have to have the same company for each), you will need your **codice fiscale** (tax code) and **Partita Iva** (VAT code) to hand before you arrange your contract over the phone. Without these two tax codes, you won't be able to complete the contract. The name on your **codice fiscale** will be the same as your passport, so you must state your full name. Also, if you come from England, Wales, or Scotland, state your country as Gran Bretagna and not Regno Unito, Inghilterra, Galles or Scozia, otherwise it will come up void.

Don't expect to be connected to the utilities instantly. When you are used to a far more efficient way of doing things, the waiting around is likely to test your patience.

With the office now set up and the hard work out of the way, the *sogno sta diventando realtà* – your dream is turning into reality.

15

Direct taxes

You may have come a long way since the start of this book and you've managed to get to grips with the very tricky situation concerning Italian taxation, but it's not time to sit back and chill out with a bowl of spaghetti and glass of locally made red wine just yet. First you have to get to grips with taxation.

TAX EVASION

Just as Italy is the land of entrepreneurs, it is also the land of tax evaders. When you are not used to the way Italians do business, this widescale practice may sound shocking, but believe us when we say that, after a while, it just becomes a part of everyday life.

Tax evasion is not a new phenomenon. As early as the sixteenth century, Italians were plotting ways to avoid being taxed. Legend has it that landowners built Trulli, the famous conical shaped dwellings in Puglia, without the use of mortar so that they could be pulled down when the tax man came. Because they weren't built using mortar, they couldn't be classified as housing and therefore the count could not levy any tax.

More recently, Silvio Berlusconi has come under investigation for money laundering, tax evasion and bribing the *Guardia di Finanza* (tax police). At the time of writing, the former Italian prime minister was being investigated for an alleged scam which it's claimed has allowed him to evade more than €60 million in taxes.

UNDERSTANDING TAXES

Paying taxes in Italy is not a straightforward affair. Taxes change on an almost yearly basis and the onus is on you to find out about them. If your Italian is good, the best way to keep up-to-date with the latest legislation and planned amendments is by reading the country's national financial newspaper *Il Sole 24 Ore*. It's not as weighty as the UK's *Financial Times* or America's *Wall Street Journal*, but it does the job. Alternatively, get friendly with the manager of the your local business bookshop and ask to be informed every time new titles relating to taxes arrive. Since good personal relationships are still key to doing business in Italy, you should find the manager readily agreeing.

If you are not fluent in Italian or don't fancy spending hours wading through the papers and books with the aid of a huge bilingual dictionary, make sure that your *commercialista* (accountant) doesn't just deal with your tax returns, but is proactive in informing you about the different taxes and what you need to pay. After all, there's nothing worse than being landed with a hefty tax bill when you don't have the money to pay it.

TYPES OF TAXES

In Italy, the tax year runs from 1 January to 31 December. Taxes change every few years so it can be difficult keeping abreast of the latest regulations. Currently, there are three main taxes affecting *professionisti*, sole traders, partnerships and corporations: IRE, IRES and IRAP. A company or individual will either incur IRE and IRAP taxes or IRES and IRAP, but not all three.

IRE (*Imposta sui redditi*) is the Italian form of income tax on individuals and replaced IRPEF on 1 January 2005. Every person resident in Italy is liable for income tax on their worldwide aggregate income and every non-resident on their income earned on Italian soil. IRE is calculated on a progressive scale and varies between 23 and 43 per cent.

IRES replaced IRPEG as the corporate income tax on 1 January 2004. Corporations are taxed at a rate of 33 per cent on their net profit or loss in the tax year. Losses may be carried forward for five years. Taxable income includes business profits, income from land and buildings, non-operating profits, capital gains from the disposal of assets (including real estate) and income earned abroad.

IRAP came into force on 1 January 1998 and replaced ILOR and other taxes. Unlike IRE and IRES, IRAP does not apply to income but to the net value of goods and services. It is paid to the *Regione* (local regional government). Any company or individual with a business activity (*lavoratore autonomo*, sole trader, partnerships and corporations) must pay IRAP. The tax rate is currently 4.25 per cent.

IRE

In Figure 15.1 below you can find the rates valid as of 1 January 2005.

Figure 15.1   IRE

| INCOME | | |
From	To	Taxation
€–	€26,000.00	23%
€26,000.00	€33,500.00	33%
€33,500.00	€100,000.00	39%
€100,000.00		43%

In practice the following table (Figure 15.2) calculates the taxation for income from €20,000 to €100,000.

Figure 15.2

Amount	Taxation	Average rate
€20,000.00	€4,600.00	23%
€25,000.00	€5,750.00	23%
€30,000.00	€7,300.00	24%
€35,000.00	€9,040.00	26%
€40,000.00	€10,990.00	27%
€45,000.00	€12,940.00	29%
€50,000.00	€14,890.00	30%
€55,000.00	€16,840.00	31%
€60,000.00	€18,790.00	31%
€65,000.00	€20,740.00	32%
€70,000.00	€22,690.00	32%
€75,000.00	€24,640.00	33%
€80,000.00	€26,590.00	33%
€85,000.00	€28,540.00	34%
€90,000.00	€30,490.00	34%
€95,000.00	€32,440.00	34%
€100,000.00	€34,390.00	34%

In Italy, you may earn up to €3,000 without paying tax so this threshold must be considered when taking into account your taxes. Be aware that the social security contributions are deductible from the income. As we saw in Chapter 8: Lavoratore autonomo, you must pay 18.2 per cent INPS for an income up to €39,297, and 19.2 per cent if your income is above this. Thus, if you earn €50,000 per year but deduct the social security contributions at a rate of 19.2 per cent, you will end up with a different taxable amount, as shown in Figure 15.3.

Figure 15.3

Income of the year	€50,000.00
Social securities paid	€9,600.00
Net taxable amount	€40,400.00
Taxation	€11,146.00

Addizionale IRE

If you are resident in Italy, you will also have to pay the *Addizionale IRE* (regional IRE surtax). The rate is fixed by each Italian region and varies between 0.9 per cent and 1.6 per cent.

The IRE applies to the following income:

1. income generated from land and buildings which are located in Italy;
2. income generated from salary as employee (*lavoro dipendente*);
3. income generated from professional activities (*lavoro autonomo*);
4. income generated from capital;
5. income generated from business (*lavoro d'impresa*);
6. other income (*redditi diversi*).

1. Income generated from land and buildings

If you buy a house in Italy as your first home the property will not incur IRE taxes. This happens only when it is a second home or you are renting the house to derive an income from it.

The income generated from land and buildings is calculated on the *rendita catastale* (national rent income) which is a nominal value from the *catasto* (land registry). To find out the *rendita catastale* you need to multiply the *consistenza* (number of bedrooms and living rooms) of your property by the *tariffa d'estimo* (the amount fixed by the *catasto* that takes into account the *zona censuaria* (location within the town) and official category of property).

The different property categories are shown below in Figure 15.4.

Figure 15.4

	Property type	
Group A		
A/1	*Abitazioni di tipo signorile*	Refined
A/2	*Abitazioni di tipo civile*	Civilian
A/3	*Abitazioni di tipo economico*	Economical
A/4	*Abitazioni di tipo popolare*	Working class/council housing
A/5	*Abitazioni di tipo ultrapopolare*	Council houses (block of flats)
A/6	*Abitazioni di tipo rurale*	Home in rural area
A/7	*Abitazioni in villini*	Small detached house
A/8	*Abitazioni in ville*	Detached house
A/9	*Castelli, palazzi di eminenti pregi artistici e storici*	Castles or listed buildings
A/10	*Uffici e studi privati*	Private offices and studios
A/11	*Abitazioni ed alloggi tipici dei luoghi*	Typical housing of the region

▶

Figure 15.4 *continued*

	Property type	
Group B	*Unità immobiliare per uso*	Accomodation units
	alloggi collettivi	for groups of people
Not considered		
Group C	*Unità immobiliari a destinazione*	Property for
	ordinaria commerciale varia	commercial use
C/1	*Negozi e botteghe*	Shops
C/2	*Magazzini e locali di deposito*	Warehouses
C/3	*Laboratori per altri mestieri*	Laboratories
C/4	*Fabbricati e locali per esercizi sportivi*	Sporting venues
C/5	*Stabilimenti balneari di acque curative*	Therapeutic spas
C/6	*Stalle, scuderie, rimesse, autorimesse*	Barns, depots, garages, stables etc.
C/7	*Tettoie chiuse o aperte*	Open and closed shelters

Practical example

A simple example to understand how it works. To calculate the *tariffa d'estimo* you need to find out the zone of the city your house is located in. Imagine you have a property in the second zone of your town. This property is a standard, no-frills apartment block and is classed as civilian housing (A/2). The *consistenza vani* is five rooms. Assuming the *tariffa d'estimo* for this house is €220,000, the *rendita catastale* is:

$220 \times 5 = €1,100$. This is the taxable amount for this property on an annual basis.

Let's say you rent the house for €500 per month giving you an annual income of €6,000. For this type of income, the taxable amount would be €6,000.

However, let's suppose that in the first year of business, you have a hard time finding tenants and the property lies empty. Even though you have not made any money, you still have to pay taxes. In this worst case scenario, you will not be liable for the full €6,000 but the *rendita catastale* as seen in the calculations above.

In the past, most landlords in Italy avoided paying taxes by not declaring their rental income. But the Italian government amended the law in 2005, making it much more stringent. Now, if the tax office has reason to believe that the rent has not been legally declared, it presumes that the houseowner has been renting out the property for four years prior to the current year (most house rental contracts are signed for a four-year tenancy). This means that the property owner must cough up five years' worth of taxes in one go, along with a hefty fine.

2. Income generated from salary as an employee

If you plan to take on staff, your *consulente del lavoro* (consultant on employment issues) will ensure taxes are deducted at source, along with social security payments.

As an employer in Italy, you will are obliged to do the following:

- keep the *libro matricola* (list of all employees) and a *libro paga* (list of the salaries given to employees);
- pay all taxes and social security contributions incurred by each employee no later than the 16th of each month;
- give employees their copy of the CUD (*certificazione unica per i dipendenti*), which is a statement of their annual salary for the tax year and the taxes you have paid on their behalf. This must be done by 15 March every year;

- declare the total amount of salaries and other relevant costs
  paid out each year.

For those people whose work is carried out in Italy, the taxation is
made using the table of IRE seen on page 167 (Figure 15.1). For
those whose work is not carried out in Italy for more than 183
non-consecutive days per year, then the taxation is calculated
using the *Decreto del Ministro del lavoro* which gives a 'conven-
tional' salary to be taxed. In other words, the Government decides
what is the salary to declare in the tax return.

Form 730
Unless your employees have another form of income in addition
to the salary that you give them (for example, declared revenue
from a rented property), they do not have to make a tax declaration to the tax authorities as you and your *consulente del lavoro*
will already have deducted all contributions at source.

Nevertheless, at some time or another, your employees may come
to you asking for help with the Modello 730 or the Modello
Unico which they can use to help reduce the amount of taxes they
have to pay.

In the past, this form could only be filled in by the Caf (*Centro di
Assistenza Fiscale* – Fiscal Assistance Centre), the government
agency which deals specifically with deductible costs. But as of
2006, accountants are also allowed to do this work. The Italian
law identifies two different types of costs: those which are *oneri
deducibili* and deductible from the total income to reduce taxation, and those which are deductible from the total amount of

taxes due. Social security payments and costs relating to your first home fall into the former category, while the latter include medical expenses (blood tests, costs for opticians, the health tariff, the cost for glasses, etc.) which are deductible only for 19 per cent of the total cost, the school fees (even state schools in Italy have a minimum fee to pay) and funeral expenses.

When an employee makes such a claim using the Modello 730, the onus is on you, as the employer, to ensure the reimbursement appears on the payslip within a couple of months. Clearly, your *consulente del lavoro* will do this for you.

The modello 730 is as shown as Figure 15.5 below.

Figure 15.5

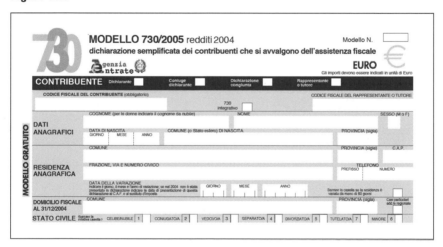

The modello Unico (the front page is shown in Figure 15.6) is the standard form to use in all the other cases.

Figure 15.6

*3. Income generated from professional activities (*lavoro autonomo*)*

As we've stated before, *lavoro autonomo* is work carried out on a regular basis which is independent (i.e. the professional has got his/her own organisation) and not related to commercial activities (i.e. the most important part is represented by the work and not by the capital).

If you are a *lavoratore autonomo*, there are two types of tax regimes depending on the amount of income you earn. The *regime forfetario* (flat regime or flat-rate regime) is rare and only applicable for those whose annual income does not exceed €10,329.14. Taxes are calculated by applying a percentage of 78 per cent to the total income and applying the relevant tax band as shown in Figure 15.1 at the beginning of this chapter.

The *regime analitico* (analytical regime) is far more common and is based on the difference between the total income and the expenses. While all the money coming from the activity is considered taxable income, not all expenses can be completely deducted. Employee salaries, telephone, power, water, interest, books and insurance can be written off at a rate of 100 per cent (see Chapter 14: Setting up the office for more detail); plane and ferry tickets, mobile phones and the costs of attending conferences at 50 per cent; company cars up to a capped limit of €18,075 at 50 per cent; and restaurants and hotels at 2 per cent of the total income.

Just as there are two types of tax regimes, there are also two types of accounting regimes: *contabilità ordinaria* (ordinary accountability) and *contabilità semplificata* (simplified accountability). The latter is the most common regime for self-employed people and is straightforward: you (along with your *commercialista* (accountant)) only need to keep the *Iva registers* (purchase book and the register of sales) and the *registro di incassi* (collections). Make sure you keep every single receipt and invoice you deem relevant. Your *commercialista* will go through these with you.

When you issue an invoice as a *lavoratore autonomo*, your invoice must show the *ritenuta d'acconto* (withdrawal tax) of 20 per cent. The withdrawal tax is not a tax, but rather an anticipation of the taxes that you will have pay in June for the previous year. The amount is deducted by the client who is obliged to pay this tax by the following month using the F24 form. This is covered in more detail in Chapter 16.

Figure 15.7 shows an example of an invoice.

Figure 15.7

DESCRIPTION	EXPENSES	PAYMENT
Dott. Mario Rossi		CB&PARTNERS SERVIZI ALL'IMPRESA businessadvisors
Date		Spett. le
Invoice, n		
Check up of the company		1.000,00
Totali	-	1.000,00
	Expenses	-
This amount is the social security + C. I. 4.0% su	1.000,00	40,00
this is the VAT + IVA 20.0% su	1.040,00	208,00
	Total	1.248,00
Withdrawing tax on	1.000,00	200,00
	TOTAL DUE	1.048,00

To illustrate how this works, imagine that you have issued *fatture* (invoices) for €20,000, plus *Iva* during the tax year. Your invoices have shown the *ritenuta d'acconto*, which amounted to €4,000 and this has already been withdrawn by your clients and paid to the government. But you have also had to pay *Iva* on this amount. In June, you are expected to pay €4,600 taxes on your €20,000 earnings. But because your clients have already paid €4,000 in the form of the *ritenuta d'acconto*, all you need to pay is the remaining €600.

As a *lavoratore autonomo*, you need your invoices paid on time so that you can deduct the *Iva* which you are paying on a quarterly basis. It is common practice in Italy to issue a *notula* (pro forma invoice) requesting clients for payment. Once you have received it, you then issue the invoice so that you can be sure you have received the amount outstanding. What counts is when your clients pay you. For example, let's say that you carried out some work for a client in October 2005 but were not paid until February 2006. This payment will contribute towards the 2006 rather than the 2005 tax year.

4. Income generated from capital

What generally happens with income generated from capital is that the company (i.e. a bank) withdraws a percentage of the capital gain as a taxation and pays it the month after to the government. This taxation can be definitive or partial payment. In the last case the right amount of taxation due, together with the other incomes, is calculated in the tax return. In the first case the income doesn't need to be declared in the tax return, as it has already been taxed.

One of the most common forms of income generated from your capital is your bank account. In Italy, the taxation is 27 per cent, withdrawn directly from the bank at the end of the period. If you decide to entrust your savings to a bank (i.e. to invest in a fund), then the taxation on the interest is only 12.5 per cent. Bonds are treated in the same way.

Dividends also have a standard tax rate of 12.5 per cent. However, if the participation is *qualificata* (qualified), i.e. more than five per cent of any kind of share quoted in the stock exchange or 25 per cent for non-quoted shares, then you only need to declare 40 per cent of the income received.

5. Income generated from business (lavoro d'impresa)

Lavoratori autonomi, whilst having an office and possibly paid employees, do not fall into this category. As a business owner, your activity is based on your activities of your organisation rather than your qualifications and if you have a *ditta individuale, Snc, Srl* or *Spa*, your income is considered income generated from the business. But, as we have mentioned in previous chapters, an Snc (partnership) or *ditta individuale* (sole trader) are personal companies rather than corporations. As such, you are liable for IRE (personal income tax) rather than the corporate tax IRES, which is reserved for an *Srl* or *Spa*.

Your *commercalista* will draw up a balance sheet in accordance with standard accounts and will then determine the taxable amount by adding or subtracting non-deductible costs. There are too many to list here now, but we've included the main ones in the section on deductible costs.

As you now know, the Italian tax year runs from 1 January to 31 December and all income and costs must be related to this period. Any invoices which were issued in 2005, but which were only paid in 2006, still contribute to the 2005 tax year.

6. Other income

This is income which has not been obtained from any commercial or professional activity. Income which falls into this category can come from selling properties, shares, bonds, any professional activities which are occasional, and any money coming from the lottery or other games.

Let's see some examples related to this form of taxation.

Case 1: Selling a house that was bought or built less than six years ago. In this case you have to pay taxes on the difference between what you have paid for the house and what you have received from the sale. This is considered the taxable amount, minus related costs such as the notary.

Of course there are some exceptions: if you have inherited a house from your parents and you sell it, or it was your *abitazione principale* (mainhouse where you lived for the majority of the year) the amount is not taxable.

Case 2: Renting a house which is located abroad. In this case, the taxable amount is exactly the same as declared in the country where the house is located. Under the Double Taxation agreement, you should not have to pay tax in both places.

Case 3: Winning the lottery. The taxation is already deducted from the amount given. The taxation on this income is 10 per cent for lottery, bingos, etc; 20 per cent for games on TV or radio or sport events; 25 per cent for all other cases (i.e. carnival competitions).

IRES

This is the corporate income tax and only applicable if you have an *Srl* or *Spa*. To be liable for this tax, your corporation must have its registered office or administrative office in Italy for at least 183 days per year.

Balance sheet

When the *commercialista* draws up the balance sheet, he or she will take into account various incomes and costs so make sure you always keep your invoices and receipts for everything related to your company. These incomes and costs include:

- *Revenue from the selling of products, goods or services.* When calculating the revenue, don't forget to include *sconti* (discounts) or returned sales. Insurance indemnities are also considered a form of revenue, as are contributions from the Italian government or any other body or institution provided that these are not related to the purchase of assets. As a general rule, all financial transactions that produce an income are considered revenue.

- *Stock inventories (rimanenze).* Inventories include *prodotti finali* (finished products), *semilavorati* (semi-finished products) and *materie prime* (raw materials). Any *lavori in corso* (work in progress such as building or road works) must also be listed in this category. The inventories can be evaluated using the FIFO (First in First out), LIFO (Last in First out) or *costo medio ponderato* (average cost method). All three methods are accepted by the tax authorities.

- *Salaries.* Employee salaries are deductible under IRES but an employee benefit, such as a company car, is taxable at a rate established by the *Automobil Club Italia* (ACI – Italian Motorcar Association) presuming 15,000 Km for personal use. This amount varies depending on the make of car. If you assign an employee an Audi A3 sportback 1.6 as shown in Figure 15.8 this will show up in his wage slip as an extra €2,443.64. You can deduct 100 per cent of the costs when the car includes personal use or is instrumental to company activity, otherwise you can only deduct 50 per cent. Figure 15.8 shows taxable rates established by ACI.

Figure 15.8

MAKE	MODEL	SERIES	Cost per Km (up to 15,000 km)	ANNUAL FRINGE BENEFIT
AUDI	a3 sportback 1.6	tiptronic 102cv	0.543031	€2,443.64
AUDI	a3 1.6	102cv mod.2005	0.512315	€2,305.42
AUDI	a3 1.6/16v fsi	115cv mod.2005	0.514801	€2,316.60
AUDI	a3 2.0/16v fsi	150cv mod.2005	0.581165	€2,615.24

◆ *Taxes and fines.* IRE, IRES and IRAP and the relative fines for late payment are not deductible, but the *imposta di registro* (registration tax), *tassa sulla pubblicità* (tax on advertising) and TARSU (refuse tax) are on the condition, of course, that your company has proved it has paid the bills. See Chapter 16 for a more detailed analysis of these local taxes.

◆ *Recurring costs.* These are costs that are not one-off but are ongoing over the years. These include advertising research and entertainment costs, along with *altre spese pluriennali* (miscellanous recurring costs). Advertising costs (included sponsors) can only be deducted if you have had a specific contract drawn up specifying any obligations between you and the advertiser or you and the company publishing your advert. These costs can be deducted in one year or spread over five years at a rate of

20 per cent each year. You can decide to deduct research costs over two, three, four or five years.

◆ *Depreciation*. The costs for depreciation are calculated following the rates indicated in the table attached to the DM 31/12/1988. This table identifies the different types of businesses and the assets they can deduct, along with their specific rates of depreciation. Figure 15.9 shows you the most important assets and their depreciation values.

Figure 15.9

Terreni (land)	0%
Fabbricati (buildings)	3%
Impianti e macchinari (plants and machinery)	15%
Attrezzature (equipment)	25%
Mobili e macchine d'ufficio (furniture and office equipment)	12%
Automezzi (lorries)	20%
Autovetture (cars)	25%

The depreciation can only be calculated from when the asset has *entrata in funzione del bene* (that is, begun to be used by the company). If you purchase an important piece of machinery in December, it is obvious that you will get far less use from it than a company which purchased the same piece of equipment in January of the same year. Nevertheless, Italian law states that in the first year depreciation must be 50 per cent of its normal depreciation rate. Depreciation can be reduced when you expect to get a lot of use from the asset. Let's say that business is going well and the machinery you bought is constantly in use 24 hours a day. Since you can document the effect that this has had on your company balance sheet, you can request that the depreciation period is reduced, thus allowing you to write off the costs over a shorter time span.

- *Ammortamento anticipato*. Under Italian tax law, companies may double the rate of depreciation in the first three tax years which is highly beneficial if your company has a high profit. Note that where assets have a value of €516.46 or less, the whole cost can be completely deducted in the first year.
- *Cars*. In Italy, the cost of cars is deductible up to a maximum limit of €18,075.99. If the company decides to lease a car instead of buying it, then the total deductible amount is proportional to the €18,075.99. If the company opts to hire a car on a long-term basis, than the maximum deductible amount is €3,615.20 per year. As we have already seen, the cost is 100 per cent deductible when the car is assigned to employees for both personal and work use, 50 per cent if this is not the case and the employee can only use it for work purposes. For sales representatives and sales managers who are often travelling, the capped limit is increased to €25,822.84 and 80 per cent rather than 50 per cent can be deducted. Where vehicles are essential to the economic activity of a business, the costs are 100 per cent deductible.
- *Leasing for tangible assets (photocopiers, PCs, faxes, machinery)*. In order to calculate the limit of the deductible cost we have to consider the economic life of the asset from a tax point of view. For instance, the period of economic life of the PC is 4 years because the depreciation rate is 25 per cent ($25\% \times 4 = 100\%$). The cost of the leasing is only deductible if the period of leasing is at least half the period of the economic life of the asset. So, in order to deduct the cost of a PC, it must be leased for at least a two-year period. The costs of leasing premises are deductible only if the lease period is fifteen years or more.
- *Provision for bad debts*. The amount deductible is only equivalent to 0.5 per cent of the debt shown in the balance sheet.

◆ *Extraordinary items*. All the costs related to previous years which have not been deducted are considered extraordinary items and thus not deductible.

Tax deadlines and calculating payments

To give you an idea of the way the taxes are calculated in Italy, we have included a profit and loss account. The starting point is the income statement (Profit before taxation). After that, we have all the non-deductible revenues/costs that have to be summed up in order to work out the taxable amount. The last step is to apply the percentage of taxation of IRES which is 33 per cent. Let's suppose that you have a profit before taxation of €30,000 and that in the tax year, you paid €30,000 for a company car. The depreciation is half of 25 per cent (because it is the first year) which is €3,750. But the deductible amount is approximately €2,250. Therefore you have €1,500 which is non-deductible. You have also paid ICI (Council Tax, see page 199) on your property for €2,000 and you paid fines for €3,200. The following example (Figure 15.10) calculates the IRES due.

Figure 15.10

PROFIT BEFORE TAXATION	€30,000.00
(Plus) Cost of depreciation of cars not deductible	€1,500.00
(Plus) Cost of taxes not deductible	€2,000.00
(Plus) Other costs not deductible	€3,200.00
Taxable amount	€36,700.00
IRES	33%
Amount due	€12,111.00

IRAP

Tassa sulle attività produttive – **regional production tax**

IRAP affects all people and companies carrying out economic activities. This tax considers the *valore della produzione netta* (net production value) and is calculated as the difference between the total income of the company less some specific costs. IRAP is calculated in a different way to IRES and IRE. The main non-deductible costs are salaries, provision for bad debts, financial costs and other provisions.

Let's take the previous example, and let's use it now in order to calculate IRAP, as shown in Figure 15.11.

Figure 15.11

PROFIT BEFORE TAXATION	€30,000.00
(Plus) Cost of depreciation of cars not deductible	€1,500.00
(Plus) Cost of taxes not deductible	€2,000.00
(Plus) Cost for salaries	€60,000.00
(Plus) Financial costs	€1,500.00
Taxable amount	€95,000.00
IRAP	4.25%
Amount due	€4,037.50

As you can see, the IRAP rules are unusual. In fact, the costs for salaries and the financial costs (i.e. interests paid to the bank) are not deductible. But what you can also see is that even when the business is running at a loss, it still has to pay IRAP. The following table (Figure 15.12) calculates the amount due when the company is making a loss.

Figure 15.12

LOSS BEFORE TAXATION	– €15,000.00
(Plus) Cost of depreciation of cars not deductible	€1,500.00
(Plus) Cost of taxes not deductible	€2,000.00
(Plus) Cost for salaries	€60,000.00
(Plus) Financial costs	€1,500.00
Taxable amount	€50,000.00
IRAP	4.25%
Amount due	€2,125.00

The EU recognised the absurdity of this situation in March 2006, declaring that IRAP was at odds with *Iva* and should therefore be abolished. At the time of writing, we do not know what the outcome will be so check with your *commercialista*.

PAYMENT
In Italy, IRE, IRES and IRAP must be paid in June and November following the end of the previous tax year (31 December). For the amounts payable in November, you can choose to start paying these in July to avoid paying a lump sum in one go. In this case, you are making monthly payments.

Payments are calculated in the following way.

Partnerships and sole trader (Snc and *ditte individuali*)
IRE
By 20 June:
Amount due + 40% of the anticipation (99% of the amount due) = Total to be paid

By 30 November:

60% of the anticipation (99% of the amount due) = Total to be paid

IRAP

By 20 June:

Amount due + 40% of the anticipation (99% of the amount due) = Total to be paid

By 30 November:

60% of the anticipation (99% of the amount due) = Total to be paid

Corporations (Srl and Spa)

IRES (for business which ends the fiscal period on 31 December)

By 20 June:

Amount due + 40% of the anticipation (100% of the amount due) = Total to be paid

By 30 November:

60% of the anticipation (100% of the amount due) = Total to be paid

IRAP (for business which end the fiscal period on 31 December)

By 20 June:

Amount due + 40% of the anticipation (100% of the amount due) = Total to be paid

By 30 November:
60% of the anticipation (100% of the amount due) = Total to be paid

TAX RETURN

Tax returns must be received by 31 October either via direct electronic submission or, if you are a *lavoratore autonomo*, *ditta individuale* or *Snc*, by filling in the declaration at a bank or post office no later than 31 July.

Most *commercialistas* use the Entratel electronic service or the electronic internet service to submit the tax return directly and for the Modello 770. To submit your tax return via the internet, you or your *commercialista* (whoever is the 'legal agent' of the company) will need to be supplied with a PIN code from www.fisconline.agenziaentrate.it. If your *commercialista* already has the Entratel system, then he is obliged to file your return using this rather than the internet service.

Complimenti for getting the hang of how direct taxes work. Now all you need to know about is *Iva* (VAT) and local taxes and you're done.

16

Iva and local taxes

Iva (*Imposta sul valore aggiunto*) is regulated by the Italian law 633/72. It is charged on the value of taxable goods and services made in Italy and therefore affects both the buying and selling of products/services in Italy.

As we saw in Chapter 2: Key figures and institutions, you must apply for a *Partita Iva* (VAT number) before your business starts trading. This means that from day one you will have to pay *Iva* to the Italian government whenever you buy or sell anything in the course of your business.

RATES OF *IVA*

Knowing the different *Iva* rates is important. If you don't know how much *Iva* you should be charging, you risk invoicing for the wrong amounts and this will lead to huge complications – you'll end up paying your *commercialista* (accountant) far more money than you should so that you can sort out where you went wrong.

Iva can be classified in four different ways:

♦ *imponibili* (taxable) where *Iva* is always applicable;
♦ *non imponibili* (non-taxable) where *Iva* is not applicable because the transactions are made between different countries (exports, intra EU sales or purchases, etc.), but which must be recorded in the *Iva* books nevertheless;

- *esenti* (exempt) where *Iva* is applicable, but with a rate of 0 per cent. In reality, what happens is that these transactions (credit, financing, insurance) have to be invoiced and recorded in the *Iva* books, even if the *Iva* is 0;
- *fuori campo Iva* or *esclusi* (non-relevant), i.e. where *Iva* is not applicable at all.

There are three different *aliquoti iva* (*Iva* rates) as shown in Figure 16.1.

Figure 16.1

Iva		
Standard rate	20%	Most services and goods
Reduced rate	10%	Plants, flowers, restaurant, meat, livestock, animal derived products, domestic energy (gas, electricity), theatrical performances
Reduced rate	4%	Vegetables and plant-derived foods, books, newspapers, first house, orthopaedic equipment

WHEN IS *IVA* DEDUCTIBLE?

You can only deduct *Iva* when you are buying or selling a good or service inherent to the activity of the company. You cannot deduct any *Iva* from the following:

- entertaining expenses (*spese di rappresentanza*);
- luxury goods (fur, yachts, cars with engines bigger than 2,000 c.c. or 2,500) – *Iva* is not deductible unless the company merchandises them;

- purchasing a house;
- maintenance costs of a house;
- food and drink;
- hotel expenses;
- motorway tolls (*pedaggio*).

But you can deduct 50 per cent of *Iva* from the cost of:

- car maintenance;
- mobile phones and mobile phone bills.

Deducting fuel costs

If you have a car that you use for work purposes (it does not have to be a company car), then you need an invoice for the fuel that you buy. In Italy, however, petrol stations do not issue invoices. But don't worry, there is a solution. You need a *scheda carburante* (petrol form), which you can buy from any *cartoleria* (stationers). Every time you fill up your car with fuel, the petrol pump attendant writes the date, the type of fuel, the amount and the price and the new km reading. They will then stamp the form. The *scheda carburante* must be filled in on a monthly or on a quarterly basis depending on when you file your tax returns.

Figure 16.2 is an example of the *scheda carburante*.

Figure 16.2

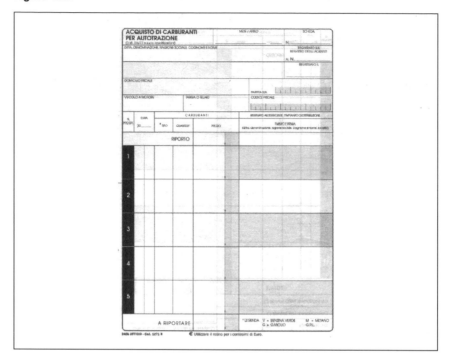

Sales and purchases

If you are in a shop, but require a *fattura* (invoice) because you are buying books or computer equipment for the company, you are required to ask for the *fattura* before starting the sale. In order for the shop assistant to give you a *fattura*, you will need to produce all your company details, including your *Partita Iva*.

Some companies are not allowed to issue invoices when they sell goods unless specifically requested. For example, supermarkets cannot issue an invoice for each customer. In these cases the law allows the so-called *commercianti al minuto* to issue a *scontrino o ricevuta fiscale* (receipt). These documents are the same from a fiscal point of view. Ensure that these include the name, address and *Partita Iva* of the shop issuing the receipt otherwise you cannot deduct the cost.

Figure 16.3 is a *ricevuta fiscale* that also can be used as a *fattura*. When being used as a *fattura*, the person issuing it should make sure it includes the progressive number and the date.

Figure 16.3

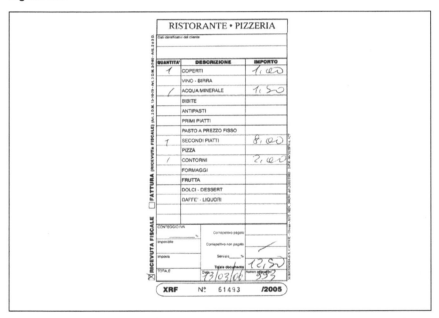

Whenever goods or services are supplied, the supplier must issue a *fattura*. This is different to the *ricevuta fiscale* or *scontrino* (receipt) which cannot be used to deduct *Iva*.

The invoice must be printed out in two copies: one has to be sent to the purchaser, the other must be kept by the seller (and recorded in the *Iva* books).

The invoice must indicate:

◆ the date;
◆ the *numero fattura* (progressive number);
◆ the name, address and other information of the customer;
◆ the *numero partita Iva* (Iva code) of the supplier and also of the seller;
◆ the quality, quantity and the kind of goods or services provided;
◆ the amount taxable;
◆ the rate of *Iva*;
◆ the total amount due by the customer.

Before you print and send off your invoices, it is worth checking that they are accurate, especially if you are invoicing in Italian. See our example (Figure 16.4) of a completed *Iva* invoice below.

Where *Iva* is not applicable, the invoice must state why by adding the specific article of the law (example: *non imponibile art.xx DPR 633/72*).

ISSUING THE INVOICE

The invoice can be issued immediately (*fattura immediata*) or subsequently. In the latter case, if you are the *fornitore* (supplier), you must issue a *documento di trasporto* (DTT – delivery note). There should be two copies of the *documento di trasporto* which should indicate the progressive number, the date and the description of the goods.

A *nota di credito* (credit note) must be issued when any goods sent by the supplier are returned and when the supplier applies a

Figure 16.4

Q.tà	Descrizione	Prezzo unitario		TOTALE	
1	Tavolo da lavoro Mod 2344	€	1.000,00	€	1.000,00
1	Sedia prof. Mod. 54587667	€	220,00	€	220,00

SPACK SRL

Via Roma 11
020100 MILANO (P.Iva 00927503092)

FATTURA N. 12   DEL   14/02/2006

Spett. Ditta Mario Rossi
        Via A. Moro 12
        020100 Milano
Tel   02/8429400

	IMPONIBILE	€	1.220,00
	IVA 20%	€	244,00
	TOTALE FATTURA	€	1.464,00

Modalità di pagamento	Assegno bancario 30gg
Note	

discount or a premium to the purchaser. The amount must be credited. Formally the credit note is like an invoice and very often the form used to issue it is the same as the one used for invoices.

PAYING *IVA*

The difference between the *Iva* calculated on invoices issued and the *Iva* calculated on the purchase invoices identifies the amount that has to be paid on a monthly basis (or on a quarterly basis in some cases).

196 / STARTING A BUSINESS IN ITALY

Payment must be made by the 16th of the following month. If you decided to pay *Iva* on a quarterly basis, you must do this by 16 February, 16 May, 16 August and 16 November.

As you know by now, Italy is a country where bureaucracy reigns and even *Iva* isn't exempt. In addition to filing *Iva* payments on a monthly or quarterly basis, by 27 December, you will also have to file an *Iva* return for your expected contribution.

The amount due can be calculated using three different techniques and it is up to you to choose which one you want to use:

- historical data procedure;
- provisional data procedure;
- actual data procedure.

Most Italian companies use the historical data procedure. You need to pay 88 per cent of the rate paid for December or for the fourth quarter. For example, if you paid €10,000 of *Iva* for December 2004, you will have to pay an *Iva* advance for January of €8,800. To avoid overpaying in January, deduct the advance paid in December and pay the difference. If you discover that you paid too much in the *Iva* advance, you will be reimbursed.

ANNUAL *IVA* RETURN

Even though you have been paying your *Iva* throughout the year, you will also have to file an end-of-year return. It may be that you discover you have paid too little. If this is the case, you have until 16 March of the following year by which to make payment.

FILING THE *IVA* RETURN

Once you have calculated the amount of *Iva* due, you will need to fill in the F24. The onus is on you to download the form from the *Agenzia delle Entrate* (tax office) website (http://www.agenziaentrate.it/ilwwcm/resources/file/eb6e16067511218/f24icimodc.pdf).

This form is long-winded but we've included the main parts here.

Below, you can see the first section of the form where you need to insert your *codice fiscale* (tax code) and the name and address of your company. If you are a *lavoratore autonomo* (self-employed worker), then you also need to fill in your date of birth.

Figure 16.5

In the second section (Figure 16.6) you have to fill in the *codice tributo* which is a specific code related to the month of the payment you are making (see Figure 16.7 overleaf). For example, if you are paying *Iva* for February and you pay on a monthly basis, the code for this payment is 6002.

Figure 16.6

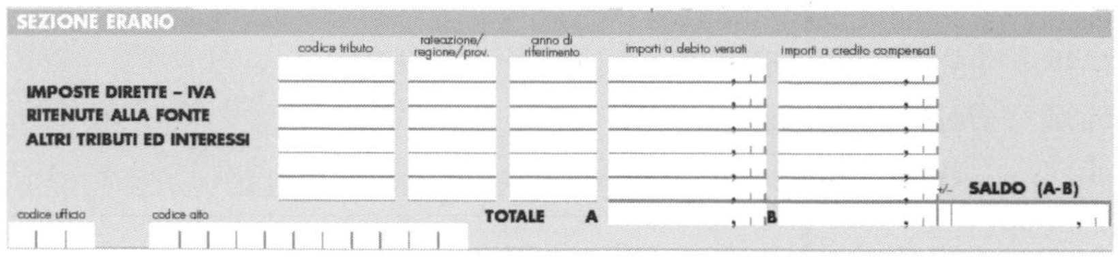
SEZIONE ERARIO

IMPOSTE DIRETTE – IVA
RITENUTE ALLA FONTE
ALTRI TRIBUTI ED INTERESSI

codice tributo	rateazione/regione/prov.	anno di riferimento	importi a debito versati	importi a credito compensati

codice ufficio — codice atto — TOTALE A — B — +/– SALDO (A-B)

Figure 16.7 lists the *codici tribute* needed to fill in the F24:

Figure 16.7

6001	Payment of *Iva* for January
6002	Payment of *Iva* for February
6003	Payment of *Iva* for March
6004	Payment of *Iva* for April
6005	Payment of *Iva* for May
6006	Payment of *Iva* for June
6007	Payment of *Iva* for July
6008	Payment of *Iva* for August
6009	Payment of *Iva* for September
6010	Payment of *Iva* for October
6011	Payment of *Iva* for November
6012	Payment of *Iva* for December

If you are paying on a quarterly basis, use one of the following *codice tributo* instead (as shown in Figure 16.8).

Figure 16.8

6031	Payment *Iva* first quarter
6032	Payment *Iva* second quarter
6033	Payment *Iva* third quarter
6034	Payment *Iva* fourth quarter

At the bottom of the form (Figure 16.9), you need to write the total due and sign the form.

Figure 16.9

LOCAL TAXES

We bet that you are getting sick of taxes by now, but before you can relax there are still another eight taxes you need to know about.

ICI

The ICI (*imposta comunale sugli immobili* – pronounced 'eechy') is a town council tax that must be paid by people and businesses who own land or property there. The taxable amount is based on the *rendita catastale* (national rent income) (see Chapter 14: Direct taxes) of the house, office, factory or land.

The taxable amount is calculated in the following way:

Rendita catastale + (*Rendita catastale* × 5 %) × coefficient.

The coefficient is a fixed value decided by the town council.

Choose the coefficient from the following table (Figure 16.10).

Figure 16.10

Category		Coefficient
Gruppo catastale	A	100
Gruppo catastale	B	100
Gruppo catastale	C	100
Gruppo catastale	D	50
Categoria catastale	C1	34

Let's suppose you own an office in the city centre. If you refer back to the *tariffa d'estimo* in Chapter 15, you can see that you fall into the *Gruppo Catastale A*. The *rendita catastale* for the office space is €880. The taxable amount is calculated as shown:

$$880.00 + (880.00 \times 5\%) \times 100 = €92,400.00$$

Now, you need to calculate the ICI due. The amount of the tax varies as it is up to each individual *comune* (council) to fix the rate, but it cannot be less than 0.4 per cent or more than 0.7 per cent. If we suppose the maximum tax rate (0.7 per cent) the amount of ICI due on the office is €646.80.

Your company is exempt from paying ICI if it is building new houses or offices, if you have a leasehold, if you are renting company premises or if you have a plot of land because there is no *rendita catastale*.

Payment of ICI

You will need to make your ICI declaration at your local *comune* by 31 July or 31 October depending on when you are filing your tax return.

Payment can be made in two different ways: you can either pay the total amount by 30 June or you can split the total amount into two parts. In this case, you must pay the first instalment by 30 June and the second instalment by 20 December. You can pay at any branch of the *Ufficio postale* (post office) or by using the F24 form if the council accepts this.

TARSU (*Tassa per lo smaltimento di rifiuti solidi urbani*)

The *tassa per lo smaltimento di rifiuti solidi urbani* (tax on rubbish) is paid to the local *comune* which sets the rate. Both individuals and businesses are liable for this tax, which is due to be abolished at the end of 2008. It will be replaced by the new tax TIA (*tariffa di igiene ambientale* – environmental hygiene tax). TIA will be applicable to each house, garage, office and warehouse which produces domestic waste. Industrial waste such as iron, oil and coal is not included.

When you start your business, you will need to send a statement to the *comune* detailing the area your property covers in square metres and the date on which you begin using the property. The statement must be received by the *comune* no later than 20 January. Payment is usually made on a quarterly basis.

TOSAP (*tassa occupazione suolo pubblico*)

Individuals or companies occupying council-owned land (whether on a temporary or permanent basis) must pay the annual *tassa occupazione suolo pubblico*. You would need to pay a one-off amount of TOSAP if you were carrying out maintenance work to your premises and needed to take up some of the pavement or road in order to do so. Similarly, if want to affix a 'keep clear' sign so that your vehicles can get in and out of your entrance, you would have to pay TOSAP on a permanent basis because, for as long as you keep the sign up, the *comune* is giving up a part of its land.

Each *comune* fixes the tax rate and calculates the amount of tax due according to the number of square metres you are occupying and thus preventing other people from using.

To find out whether or not you eligible for TOSAP, contact the *Ufficio Tributi* at your local *comune*.

Payment can be made either at the *Ufficio postale* or with the F24 via the internet but, again, you will need to check the preferred method. Payment must be made by 31 January each year.

Imposta comunale sulla pubblicità

This tax is applicable to all forms of advertising – signs, bill-boards, and adverts on the sides of vehicles are just three examples. The *comune* takes into account the size of the advertising when calculating the amount due. However, when they are less than 300 square cm (for example: 10cm × 30cm) then you do not have to pay.

To give you an idea of the different costs, you can see the amount charged in Turin. If you want to put a *striscione* (banner) above a road in Turin the tax costs €4.20 per square metre per day. If you want to use an airship (*dirigibile*) than you pay €111.94 per day. If you want to distribute flyers (*manifestini*) the tax is €11.67 per day. For billboards in Turin, Figure 16.11 sums up the costs.

Figure 16.11

	PUBLIC AREAS	PRIVATE AREAS
POSTER 6 square metres	€517.29	€323.30
POSTER 12 square metres	€1,546.86	€982.17
POSTER 17 square metres	€2,552.36	€1,620.61
POSTER 17.5 square metres	€2,652.91	€1,684.45
POSTER 18 square metres	€2,753.46	€1,748.30
Source: Comune di Torino		

If it is a one-off payment, you can make it at the local *comune*. However, if you will be paying it on a regular basis, you can do so at the *Ufficio tributi* or *Ufficio postale*.

Diritti sulle pubbliche affissioni

This tax is only for a *comune* with more than 3,000 inhabitants. It is levied on the *affissione di manifesti* (putting up of posters) and the amount of the tax varies depending on the size of the poster and the type of business/institution wishing to use the service.

The payment is made in the same way as the *imposta comunale sulle pubblicità*.

Imposta di registro

The registration tax affects all legal acts or deeds which must be legally registered. This tax will affect you if you are purchasing a home from which you will be running your business or if you are purchasing company premises.

If you are buying your designated first home in Italy, the rate of taxation is 3 per cent. If you are buying a second home or company property, it is 7 per cent. Buying real estate incurs an 8 per cent tax. You will normally be required to pay the tax on the day the legal act is drawn up by the notary. The notary will help you do this.

Imposte catastali ed ipotecarie

The *cadastral* (national rent income) and mortgage taxes are linked to the selling or modifying of properties and is normally paid at the same time as the registration tax. The rate of the *imposta catastale* is normally one per cent. However, mergers between companies, and transactions subject to *Iva* incur a fixed charge of €168.

The *imposta ipotecaria* (mortgage tax) is due to the registration of some guarantees or rights on the properties. For instance, if you need a mortgage in order to buy a property, the bank is likely to ask you for a guarantee. This guarantee is the *ipoteca* and must be registered in the public archive. To do this, you must pay the *imposta ipotecaria*.

The tax is normally charged at 2 per cent unless you are buying a first house when you will be asked to pay €168. Payment for both taxes is via the Modello 23. Again, a notary will help you with this.

Imposta di bollo

Each official document, cheque, bill of exchange and statement of account are subject to the *imposta di bollo* (registration tax). This tax varies depending on the document. For example, your bank account statement attracts an annual tax of €34.20. For each cheque, there is an *imposta di bollo* of €0.26. But, in the majority of the cases, the amount is fixed at €14.62. If the document is subject to *Iva*, then you do not have to pay the *imposta di bollo*.

For all invoices or receipts which are over €77.57 and *Iva* exempt or with a 0 per cent rate, you need to add a *marca da bollo* (tax stamp). If you are issuing the invoice, don't forget to spoil the tax stamp with a small scribble. If you don't do this, the stamp can be reused and you could be caught for tax evasion. Together with the tax stamp there is another way to pay the *imposta di bollo*: the so-called *punzone* which is an embossed stamp.

Mario's Pearl of Wisdom

There are so many tax laws in Italy that it is impossible to follow every one of them all the time. Let's compare it to driving a car along the road. Sometimes the speed limit is 50km per hour, sometimes it is 80. Motorists who regularly use the road know this, but they also know that more often than not, no one is checking. But when motorists know a speed trap is coming up and that the police are waiting in a lay-by to trap offending drivers, they slow down to the required limit because they know that in this case, they will be fined even if they are 5km over the limit. It is the same with tax legislation in Italy. People follow the law to the letter in some instances and turn a blind eye to others, knowing that they are not going to be caught.

Now you know all about the official legislation in Italy and what you need to do. But do you know how to deal with Italians on a day-to-day basis? Well, after your next *cappuccino*, you are about to find out.

17

Culture clash

As we've said all along, we've been making the mistakes so you don't have to. Back in 2002, Emma was a fashion and textile journalist in Milan. Her first task was to interview the owners of spinning mills in the tiny town of Biella in Piedmont. She turned up 15 minutes late which didn't impress the people she was meant to be meeting.

Fast-forward to 2005 when Emma was living in Sardinia. She had an interview to do some freelance writing work with a local company and the meeting had been set up by a mutual acquaintance for 3pm. She turned up 10 minutes early. And she waited. And waited. And waited. After a while, she got her book out of her bag and started reading. Half an hour later still no one had shown up and Emma was wondering if one of them had got the wrong day.

TIMEKEEPING

Italians are lively, sociable people who believe finishing conversations with a colleague or friend is far more important than breaking it off in order to be punctual for the next business appointment.

Richard D. Lewis is the chairman of Richard Lewis Communications, an international institute of cross-cultural and language training. In his book *When cultures collide, leading across cultures* he cites what happens when a German and an Italian meet. 'Why are you so angry because I came at 9.30am?'

he asks his German colleague. 'Because it says 9.00 am in my diary,' says the German. 'Then why don't you write 9.30 am and then we'll both be happy?' is a logical Italian response'.

On another occasion, Emma was leading a Weaveaweb social business networking event in Cagliari and only a few members had turned up for the 5pm start time. At 5.15pm they were still in the hotel lobby waiting for the others to arrive so Emma suggested that they should move over to the bar area and have a drink. 'But it's only 5.15pm', one member said looking at her watch. 'Let's wait another quarter of an hour before starting'. It was another slip-up on Emma's part, which proved that she still had a way to go before being truly comfortable with the Italian way of doing business.

Of course, Emma's experiences in Cagliari are not true for the whole of Italy for, as we have said before, there is a strong cultural divide between the north and south. Even so, the Milanese will be approximately five minutes late, a Roman will be around 20 to 30 minutes late, and in the south and the islands there is a much more flexible timescale.

MEETINGS

The clash of cultures can often rear its ugly head at meetings because each country has a different way of doing things. For example, whereas Brits, Americans and Australians can concentrate for around 30 minutes in a meeting, the Italian concentration span is much shorter – around 20 minutes, even though they have much longer meetings.

After two years spent in Dusseldorf as the head of a German team for IT Holding, Mario had become used to the rather formal, precise and serious way of doing business. Even arriving a couple of minutes after the arranged time was considered late. You can imagine his shock as he settled back into an all-Italian team in southern Italy.

He scheduled meetings and, used to the ultra precise manner of the Germans, started to get impatient when staff hadn't turned up after five or ten minutes. People would tend to arrive in dribs and drabs, checking to see who was there and who wasn't. Then they disappeared again, only coming back when a larger crowd had gathered.

WRITTEN AGENDAS

Both of us have gone to meetings with full agendas, but these haven't always been followed. If a foreigner was a fly on the wall, they would certainly be surprised by what they saw: lots of waving of arms and hands, conversations getting louder and louder and colleagues talking over one another without making progress. But again, it would be wrong to assume that this is rowdy and unprofessional. It is just the way business is done. Italians (southern Italians especially) do not like following written agendas because they think that something vital has probably been missed out and, if there is a written agenda, they will attach no order to the points.

NEGOTIATIONS

In northern Italy, your business colleagues will not want to be kept waiting as they have other matters to be getting on with. Keep what you have to say concise and to the point and your argument will be listened to and considered. South of Rome and you would be wise to pay as much attention to your image, your body language and the message you are putting across as to the matter in question.

No matter how good the deal, Italians will only do business with you if they decide you are a *persona per bene*, i.e., a person with good intentions. Before launching your assault, strike up a good rapport by talking about family and hobbies over a *cappuccino*.

BUILDING TRUST

Italians are world famous for their gregarious nature and their ability to befriend you in an instant. Don't fall into the trap though of thinking the friendship runs deep. You may be invited to the pizzeria on a regular basis but Italians take a long time to turn a *conoscente* (acquaintance) into an *amico* (friend) and then a *buon amico* (good friend). According to an old Italian proverb, *chi trova un amico, trova un tesoro* (he who finds a friend, finds a treasure). Italy is a low-trust society and natives are, on the whole, deeply suspicious of people they don't know, especially in the business arena. You will often win contracts in Italy after having been recommended by a friend who then becomes the *tramite* (go-between) and subsequently arranges all the meetings between you and your potential client until you get to know them better.

To build trust with your Italian business colleagues show compassion, be loyal and help them out wherever possible. Be prepared to do this in face-to-face meetings rather than over the phone or via email even though you will be losing valuable time. Italians are still rather wary of email communication. The estate agents that Emma deals with for How to Italy's relocation work are always bemused that she can conduct business with Americans over the internet and arrange for leases to be signed with people she has never met and probably never will. This lack of trust in strangers also extends to products and services. For example, Italians are still wary of e-commerce and few are willing to make online payments, especially for goods or services they have not yet received.

FREQUENCY OF COMMUNICATION

It is very important to make the effort to *farti sentire* (get in touch) on a regular basis. As busy as you may be, find the time to ring your business acquaintances and clients. When you know you are going to be passing their work premises, get in touch and invite them to have a coffee with you in the local bar or if you are in Milan, invite them after work for an *aperitivo*. This gesture will also confirm your trustworthiness and your willingness to cement your business relationship.

Both of us have had huge pay-offs from this approach. Emma has been offered projects three years down the line as a direct result of having kept in touch with someone she once worked with for two months and Mario regularly socialises with past clients.

FLEXIBILITY

It is often said that the only law Italians fully respect is the one banning smoking in all public places, which came into effect on 10 January 2005. The rest of time, Italians have a far more laid-back approach and, for the most part, regard those who obey the letter of the law as rather old-fashioned and a bit naïve. Don't judge the people who do take short cuts in Italy because it is part of the culture.

Southern Italians are far more flexible than their northern cousins, particularly when it comes to payments. On the *fattura* (invoice), it might state that the amount must be paid in full after 60 days, but in the south people (including expats who adapt to the lifestyle) will assume that the 60 days is for official records only and that it is fine to pay after 80, 90 or even 100 days. The further south you go, the more difficult it will be to ask for the payment as it is considered *una vergogna* (an embarrassment) to do so. Where you have been introduced to the debtor by an Italian friend, ring them and explain the situation. Your friend will then take it upon him or herself to find out from the guilty party when you can expect payment. He or she will then relay this back to you without either party losing face.

LANGUAGE

Italians place great emphasis on the ability to speak and write eloquently so don't expect every piece of writing you read to be concise or to the point. The most important nugget of information is likely to be contained in the last paragraph.

COMMUNICATION SKILLS

Let's be clear here. Italians talk. A lot. Ballerò and Alice are two television shows which host different politicians each week. To untrained foreign eyes, it seems that the shows' guests go out of their way to be rude as they constantly interrupt the person being asked the question and begin to speak over them. This is very much a part of Italian life and whether you are in a restaurant or in a meeting, your Italian colleagues won't always wait patiently while you finish your monologue. If they think you are wrong, they will voice their opinion vociferously. Similarly, if you are listening to an Italian speak, don't sit there in silence as this will be taken for boredom and lack of interest.

BODY SPACE AND BODY LANGUAGE

Generally speaking, Brits, Australians, New Zealanders, South Africans, Canadians and the Irish have a 1.2 metre personal space bubble around them. Only friends and family are allowed to enter this space.

But the sociable Italians like to be standing less than 80cm away from the person they are talking to and possibly even closer so that they can, horror of horrors, touch you. But whatever you do, don't become defensive and back off from your Italian counterpart as you will seem rude and stand-offish and, even worse, give the idea that you do not want to do business with them. Emma used to go all wooden when people she didn't know started touching her on the arm or on her shoulder, but now she is used to it and even does it herself.

HAND GESTURES

Just as Italians talk a lot, they are also rather fond of body language and entire conversations can be visual. When you're not familiar with the gestures, it can be quite confusing. Italians regard northern Europeans, Americans and Canadians as somewhat rigid because of their tendency to keep their arms still when they talk. Try using your hands to punctuate your conversations. You may feel rather self-conscious initially, but you'll soon find yourself using them all the time.

Case study

German, Nicola Shroeder, grew up in New Jersey and moved to Lucerne, Switzerland, when she was 17. She has lived in Sardinia since March 1991. Together with two business partners, she set up Centro Mediterraneo Pintadera, a small Italian language school in Alghero, in February 2004.

Emma: Nicola, Sardinia is not Tuscany or Umbria or any other traditional expat beat. How come you ended up on the island?

Nicola: I followed my heart. My companion, who I met in Florence, is from Sassari and happens to think that Sardinia is the best place in the world.

Emma: I agree, but I'm biased living there myself. Were you familiar with Italian culture before moving?

Nicola: I did an Italian language course in Florence one summer many moons ago. It was back in 1979 when I had finished high school. I stayed three months and it was a fantastic experience.

Emma: Did you visit Italy any more times before moving to Sardinia?

Nicola: Yes, ever since my Florence language immersion, I spent as much time as possible in Italy and in the Italian part of Switzerland. I was working for a Swiss marketing firm when I was transferred to Rome in 1987 so, initially, I had the security of a Swiss salary while living in Rome.

Emma: Lucky you. How easy or difficult did you find it to get to grips with Italian culture?

Nicola: It was all very gradual for me. I worked on the marketing and organisation of the Italian World Cup in Soccer in 1990 for the Swiss company and it was an international but Italian-flavoured experience.

Emma: Has it all been plain sailing?

▶

Nicola: No. I am very direct and this has led to my being criticised for 'lack of tact'.

Emma: What about your experience with Italians and timekeeping?

Nicola: Now this is something I haven't quite come to terms with. Seeing I am not able to impose punctuality on Sardinians, I have had to adjust.

Emma: Anything else you have had to adjust to? What about Italians and their way of taking short cuts or bending the law?

Nicola: Seeing that '***flessibilità***' (flexibility) is seen as a virtue here, I have had to adjust.

Emma: You speak Italian. Does this help you integrate better into Italian society in terms of culture?

Nicola: You must learn the language and I am not just saying this because I run an Italian language school. If you cannot communicate, you will always be an outsider.

---

*Mario's **Pearl of Wisdom***

We Italians don't really get understatement and we often change our minds. We may sound really keen about your proposal but don't necessarily think that we are telling the truth. If we thought it was a terrible idea and we told you that, we'd risk making a ***brutta figura*** (a bad impression). Our only other option would be to use Anglo-saxon coded language such as 'that sounds interesting' which we don't do. Listen out to key words when we speak. If we say something like 'send me an email with the details' or 'Give me a ring next week to talk about it', then we probably mean business.

If you are not familiar with the Italian culture, you will probably end up in all kinds of bizarre situations, which are amusing at best and frustrating at worst. When things do go wrong or a culture clash occurs, don't take it personally. It happens to everyone when they are in a new country. But no matter how annoyed or upset you feel, it is important not to vent your feelings on the Italians as this will leave you feeling bitter. Shrug it off and have a laugh as this is the best way of diffusing any tension.

18

Business etiquette

As with all other areas of Italian life, the importance of the '*bella figura*' cannot be stressed enough. In *The dark heart of Italy*, British journalist Tobias Jones writes: '*That obsession with outward appearance is at the root of the word figura ... Fare una figura, to make a bad impression, is an error not necessarily of morals but of presentation.*'

Thus, it is vitally important to cut the right figure in the business environment. In Italy, first impressions count more than anywhere else in Europe. Whatever you do, don't think that that cursory two-minute glance in the bedroom mirror before leaving the house is sufficient to check whether or not you are presentable to the rest of the world. It won't be. Fashion counts a lot in the workplace and that goes for men as well as women.

WOMEN

Smart trouser suits are a common sight in Italian offices and are replacing the skimpy outfits of yesteryear. Make sure yours is modern and as expensive as you can afford. Wearing a suit with a jacket that comes past your hips will mark you out as non-Italian instantly. Although blue and grey suits are perfectly acceptable, many Italian women prefer black ones. Use a blouse or fitted jumper under your suit jacket: cream, light blue, pink and yellow are all acceptable colours. In the summer, opt for linen trousers and a smart sleeveless top.

Tights

Tights should be worn all year round, even in summer. Make sure you wear black tights in winter and nude/transparent ones in the summer. Be warned that Italians always enjoy a laugh at British women's expense for the trend of wearing skirts *all'inglese* in winter: in other words, bare-legged. Make sure legs are hair free at all times. And be warned, Italian men and women are trained to spot cellulite at a distance even in places you didn't think you had it.

Shoes

Italian women normally wear pointy-shoes: wearing high heels is *de rigueur* so forget comfort, be prepared to put up with blisters and go for glam. Heels for the office are normally no higher than 7cm (2.75 inches), although you can swap your shoes for a higher pair if you have a business dinner in the evening.

Grooming

Women tend to be immaculately groomed both in and out of the office. Particular care should also be paid to hair and make-up. The average Italian woman goes to the hairdressers at least once a month (some even go once a week) to keep her hair in check. While this may seem excessive, it is worth noting that Italian women do not suffer the same bad hair days that are the bane of her Anglo-saxon cousins. They will also never leave the house with wet hair. If you are running late for an appointment, do not even consider letting your hair dry on the way to the office. In this situation, it would be better to make an excuse and turn up late.

Eyebrows

A lot of attention is placed on the aesthetic appeal of a woman's face and never will your eyebrows have received so much attention. Eyebrows can be thin or *au naturel* but they must always be tidy. If you've never had your eyebrows professionally plucked, waxed or threaded before, now is the time to start. In between sessions, use an eyebrow gel or pencil to keep them well-defined.

Make-up

Make-up should also be worn, and it would be better to forfeit the no make-up look altogether unless you have immaculate skin – as is the case with most Italians.

Hair cut

That immaculate coiffed-to-Hollywood perfection look that Italian women always pull off doesn't happen by accident. They suffer bad-hair days as much as the rest of us. However, they would rather set the alarm three hours earlier than leave the house looking less than amazing. Monthly hair cuts and will ensure you look equally amazing.

By bringing together all of these pointers, you will have the same self-assured and self-confident manner as Italian women.

MEN

Men will be forgiven now for thinking that the sartorial rules are more lax for them, but, in Italy, image in the workplace counts for both sexes.

Suits

Grey is the most popular colour for suits and can be made from any material just as long as it is natural rather than synthetic. If you feel uncomfortable wearing suits or are on the road a lot, consider a tweed or blue felt jacket that can be worn with a pair of chinos or smart jeans. Unless you will be doing business with top managers, this is a perfectly acceptable alternative.

Ties

Ties are no longer the office essential they once were and you can choose whether or not to wear one. This is particularly true in the summer when many men skip the formal suit jacket because it is just too hot.

If you do choose to wear a tie, don't make the mistake of thinking any tie will do – it won't. Ties, like suits, should be of a high quality. Cartoon prints are strictly out as this will give the impression of someone who likes to fool around rather than someone who takes his work seriously but also has a sense of humour. Sporting a tie from any of the Italian fashion heavyweights such as Valentino, Ermenegilda Zegna, Gucci and Versace will prove that you are a man worth doing business with. The knot of the tie is normally wide.

Socks

Socks should match the same shade as your suit (pull out any businessman's sock drawer and you are likely to find dozens and dozens of pairs of socks neatly colour coded, along with several pairs of new socks should any emergencies arise). Whatever colour you do opt for, your socks (yes, your socks!) should match.

Shoes

There is also a strict rule regarding shoes. Italian men have both black and tan shoes in their wardrobes. Black is normally used in the winter, whereas tan shoes are often worn in the summer with lightweight suits. Shoes should always be polished and shiny.

By following all of these rules, you will be the sophisticated, trustable businessman who has cut the *bella figura*.

IMPORTANCE OF TITLES

Italians are much more formal than Americans or the British when it comes to the workplace. A university degree still carries prestige. As such, a graduate holds the title of *dottore* if he is a man, and *dottoressa* if she is a woman. If your business acquaintance has an engineering degree, then *ingegnere* is the correct title. If they are law graduates then *avvocato* would be the correct title. If the person does not have a title, address them as *signor* for a man and *signora* for a woman. If the woman is in her early twenties, you can also address her as *signorina*. After the title, always add the person's surname. So Mario Rossi the lawyer becomes *Avvocato Rossi*. Mario Rossi the engineer becomes Ingegnere Rossi, Mario Rossi the graduate becomes *Dottor Rossi* and Mario Rossi who is none of the above is *Signor Rossi*. However, always err on the side of caution. If you are unsure of how you should address someone, then be honest and say so. Not only will they be flattered, it will also demonstrate that you are an honest person that takes time to get things right. If you are mistakenly given the title higher than your own, correct the speaker at the outset and without cracking a joke. However, if you are called *signor* or *signora* when you have a university degree or higher, do not pass comment.

Figure 18.1 below shows you the professions in English and the corresponding term of address in Italian.

Figure 18.1

Title	Male	Female
None	*Signor Rossi*	*Signora Rossi*
Teacher	*Professor Rossi*	*Professoressa Rossi*
Graduate	*Dottor Rossi*	*Dottoressa Rossi*
Architect	*Architetto Rossi*	*Architetto Rossi*
Surveyor	*Geometra Rossi*	*Geometra Rossi*
Engineer	*Ingener Rossi*	*Ingener Rossi*
Head of local government department	*Assessore Rossi*	*Assessore Rossi*

Normally, the younger person is introduced to the older person, the man to the woman and the least important person to the most important one. To introduce someone say '*le presento il Dottor Rossi*' or in the case of a woman, '*le presento la Dottoressa Rossi*'. If there is no one to introduce you, say '*Buongiorno, sono ...*', followed by your name and surname.

USE OF *TU/LEI*

The use of informal *tu* and the formal *lei* is a minefield. The general rule is to follow your Italian colleague's example. So, if they use *lei*, so do you; if they use *tu*, follow suit. However, as with all aspects of Italian life, there are no hard and fast rules and they can be overridden if your Italian colleague says '*ci possiamo dare del tu or ci diamo del tu?*'.

HIERARCHY

Italians are formal creatures in the workplace and company hierarchy is rigidly observed. The *dirigenti* normally eat with the bosses and external consulants, while lower-ranked workers eat together. Socialising together outside of work is rare.

PLEASED TO MEET YOU

It used to be pretty standard practice to say *'piacere'* or 'pleased to meet you' on shaking hands with a new business acquaintance and you will still hear this on some occasions. However, these days, instead of saying *'piacere'* simply state your name and surname while shaking your colleague's hand.

GREETINGS

As a general rule, remember that *salve*, literally meaning 'greetings' is formal, while *ciao* is much less formal and should generally not be used in initial conversations or emails. *Buongiorno* (good morning) or *buonasera* (good evening) *avvocato, ingegnere, architetto* etc may seem pompous and old fashioned to a foreigner used to being on first name terms even with the boss, but Italians appreciate the effort. When you are leaving, use *arriverderla* (goodbye), or *arriverderci* if you have switched to using *tu*.

EXCHANGING BUSINESS CARDS

This always happens at the beginning of a business meeting rather than at the end. As a general rule, this exchange takes place straight after introductions and pleasantries are out of the way. The first person to offer their *biglietto da visita* (business card) is the person who has invited you to their offices. If a number of people give you a card, try to remember the order in which you receive the cards and follow it when you hand out yours. The order may seem insignificant to you, but in Italy there is a strict business hierarchy and you would be wise to follow it initially. Business cards are not slid across tables or given in multiples to the nearest person for him or her to then distribute these to his or her colleagues. Use both hands if possible to press the business card into the hands of the person receiving it.

Details

If you are conducting a deal in both English and Italian, one school of thought is to have one language on the front and one on the reverse of the card. However, even the most idiot of idiots can recognise an email address and telephone number in either language, and as for business titles using English terms is now fashionably trendy. Whatever rule you plump for, remember that the more senior the business executive, the less information there tends to be on the card.

Unless you do a lot of travelling and are frequently out of the office, do not include your mobile number on your business card. Adding your mobile number by hand in front of the person you are giving the card to is particularly appreciated. What is not appreciated is the giving out of business cards with DIY amendments scribbled previously. This is known as *rattopatto*, literally 'patched up', and is considered seriously bad form. If your details have changed, it's time for a new *biglietto da visita*.

Italians like everything to be ordered and for people to appear in control even when, perhaps, they aren't. Have two sleek holders for your business cards – one for the cards you are doling out and one for the cards you will receive.

BUSINESS LUNCHES/MEALS

If you have a meeting scheduled for mid-morning, bear in mind that it is only a couple of hours away from lunchtime and thus you may want to consider extending the meeting over lunch – this is especially popular in your initial dealings with a new business acquaintance. Chatting over lunch might seem cosy and relaxed, but its sub aim is to create an atmosphere of trust – vital to an Italian before he or she will even consider doing business with you.

Buon appetito

Wishing your fellow diners *buon appetito*, or a good meal, is now strictly passé and has been replaced with a smile. However, given that it was also the signal for everyone to begin eating, it now means people are not always sure when to begin. In general, the woman should start eating once her fellow diners have received their meals. If there is no woman, then the guest of honour, normally seated at the head of the table (*capotavola*), will start eating and give the signal to the other diners. If there is no *capotavola*, the person who organised the dinner should start.

Use of cutlery

Dining is an indulgent but relaxed affair in Italy and this is reflected in the informal use of cutlery. The fork is often used to eat everything apart from steaks and, if no meat is being eaten, Italians will often dispense with the knife altogether. When using a fork in your right hand (for pasta, vegetables and small pieces of meat), the prongs point upwards; when using a fork in your left hand they point downwards. When eating meat and vegetables, bread is often used as a substitute for a knife. Break the bread into small pieces as and when you want to eat it and take it in your left hand. Use it to push the food up onto your upturned fork.

If you are eating spaghetti, tagliatelle or any other type of fiddly pasta, don't be embarrassed to ask for a spoon. This will ensure you keep up with the rest of the diners and won't suffer the same fate as Emma. Newly arrived in Milan, she was trying (and failing spectacularly) to eat a plate of *spaghetti al pomodoro* with just her fork. The little girl sitting at the table next to her, cried out 'Look *signora*, I can eat spaghetti better than you. This is how you do it', as she expertly twirled her pasta around her fork.

BUYING PRESENTS

Some Italians may want to curry favour by presenting you with lavish gifts – or it may simply be a display of their generosity and showing that they are delighted to do business with you. If you feel that you cannot accept the gift, the best thing to do is to turn it down politely citing your company's ethical policy – of course, if you don't have one, you could always make it up.

The best way of really understanding the *bella* and *brutta figura* is by people watching. The next time you are in Italy, head for a bar frequented by businessmen and women, grab yourself a *latte macchiato* and take note of how everyone is behaving. It sounds simple but it really is an effective way of absorbing the Italian culture around you.

Mario's Pearl of Wisdom

In this chapter, we may have stressed the importance Italians place on business etiquette and the **bella** and **brutta figura**, but don't worry, we (Italians, not Emma and I) know that more often than not foreigners have no idea how to dress well so we don't expect you to and we don't expect you to know the ins and outs of our business etiquette. You won't lose any brownie points by forgetting some of these pointers.

If you really can't spare the time for lunch, then a quick **panino** at the local bar or even a very quick bowl of soup or pasta is perfectly fine. But if you don't know your colleagues very well or need to create a good impression, take us to lunch and don't talk business: the emphasis is on eating and drinking well in a seriously chic location. Take us up in the mountains, wow us with a sea view or wine and dine us in a place steeped in history.

19

Networking

By now you should be raring to go. There is just one problem: you don't know anyone in the area in which you are planning on setting up a business. Emma knows exactly how you feel. Before she moved to Milan, she knew she had a busy task ahead of her if she wanted to make reliable contacts in the textile industry – when you think she was covering the whole textile chain from the raw wool through to the weavers, the spinners, the machinery makers and the designers, that's an awful lot of people. But ever up for a challenge, she threw herself into it with relish. Initially it was great because building up networks is what Emma is good at.

But as she immersed herself in her job, she realised the *Dolce Vita* she had been hankering after ever since studying media and politics at the University of Bologna was nowhere to be found. She was imprisoned in her fourth-floor studio flat (she worked from home) in the centre of Milan. Admittedly, the location was glamorous, but she had no time to enjoy it and the vicious circle of working all hours because she had no social life began. In the end, Emma found herself in a catch 22 situation: the more she worked, the more she needed a support network but, ironically, the more she worked, the less time she had to build one.

It is little wonder that Emma was miserable and felt a failure. Stressful days weren't dealt with by meeting friends for an *aperi-*

tivo and a gossip during Happy Hour but by knocking back G&Ts in her apartment on her own.

COMPARE THAT WITH SARDINIA

The only similarity between moving to Milan and moving to Sardinia was that when Emma moved she didn't really know anyone. This time round though, she didn't have a job either. After spending several afternoons sobbing in various piazzas in the burning heat of the afternoon and convincing herself she would become just another unemployment statistic, she decided she had to take action.

But she turned that to her advantage. Because she didn't know anyone, she spent her days networking. At first, this was done over the internet. In order to combat the loneliness that always accompanies the move to a new place, she aimed to contact at least 20 people per week. At this point, these were mainly English-speaking expats around the world who were leading lives that she herself wanted to lead.

Eventually, she found a stop-gap job teaching English three hours a week as maternity cover. This proved vital as her students were a link between her own little world and the 'real' Italy going on in the rest of Cagliari.

The next step was to set up a networking association for professional women in Cagliari. This was more difficult than it seemed considering that Emma still didn't know very many people and certainly not enough to form a professional women's association. The few people she did share her idea with looked at her as if she were mad. But having seen networking associations thrive throughout the rest of the world, she stuck to her guns and did it anyway.

Case study

Jonathan McGuinness

Jonathan McGuiness is married to an Italian and lived between Milan and Cagliari for three years. In Milan, he set up the group Business and Social Networking.

Emma: If you network you must have good Italian skills. Is that true for you?

Jonathan: Networking is about communicating with other people to help them and let them help you, so any tool that facilitates that communication has my full backing. Communication is about the response you get. If you want to be sure that someone else understands something, it needs to be communicated in a way that they can and even more, that they want to continue being involved in the idea you are talking about by being motivated. Can this be achieved through English? Sure. Can it be achieved so much better through the other person's language? Yes!

Emma: So did you speak Italian before you moved?

Jonathan: A couple of words, literally. It became a block between other people and me, so the block had to go. Bit by bit, I chewed my way through the language, enjoying making mistakes which others enjoyed too.

Emma: I know that feeling of coming out with complete rubbish. Still, you get there in the end. So tell me how you developed Social and Business Networking.

Jonathan: When moving to Milan, socialising was among the group of people that I got to know from work and those usually most available to meet up were non-Milanese, those people foreign to Milan, people who spoke my native tongue of English and Italians not from Milan but Rome, Bari and many other places.

Emma: Right, okay. And where did you find them?

Jonathan: On several occasions, I did a search on Ecademy for other people living in Milan who would be interested in meeting up, as there was – and is – a belief driving me that in meeting another person, another world opens up to me. I remember being with some friends from work and going to meet an English couple living just outside of Milan for a classic *aperitivo* and getting to know each other which turned out to be an enjoyable evening. This idea then took force with 'that was good, let's do it again'. So to answer the original question, Business and Social Networking was an extension, an added way, to my normal activities and this part was taking structure.

Emma: Business and Social Networking sounds interesting. Tell me more.

Jonathan: It was a group of four people as a core team all with different perspectives and agendas who commonly enjoyed, and benefited from, the activity of networking in Milan. It also took a natural course in the way it formed. We met individually with many people and brought them together for the bigger meetings and events that we had which accumulated into quite a number resulting in the following http://www.ecademy.com/node.php?id=22464. It gave extra stimulus to the growing momentum.

Emma: You built up quite a network. It's fair to say you're a bit of an expert. Did it take a lot of effort?

Jonathan: Effort, yes, plus the curiosity to meet new people and learn new things drove me to introducing myself to many people. It then took on the multiplier effect because I teamed up with people who had a similar (no one is the same) satisfaction from these activities taking place all with their own agendas as per life.

Emma: Given your success, what do you think is the best way to network in Italy?

Jonathan: The concept of a best way can hurt. Networking is about being flexible and having many ways to be able to communicate with people. The ways need to be adapted to the audience that you wish to appeal to. To answer your question, if there is any best formula to have it is to be adaptive and have a clear mission. Networking is a living organisation that needs to change for people, for the environment and be directed towards a common goal which is clear and simple.

Emma: Do you think it is more important to network with expats or with Italians?

Jonathan: Neither and both. Networking can be viewed as an activity to help achieve your business and social agendas. Setting a bias to whom can satisfy those agendas is the act of self-imposing limitations and you may be right and you may be wrong. An optimal approach is to focus on people more likely to satisfy your needs by their occupation, connections and ability to communicate.

Emma: What advice do you have for expats new to networking in general or networking in Italy?

Jonathan: Try it and try it several times. Do not judge initial results to summarise the activity as a whole. Be careful, though, as you may not ever want to stop!

NETWORKING IN ITALY

Although you may not know many people in Italy yet, take heart. Italians, like the Spanish and Portuguese, are natural networkers. In countries where nepotism still exists, it is the only way to do business. Social relationships transform effortlessly into business relationships, just as *aperitifs* merge seamlessly into dinner.

However, one very real problem to overcome is that of *raccomandazione*. Or, in plain English, you do a favour for me and I'll do a favour for you. In southern Italy especially, the idea of professional networking is still looked on suspiciously but times are changing. One of Mario's business colleagues rang him excitedly at midnight to tell him that he had been talking to someone from the British Chamber of Commerce and that they were as enthusiastic about this concept of networking as us.

Joining a professional networking association

The potential value of networking is immense. If we remember that we are only seven people away from any other person on the planet, it makes sense to network professionally and socially, with expats and Italians. After all, you never know where your next work lead might come from.

There are four professional national and/or international networking associations in Italy:

♦ **LinkedIn**
www.linkedin.com
LinkedIn is an English-language online network of more than five million experienced professionals from around the world, representing 130 industries. When you join, you create a profile that summarises your professional accomplishments. Your profile helps you find and be found by former colleagues, clients, and partners. You can add more connections by inviting trusted contacts to join LinkedIn and connect to you. Basic membership is free. The Business account costs USD19.95 per month, Business Plus costs USD50 per month and Pro costs USD200 per month. Offline meetings are held in Italy on a monthly basis.

◆ **Ecademy**

http://www.ecademy.com

Ecademy started out in the UK in 1989. It has more than 70,000 members worldwide and, as of February 2006, 858 in Italy. You can either take out a monthly or yearly subscription. In 2006, it cost GBP25, USD25 and €25 for basic GreenStar membership, and GBP120, USD170 and €168 (for developing and emerging countries there is a special annual rate of USD60) for Powernetworker proactive networking membership. Prices will remain the same for 2007. Ecademy is an English language networking forum. However, Ecademy Italy, the country club for Italy, is bilingual and there are plans in the pipeline for the whole of Ecademy to become multilingual in 2008.

◆ **OpenBC**

www.openbc.com

OpenBC makes contacts of contacts visible to members and integrates these contacts within a member's own network. OpenBC stands for an open and secure network and connects entrepreneurs, business managers, freelancers and the managers of the future by finding new business contacts or cooperation partners, opening up new markets and maintaining existing business relationships. Because Italian is one of the platform's languages, OpenBC attracts lots of Italian users. If Italians are your potential clients, then this is a good site to use. Basic membership is free, Premium Membership is €5.95 per month.

◆ **Biz Bureau**

www.bizbureau.org

Biz Bureau bills itself as the first Italian social network. Members come from all different sectors and meet on the last Tuesday of every month to discuss opportunities arising from the digital economy. Each month, members meet at another member's workplace and can also invite guests. Every month there is also an outside speaker. The person hosting the event has the opportunity to present him or herself, providing a promotion opportunity. It is linked to LinkedIn (www.linkedin.com).

Other Useful Associations:

◆ **American Business Group**
www.americanbusinessgroup.it
The group is made up of executives from the American business community but the American Business Luncheon is open to all those having interests or business dealings with North America and North American companies. Participation is by invitation only. The group is not registered and has no membership fees or other costs other than that of the luncheon.

◆ **American Chamber of Commerce in Italy**
www.amcham.it
AmCham's mission is to develop and promote economic relations between the USA and Italy, to promote and protect the interests of its members within the framework of their business operations between the two countries, and to inform the Chamber's members of its activities. AmCham's Italian headquarters are based in Milan, with secondary offices in Rome. There are also honorary representatives in Trieste, Turin, Genoa, Bologna, Florence, Rome and Naples. It has monthly meetings and provides good networking opportunities.

◆ **British Chamber of Commerce for Italy**
www.britchamitaly.com
The Chamber was founded in Genoa in 1904 but its headquarters are now in Milan. There are additional branches in Emilia Romagna, Tuscany, Lazio, Piedmont, Veneto, Friuili, Puglia, Campania and Sardinia, along with Area Secretaries in

Bergamo, Brescia, Padua, Pordenone, Taranto, Venice, Verona and London. It has close ties with the British Embassy, the British Consulate General in Milan and the posts in Naples and Florence, and represents the interests of the Confederation of British Industries and the British Standards Institute in Italy. The BCCI also has ties with the Department of Trade and Industry and the Association of British Chambers of Commerce. Throughout Europe, it is linked with COBCOE, the Council of British Chambers of Commerce in Continental Europe. The Chamber holds a monthly networking lunch in Milan. Other branches also hold their own events during the year.

♦ **Australian Business Network in Italy**
www.australianbusiness.it
The Australian Business Network in Italy is a local forum which brings together Australian organisations doing business in Italy and Italian organisations doing business with these companies or with companies in Australia. It has regular networking meetings.

Setting up a networking association

Do you want to know the reason why there isn't a networking association in the Italian town you are based or want to be based? The answer is simple: probably because someone is waiting for someone else (i.e., you!) to set it up. By establishing the network, you will automatically be seen as creative, inspirational, a leader and a self-starter. And if that isn't a good enough reason, you will be in control of the network and so have a huge group of ready-made contacts. Since Emma started up Weaveaweb, she has been given all kinds of work offers – from teaching to translating, to international PR for Italian companies to advising Italian schools on

English. Some of the offers she took up, some she didn't. But that doesn't matter. The point is, that she was in a position to choose.

Before setting up the networking association, think about who you want to aim it at. All expats? Young expat mums? Expat entrepreneurs? Expat professional women? Expat teachers? American Expats? British Expats? Professional Italian women? All Italian professionals? Young Italian-speaking professionals? The list is endless. You may not think there is any interest, but if it meets your needs, the chances are there is a gap in the market and other people are also crying out for the same group.

Getting the group off the ground

To get your group up and running, think small. To start with, you don't even need a website. Putting up a poster in the window of a local shop or leaving flyers at the local gym will be enough to get it going. At the first Weaveaweb meeting, there were only five women, cobbled together from anyone Emma could find. But that way, Weaveaweb had officially started and from there it could only get bigger, as in fact it did.

Think location, location, location

If you live in a small village in southern Italy, the chances are you will soon know everyone anyway. In that case, it may be better to hold it in a town nearby in order to increase the catchment area of the potential networkers.

You also need to think about where you want to hold the meetings and their format? In a bar for aperitifs? In a restaurant for a pizza? In Milan, where Happy Hour is a firm tradition, meeting for an aperitif works much better than meeting for dinner because people are free to drop in at any time, and food is always available. In Cagliari, on the other hand, having an aperitif doesn't work because aperitifs don't come with the hot and cold buffet you get in Milan and people are more tied up to the custom of going home after work, having a shower and beautifying themselves (men as well as women) before going out for the evening. As a result, dinner tends to start at around 9.30pm. There are no right or wrong answers so play around with the format until you get one that suits you.

Meet regularly

By holding the networking event on the same date every month, people can plan ahead, meaning that if they can't attend one of the meetings, they at least know when the next one is. This also makes your job easier as coordinator, as you don't need to send out as many reminders about the event.

Formal or informal?

Do you want a large event where people need to have a name badge and need to do a lot of small talk and walk up to potential strangers? Or do you want a more intimate event which is socialising in the bar on a local basis? Do you have to be a member of a club or is it a more drop-in-and-bring-your-friends event? It's your club, it's up to you. But remember that Italians like to have a warm environment conducive to establishing relationships.

How to be a good networker

There are a lot of misconceptions about networking and how you have to walk a room dealing with snobby strangers who don't want to talk to you. But networking isn't about schmoozing a room of 1,000 people who are all busy airkissing each other and pretending to be nice. Done right, networking finds you friends, colleagues and customers, helps with setting up a business and enables you to get to the top.

To excel at networking, confidence is crucial. But we're not talking about being extrovert. What we mean is having confidence in yourself and the confidence in your business. Richard Branson, the CEO of Virgin, is famously shy as was Carole Stone who now has more than 40,000 names in her address book.

How to attract members

As we've already said, networking as a concept is still relatively new in Italy so don't expect that your new club will be a success straight away. Italians love foreign concepts but remain suspicious of what they don't know. To increase the number of networkers in your club, stage an event with other organisations such as Open BC or Ecademy. At the event, have a mini networking expo where the participants can showcase their businesses – this can pay dividends as everyone likes having free publicity and it means the rest of the evening can be more relaxed and not 100 per cent focused on business. Other tricks include sending press releases out to the local media until they start publicising your event. Of course, if you can persuade an Italian journalist to cover the meeting, even better.

Here's a copy of the press release that Emma sent to Sardinia's regional newspaper *Il Sardegna* when she launched Ecademy Sardegna:

'Si chiama Ecademy Sardegna ed è un'associazione che raggrupa professionisti, italiani e stranieri. 'Networking non ha niente a che fare con il vecchia sistema di raccomandazione' spiega Emma

Bird, giovane ragazza inglese che coordina il gruppo. 'Lo scopo è di creare una rete di contatti tra imprenditori, liberi professionisti e manager in azienda nell'isola per scambiare idee, esperienze e contatti di lavoro non solo in inglese ma anche italiano. E' un luogo dove crescere le competenze professionali e si può accedere ai servizi offerti dai soci. In più, c'è la possibilità di fare networking a livello nazionale ed internazionale.'

It worked. The press release got published and the next day, the Ecademy Sardegna home page received a higher number of page hits than normal and a couple of people even signed up. Maybe that will happen to you, too. There's only one way to find out.

Mario's Pearl of Wisdom

When networking, it's the givers that receive the most. Concentrate on making a proper connection with a person, not just on a business level. This is especially important in Italy because we like doing business with people we know and trust. If we are not doing business with close friends and family, we prefer to work with people we actually like and would class as a friend. When you meet someone in Italy, be genuinely interested in that person and what they do and take time to cement the relationship. I know Italians and foreigners who have got confused about networking. They think it's all about the here and now and forget that the benefits will often boomerang back to you six months or more down the line. Also remember to cast your net (I like that English phrase!) as wide as possible. Don't just network with people in your field, network with everyone, Italians and other expats, as you never know where your next client or potential lead may come from.

20

Women in business

In a land where *veline* (showgirls) still wiggle their provocatively-clad bodies on sports programmes and the nightly current affairs show *Porta a Porta* brings on well-endowed topless models when discussing plastic surgery, it probably doesn't come as any surprise to learn that few women reach the upper echelons of Italian power. Although Italy has yet to produce a female prime minister, Letizia Brichetto Arnaboldi Moratti is a notable exception. She was the Minister for Education in Silvio Berlusconi's cabinet but before playing with the big boys in politics, she was also a prominent businesswoman. Between 1994 and 1996, she was the president of RAI, the country's state television channel.

Whilst the glass ceiling has been successfully shattered in the USA, UK, Australia, New Zealand, and Canada, the *soffitto di cristallo* is still firmly in place in Italy. Not surprisingly given Italy's strong Catholic influence, women's rights lag behind the rest of Europe. Italy only granted partial voting rights to women in 1925 and full rights in 1945 (New Zealand women were the first in the world to be given the right to vote in 1893, Australian women in 1903, American women in 1920, UK women in 1928, South African women in1930 and Canada in 1950), divorce was legalised in 1970 and abortion followed in 1978. Italians also voted against legalising IVF treatment in the May 2005 referendum and, in February 2006, the *Cassazione*, Italy's Supreme

Court, declared that a 14-year-old girl being raped by her step-father was 'a less serious' crime than it might otherwise have been because she already had sexual experience. As you can see, a woman's life in Italy is not the *dolce vita* it might initially seem. When even journalists for Italy's national financial newspaper *Il sole 24 Ore* state Italian women that would be better off setting up their own businesses, it's surely time to take notice.

THE CURRENT SITUATION IN ITALY

Female entrepreneurs tend to be highest in the Italian regions worst hit by unemployment. More female-run businesses (36.8 per cent) are concentrated in southern Italy and the islands than anywhere else in the country.

As of October 2005, there were 1.2 million companies run by women in Italy. The majority of these (73.9 per cent) were sole trade companies, with joint stock corporations in the minority (5.3 per cent). According to the *Osservatorio sull'imprenditoria femminile di Unioncamere-Infocamere,* in the first semester of 2005 the number of women-run companies in the country had risen by 2.4 per cent compared to the same period in 2004, whereas the overall rise in businesses was just 1 per cent. The industries recording the biggest rise in female entrepreneurship were manufacturing, real estate and the services.

WOMEN AND MANAGEMENT POSITIONS

Even though there are more female than male graduates in Italy, few women reach management level and even fewer can be found in the boardrooms. Only 3 per cent are senior managers and only 2 per cent sit on boards (*source*: Egon Zehnder International, data collected in March/April 2004). The few prominent women in Italy tend to come from powerful families. Marina Berlusconi the daughter of the former prime minister Silvio Berlusconi is the vice-president of Finivest and Jonella and Giulia Maria Ligresti are chair and vice-chair respectively of Fondiaria-Sai, the insurance company of which the Ligresti family owns 41 per cent of the shares.

MATERNITY RIGHTS AND CHILDCARE

Italians attach much importance to the women staying at home to bring up their children and this is reflected in the country's maternity and childcare legislation. Italian women enjoy some of the best maternity conditions in Europe and from the time a woman is pregnant through to the first birthday of her child, she cannot be sacked or made redundant.

LEAVE OF ABSENCE

Maternity leave is equivalent to 80 per cent of the normal salary. The pregnant woman/mother must take a total of five months leave. Normally, two months are taken before the birth and three months after the birth. However, if there are no complications with the pregnancy, she can work up to one month before the birth and take four months off afterwards. If the woman's role includes dangerous work of any kind, maternity leave can be extended for an additional two months. If there is a risk of miscarriage, then a woman will often be signed off work by a doctor three months into the pregnancy. A woman can also choose to take an additional period of unpaid leave up to a total of six months. If she is a single mother, she may take ten months unpaid leave.

MATERNITY PAY FOR ENTREPRENEURS AND CONSULTANTS

Female consultants and entrepreneurs are entitled to 80 per cent of five months of their annual salary. The exact amount is calculated according to the total amount declared in the tax year two years prior to the one in which she falls pregnant.

BREASTFEEDING RIGHTS

During the baby's first year, the mother is entitled to paid leave during the day to breastfeed her child or to rest. New mums working full-time are entitled to two hours' paid leave per day, while for mums working part-time (less than six hours per day), one hour of paid leave is granted. In the case of twins, triplets etc, the amount of paid leave doubles for each additional child.

CHILDREN'S ILLNESS

Both parents can take unpaid leave when their children are ill. In the case of children aged two and under, parents have the right to stay off work for the entire duration of the illness. In the case of three to eight year-olds, unpaid leave is restricted to a total of five days.

CHILDCARE

The provision of *asili-nido* (childcare facilities) for children aged between three months and two-and-a-half years varies considerably depending on the area. The north-east of Italy has the highest number of places available and the south and the islands have the fewest. This is not surprising given the high unemployment rates among women in the south and the prevalence of the tradionally-held attitude that a woman's place is in the home.

Childcare in Italy is not over expensive. In 2005, the average cost for a full-time place was €288 per month and €215 part-time. Calabria was Italy's cheapest region, with a full-time place costing an average of €167 per month. Trentino Alto-Adige was the most expensive region with a full-time place costing an average of €410. In terms of cities, the answers are different to what you might expect. Despite being the Italian capital, Rome had the cheapest costs in 2005: a full-time place cost just €146 per month. Lecco, in Lombardy, registered the highest prices at €572. The website: http://www.zerodelta.net/it/studiare-nidi_scuole_infanzia.php provides a comprehensive list of *asilo-nidos* throughout Italy, along with their opening hours.

IN-COMPANY CRÈCHE FACILITIES

As a result of the lack of childcare in Italy, the Italian government has offered financial incentives to companies setting up crèches. Between 2002–2004, €10 million was set aside for such schemes. Tiscali, the telephony and internet giant, is one company that provides in-house facilities. The service was set up in September 2003 when the company's new premises were opened just outside Cagliari. In 2005, there were 31 children on the books aged twelve months to five years. The crèche is open from 8.30am until 7pm and costs on average 50 per cent less than a private nursery in the city.

If you wish to apply for funding to set up a *micro-nido* in your company, the following criteria apply:

◆ the nursery must be on work premises or in the immediate vicinity. No more than ten children can be looked after;

- each child requires seven square metres of space;
- there must be one area entirely for the children plus one area for the nursery workers. There should be separate bathroom facilities for each;
- the nursery opening hours must be decided between the employer and employees who wish to take advantage of the facilities;
- there must be a ratio of one qualified nursery worker for every seven children;
- children must be aged between three months and three years.

Funding allocation varies on a year-to-year basis and region to region. Contact the *Amministrazione Provinciale Servizi Sociali* (the social services department) of your local *Regione* (regional council) for guidance.

WOMEN AND NETWORKING

Compared with Britain, the US, Canada, Australia, and New Zealand, Italy does not have well-developed networks focussing on women's needs. Dinner Girls, Women who Lunch and A Woman's Place (part of the Ecademy network) simply do not exist in Italy. The best alternative is to join one of the professional women's associations located in the main Italian towns. Two of the best ones are:

- PWA Milan
  www.pwa-milan.org
  The Professional Women's Association (PWA) in Milan is one of the most active women's networks in Italy. It was launched in

1987 and brings together professional (mainly entrepreneurs and managers) English-speaking women in an international environment.

PWA is also part of the European Professional Women's Network (with offices in Paris, London, Amsterdam, Milan, Athens and Vienna).

◆ International Women's Forum, Bologna
http://www.iwfbologna.com/
Women from 16 different countries meet once a month, but there are also several small groups organised according to members' interests. The association was launched in 1998 for English-speaking women of all nationalities.

International networking:

◆ WIN
www.winconference.net
The Women's International Networking (WIN) Global Leadership Forum is staged every October. It brings together nearly 500 women from all over the world for the three-day event. The conference provides the possibility to gain relevant skills and knowledge via specialised workshops; the chance to make new business and personal contacts and to renew existing ones; and the opportunity to gain inspiration and new ideas through plenary workshops and speaker debates. This is a good event for women doing business at an international level (and an opportunity to network with English-speaking Italian business women). Emma knows women who attend every year and they say it is vital for growing their business on a global level.

WOMEN AND FINANCING/GRANTS

Central government actively promotes women-run businesses in Italy and offers large financial grants as an incentive. In 2004, the government allocated €88.5million in grants. In addition, regional governments have allocated a total €12million.

The *bando* (call for application) for applying for grants normally comes out in December each year and tends to be in the form of half-grant, half loan – 50 per cent of which must be paid back within 10 years of being awarded with an interest rate of 0.5 per cent. Projects which the money is awarded for must have been completed within 24 months.

Case study

Valerie Ryder is American. She is the director of Valerie Ryder Associates, a coaching company with offices in Milan, Boston and Paris. She was also the president of the Professional Women's Association in Milan for the year 2005-2006. Prior to moving to Lissone, just outside Milan, with her Italian husband in 2003, she lived and worked in Paris.

Emma: Valerie. How is running a business in Italy different to your other career positions?

Valerie: It is entirely different, for two major reasons. It goes without saying that running your own business is fundamentally different than working in the corporate world, whatever country you're located in. Then there's the Italian factor. In Italy, it is more difficult for a woman to advance to high-level corporate positions than it is, say, in France or the US. Women entrepreneurs and independent professionals are gaining ground more quickly; in the decade from 1993 to 2003, the percentage of women as compared to men in these fields went from 17 to almost 25 per cent. The sheer number of women business owners and independents increased by 152 per cent, whereas for men the increase was only 63 per cent. In any case, for both men and women, whether you're in business on your own or working for a company, in Italy you **must** have a reliable network of contacts to succeed.

Emma: At which levels are women least active?

Valerie: Italy has a conspicuous lack of women at the uppermost levels of business and politics, on boards of directors of corporations, in top management and in key decision making political roles.

Emma: If I understand correctly, what you're saying is that it's difficult for women to get to the top of their careers in Italy.

Valerie: In short, I would characterise the situation regarding **donne in carriera** as one currently fraught with barriers: male-dominated power structure; lack of an old-girl network to counter that of the old boys; attitudes towards women's 'proper place' and it's not at the top levels of companies; inadequate infrastructure for childcare; little or no assistance by male partners in childrearing and household duties; lack of political sponsors and role models for women. The list goes on.

Emma: How important is networking and peer-to-peer mentoring for women in Italy?

Valerie: Networking is crucial to the professional success of women in Italy, for the reasons I've already mentioned above. Through mentoring, also critical, women can learn from the experiences of others; establish further connections; and identify role models as well as possible political sponsors. Overall, mentoring can provide women with greater tools, knowledge and power, necessary to their advancement.

Emma: Turning to your activities as the president of the PWA in Milan: what have you achieved and what do you want to achieve?

Valerie: I became president because it is a concrete way in which I can help the professional women in Italy advance in their careers through *networking, gaining new skills and accessing more professional opportunities.*

Emma: Valerie, what advice would you give to expat women thinking of setting up a business in Italy?

Valerie: Learn the language, do your homework in terms of what the professional opportunities are for women in the geographical area you're looking to move to, be realistic in terms of your expectation, establish a strong network of contacts, join networking organisations and professional and industry associations, have a good support structure of friends, family and colleagues and persevere.

USEFUL WEBSITES FOR PROFESSIONAL WOMEN IN ITALY

These Italian language websites post listings of courses and seminars for female business owners and aspiring business owners so check regularly:

+ www.osservatoriodonna.it
+ www.italiadonna.it/
+ www.women.it
+ www.if-imprenditoriafemminile.it/
+ www.assodonna.it

When you find yourself surrounded by Italian women who have far more traditional views than your own, don't alienate yourself too much. You might not have the same outlook, but you can go out with them, stroll round town with them or just hook up now and again for a coffee or an ice cream.

Mario's Pearl of Wisdom

'Mamma mia' – this famous Italian expression says it all. From Mary the mother of Jesus through to *la mamma italiana* making fresh ravioli in the kitchen, women were always the matriarchs of family life in Italy. But today 50 per cent of mothers are also working women and this has led to a relaxation of women's roles in Italian society. As women become increasingly independent, they are opting not to settle down and have children straight away. Many *convivono* (live with their partners) instead of getting married and have children at a much later age, if at all. This has inevitably led to a near-zero birthrate.

21

Taking on staff

At this point, your business is probably already up and running or, if not, it soon will be. But don't skip this chapter. Even if you don't need to hire staff immediately, there is likely to be a time in the future when you will need to have at least one person working for you so that you can concentrate on growing the company.

In the 60s and 70s, Italian trade unions worked hard to secure workers' rights. One of the most important laws still in place today is the *Statuto dei Lavoratori* (Workers' Statute), which was passed on 20 May 1970. It guarantees the freedom and dignity of workers, the freedom of the trade union activity at work and lays out the rules to follow when hiring employees.

The law bans the following:

- restricting workers to express their ideas and opinions at work;
- filming employees at work to monitor their behaviour;
- investigating the religious and political views of employees in order to establish which trade union they belong to;
- moving employees sideways or downwards to do a job different to the one stated in the contract.

In addition to the *Statuto dei Lavoratori*, workers are also protected by the CCNL, *contratto collettivo nazionale di lavoro* (national employment contract). This contract details the general rules relating to salary, holidays, disciplinary warnings and workers' duties and rights. The CCNL is renewed regularly and all the modifications must be accepted by each company and communicated to the workers.

STRICT LABOUR LAWS

Until recently, Italy had one of the most rigid labour markets in the whole of Europe and, unless employers were careful, when they took on staff, they tended to take them on for life. But that started to change in 2002 when economist Marco Biagi was advising the Italian government on much-needed reforms to article 18 of the 1970 Workers' Statute. Article 18 protects Italian workers from dismissal, whether unfair or otherwise. If an employee is fired, the company must prove a *giusta causa* (just cause), such as breaking the law, stealing from the company or fighting with colleagues on work premises. Nevertheless, the employee is protected by the Workers' Statute to such an extent that even in these cases, the incident doesn't always result in dismissal.

In 2004, a number of baggage handlers at Milan's Malpensa airport were found stealing valuable objects from travellers' luggage. If you are expecting us to tell you that they were instantly sacked, forget it. We'd love to be able to tell you that that was the case but, this being Italy, of course they weren't. The baggage handlers were arrested but because the court case hadn't yet started, the *datore di lavoro* (the employer) was unable to sack them. Just to prove that this isn't a one-off case, four years previously a cashier was caught red-handed as he took 'a loan' from the till. When the case came to court, the judge declared the employee was suffering from depression and ruled it illegal to sack him. The company had no choice but to continue to employ him.

Riforme Biagi

On 19 March 2002, Biagi was shot dead outside his home by the armed leftist group the *Brigate Rosse* (Red Brigade) even though his controversial reforms to labour legislation had not yet been pushed through parliament. In a nutshell, these included short-term contracts for projects allowing employers to skirt around the stiff labour laws which were still in place. Despite staunch opposition from workers and Italy's major trade unions, the reforms finally came into effect in 2003.

CENTRO PER L'IMPIEGO

The *centro per l'impiego* (local employment office) has a data-base containing the *scheda anagrafica* of all workers. This *scheda anagrafica* records a person's work history (including whether or not he or she has been fired or made redundant), education, additional qualifications, skills, address, residency and date of birth.

The *centro per l'impiego* also keeps a copy of an employee's work contract. Once you have drawn up the contract and both you and the employee have signed it, you must send it to the *centro per l'impiego* (local employment office) within five days either by post or fax.

CONTRACTS

In Italy, work contracts are fairly short documents. This is because what is not written in the contract is contained in the general contract drawn up by the relevant trade union – CGIL (*Confederazione Generale Italiana del Lavoro* (www.cgil.it)), CISL (*Confederazione Italiana Sindicati Lavoratori* (www.cisl.it)) or UIL (*Unione Italiana del Lavoro* (www.uil.it)). Each industry sector and subsector has its own union contract and regulates holiday, maternity and sickness pay, pensions, working hours and overtime. Given that each document is lengthy (over 100 pages each) we can't include them here. However, they are available in PDF format from the respective trade unions. See the urls as before.

Different types of contracts

In Italy, there only used to be two types of contracts – the *contratto a tempo indeterminato* (unlimited duration contract) and the *contratto a tempo determinato* (fixed-term contract). But the Biagi reforms have changed this.

Contratto a tempo indeterminato

These are the contracts that are like gold dust in Italy and one of the reasons why employees are reluctant to move onto new jobs. An unlimited duration contract equates to what the Italians call the *posto fisso* (job for life) because working conditions are excellent and, as we have already seen, you will find it very difficult to dismiss an employee on such a contract.

If you hire a worker on a *contratto a tempo indeterminato*, you will have to ensure that:

- the normal working week does not exceed 40 hours;
- he/she is paid overtime (in accordance with the CCNL) for working weeks over 40 hours;

- he/she does not work more than six days in a row;
- if redundancies are on the cards, you have enough money to pay him/her. It is not unusual in Italy for employees to get pay-offs equal to a year's salary;
- female workers have full maternity rights which are among the best in Europe (see Chapter 20: Women in business).

Contratto a tempo determinato

Employees on a *contratto a tempo determinato* (fixed-term contract) enjoy many of the same conditions as those workers on a *contratto a tempo indeterminato*, although obviously on a pro rata scale. The law states that if a fixed-term contract is renewed it then becomes an unlimited-term contract. However, many employers in Italy avoid awarding workers holiday pay. Once the fixed-term contract has expired, employers wait for a period of three weeks before effectively hiring the worker on a different contract.

EMPLOYING STAFF
La somministrazione di lavoro

In Italy you do not take on staff directly, but go through a temping or employment agency which decides whether or not to give workers unlimited term or fixed term contracts. In Italy, it is illegal to use temping agencies to cover workers exercising their right to strike or to replace staff who you have made redundant six months ago or less. Temporary workers in your workplace will have the same rights to social assistance as your permanent staff.

Temps must receive at least €350 per month in their wage packet.

Il distacco

If your company has branch offices or factories and you need to temporarily transfer staff between the two or if your company needs to 'borrow' a worker from another company on a temporary basis then you can take advantage of the *distacco* (literally 'separation'). For the employee, not much changes – in the case of there being two companies involved, he/she will continue to be paid by the original employer who will then invoice the second company.

However, if the employee needs to transfer to another Italian town more than 50km away, you, as the employer, must demonstrate why you cannot hire a local worker. Once the period of *distacco* has finished, the employee will return to his/her original workplace.

Il lavoro intermittente (o lavoro a chiamata)

You can use this contract when hiring staff for given time periods, such as weekend working or Christmas, Easter and summer holidays. In order for the contract to be valid, the employee must agree to work a set number of days per week and must agree to being available to work an additional number of days per month with only a day's notice. If the employee signs this type of contract, he/she cannot decide not to work on the day requested due to other commitments. If you do not need the employee to work on the additional days, you must still pay them a retainer fee equivalent to 20 per cent of their daily rate.

This contract was originally introduced in order to combat Italy's high unemployment levels and can be used for unemployed people aged 25 and under or aged 45 and over.

You must not use this contract to substitute employees on strike or to replace staff who have been made redundant.

Il lavoro ripartito

Job-sharing is innovative in Italy and is a contract between you and the two employees who can decide how to share the workload between them. They can replace each other in any given moment, providing they complete the required work.

If you have reason to fire one of the job sharers, the other employee will automatically be out of work unless you ask him/her to take on the role on a full-time basis and he or she agrees.

Il lavoro a tempo parziale

There are three different types of part-time contracts: horizontal part time, vertical part time and mixed part time. In horizontal part time, the employee only works part of the day but every day, for example, from 9am to 1pm. In vertical part time, the working hours are the same as in a full-time job, but the employee works only some days of the week, or only in some months, for example from Monday to Wednesday or from May to September. Mixed part time is a mix of horizontal and vertical part time. However, that does not mean that you cannot increase the number of working hours if it is limited to a specific period and for a specific reason.

You can, at any time, turn the part-time contract into a full-time contract and vice versa, provided that the employee is in agreement.

In terms of salary, holiday, sick and maternity pay and working conditions, you need to adhere to the legislation for the *contratto a tempo indeterminato*.

Il contratto di apprendistato

This apprentice's contract can be used when hiring young people between the ages of 15 and 29. There are three types of contracts (Type A, Type B, Type C) for apprentices and a contract must not last for more than six years. Before taking on an apprentice, you must specify which type of contract you are offering.

Type A is for workers aged 15 and over and is suitable for all industry sectors. It must not last more than three years. You must specify how many hours of training the apprentice will receive and what educational or professional qualifications will be given on completion of the apprenticeship. An in-house tutor must be present to carry out the training. Wages must be standardised and cannot be paid on the completion of specific objectives.

Type B is for workers between the ages of 18 and 29 and is suitable for all industry sectors. The CCNL helps decide what type of qualification can be awarded at the end of the apprenticeship which must be a minimum of two years and a maximum of six years. You must guarantee a minimum of 120 hours training per year and this must be carried out by a qualified in-house tutor.

Type C is for workers between the ages of 18 and 29. However, if the apprentice already has a professional qualification recognised by the Law 53/2003, he/she can begin the apprenticeship aged 17. The length of this training period depends on the region where your company is based. This apprenticeship is applicable to all industry sectors.

Whichever type of apprenticeship you offer, the law states that you must not have more apprentices than employees at any one time. The exception is if your company has less than three employees. In this case, you may employ up to three apprentices.

Il contratto di inserimento

In English, the *contratto di inserimento* is the insertion contract, which clearly demonstrates its aims: to integrate or reintegrate people into the workforce. The contract aims to insert various types of people into the workforce. The categories are shown in Figure 21.1.

Figure 21.1

Contratto di inserimento	
Age	Category
18–29	All
29–32	Unemployed
> 50	Unemployed
All	Unemployed in the past two years
All	Women resident in areas with high unemployment rates
All	People with physical/mental disabilities

The contract must be for a minimum of nine months and a maximum of 18 months and must be clearly titled *Progetto di inserimento*. When the contract expires, you are legally bound to convert at least 60 per cent of these contracts into *contratto a tempo indeterminato* (unlimited-term contracts).

As an incentive to take on workers in the above categories, your company will pay lower social security taxes (except for workers aged 18–29).

Il lavoro a progetto

With this kind of contract, you have the chance to take on a person for a particular project. It is unpopular with workers because they do not get sick, maternity or holiday pay and can be dismissed on the condition that you have given a week's notice. As you can imagine, it is extremely popular with employers for exactly the same reasons. There is no salary and you pay the employee for the quality and quantity of the work carried out.

You can use the *lavoro a progetto* if the job the worker is being hired to do is either a specific project, a phase of a particular project, or a particular work programme which has a predefined lifespan. If you do not have a strict project or work phase in mind, the employee can go to a lawyer and has the right to change the *lavoro a progetto* into a unlimited-term contract. You can get around this by defining a series of short-term projects and therefore you can continually renew the contract – in fact, there is no limit to the amount of times you can renew the contract as long as there is a new project to work on each time.

However, one aspect to bear in mind is that the worker must be given total independence to do the job as and when he/she wishes so you are unable to impose strict starting and finishing times. Again, if a judge rules that this isn't the case, the *lavoro a progetto* will be turned into an unlimited-term contract and backdated to the start of employment.

In a nutshell, these short-term contracts for projects allowed employers to skirt around the stiff labour laws which were still in place. In the case of sickness or where a female worker becomes pregnant, you have the right to suspend the contract (without pay) until he/she is ready to return to the workplace.

Il lavoro accessorio

This contract is specifically for occasional work and can be used when hiring people who have not yet entered the workforce or those that are leaving it. Housewives, students, pensioners, drug addicts in rehabilitation, people who have been unemployed for more than one year and non-EU workers who have been resident in Italy for more than six months after losing their job all fall into this category.

The following activities are classified by the Italian law as *lavoro accessorio*: gardening; cleaning and maintenance of buildings and monuments; private teaching; 'emergency' work with charity organisations and domestic work, including caring for children, the elderly and people with physical and mental disabilities.

This work is strictly limited to 30 days per year and the pay must not be more than €5,000. This work doesn't affect a person's unemployment status.

CATEGORIES OF WORKERS

In Italy there are four categories of workers (*dirigente* – senior management; *quadro* – junior management; *impiegato* – office worker; *operaio* – factory worker or labourer) and the salaries of each category are established by the state and published in *tabelle professionali* (professional ratings). Employees who have never worked before usually earn the minimum wage for their sector but they rarely progress to *dirigente* status. There are two reasons for this: one is that most employees prefer to hang on to their job for life (and therefore remain on the same rung of the career ladder until they retire), whereas the *dirigenti* have left the security of their *posto fisso* in order to gain international experience in as many companies as possible. The second reason is that *dirigenti* do not enjoy the same protection as the other categories of workers. Because they can be dismissed at any time, their salaries are far higher and employers also have to pay much higher social security contributions. To avoid doing this, employers give their *quadri* (junior managers) senior management responsibilities but without the training and the pay.

WAGES

In Italy, employees receive paychecks or bank transfers 14 times every year rather than once a month as in most other countries. Employees are paid monthly with the *tredicesima* (thirteenth paycheque) just before Christmas and the *quattordicesima* (fourteenth paycheque) during the summer. If you hire staff on *contratti a tempo indeterminato*, they will expect you to pay them in the same way.

HOLIDAY LEAVE AND PAY

Italian employees are normally entitled to 26 days per year (including Saturdays), although apprentices aged 15 and 16 must be given at least 30 days holiday. Small companies often close at Christmas and in the week either side of 15 August and staff are expected to take their holiday at this time. However, if the company doesn't close, employees are not obliged to take their leave at this time. In the past, companies had to pay employees indemnity pay for holidays that were not taken or force them to take three months of leave at one time. This changed in 2004 with the Law Dlgs 213/04 which states that employees must be given at least four weeks' holiday per year and that two of these must be taken consecutively. Indemnity pay is no longer given and if employees do not use up their allocated holiday in the given year, they have until June of the following year to use this. *Dirigenti* are the only category of workers who can choose when to take their holidays, if at all.

Case study

Graham and Lin Lane are the directors of La Porta Verde, in Umbria and help people find property in Umbria. We met them in Chapter 11: Srl.

Emma: Graham, you have lots of staff working with you. How long did you wait before taking them on?

Graham: Caroline started with us after about a year. She knocked on the door having heard about us through a friend and she offered her services just at the time when we needed someone. Sophie came on board last summer and her husband Michael maintains our computer and communication systems.

Emma: Are they employees of La Porta Verde?

Graham: They are self-employed and this was their choice and one which we are in favour of as they work for other people as well. They are membes of the After Sales Team

Emma: You have a mixture of Italian and expat staff. Why?

Graham: My wife and I are English and our core staff are Dutch and German. It just happened that way. Our After Sales Team is made up of a variety of nationalities, all of whom hae lived here for some time and

▶

*have some help to offer. In addition, we use **geometras** (surveyors), builders, electricians and the like, so they tend to be Italian.*

Emma: Italy is known for its rigid labour market. What is your take on it?

Graham: Historically, Italy had many small businesses and still does. The labour laws are so biased towards the worker that companies think very hard before taking on extra staff, which I feel is counter-productive. Because of these laws, they prefer to employ members of the family rather than outsiders so it is difficult to get a job as an Italian, let alone a foreigner.

Emma: What advice would you give to expats in Italy looking to hire employees?

*Graham: Don't do it unless you have to but if you do, engage a good **commercialista** and take his advice.*

FINDING STAFF

Rather than taking out adverts in the local or national or trade press, most employers make use of their personal networks to find suitable candidates, but this method may not be suitable if you are recruiting for management or specialised positions. Where this is the case, think about outsourcing the task to a *cacciatore di testa* (headhunter). Praxi (www.praxi.it) is one of the largest recruitment companies in Italy and can organise executive searches, temporary management and personnel selection on your behalf. Praxi has offices in Bologna, Cagliari, Florence, Genoa, Milan, Naples, Padua, Rome, Turin and Verona. Michael Page International (www.michaelpage.it) has offices in Bologna, Milan, Rome and Turin, but operates recruitment and headhunting services countrywide. Taking on staff is a minefield in Italy. As you can see, there is a lot of information to take in here and once again you can also see how quickly employment legislation is changing in Italy. This will no doubt continue because the Italian Parliament and the trade unions will continue to disagree with each other over the best way to reduce unemployment and to provide job security.

Where possible, we advise you to find a good *consulente del lavoro* (consultant on employment issues) (see Chapter 2: Key figures and institutions) who will be able to deal with all the paperwork and red tape relating to personnel issues.

Mario's Pearl of Wisdom

When taking on staff, please double check their employment history and make sure you feel comfortable about hiring them. If your employee has close links with trade unions, they will be asking for significant time off work and you will have to give it to them. The other aspect to bear in mind considering that the probation period is generally not more than one or two months, is that this period is not sufficient to understand if the employee is good or not, and in this case I suggest a fixed-time period e.g. a **contratto a tempo determinato**, of at least six months, in order to ascertain the skills of the employee.

$$\widehat{22}$$

Setting up and running a B&B

B&Bs first arrived in Italy in 1999 and are becoming more and more popular. Official figures from Anbba, the national association in Italy for B&Bs, show the demand from tourists rises by 10 per cent year on year.

With just one extra room, a guest bathroom, and a set of bedlinen, you can earn up to €110 per night, so it's little wonder that everyone from parents to young singles are getting in on the act.

And don't worry if you don't live in Expat Central of Tuscany or Umbria. These days, B&Bs are also in demand in the big cities, such as Rome, Milan and Turin. Given the current pessimistic economic situation in Italy, many Italian professionals prefer to cut costs by staying in a B&B rather than a hotel. B&Bs in Veneto command the highest prices – an average of €85 per night – while Trentino and Umbria have some of the lowest (€50 and €53, respectively).

DEALING WITH OFFICIALDOM

Here's the news we know you want to hear. Running a B&B that is also your home is one of the simplest types of business in Italy and doesn't require you to join associations or have a *Partita Iva* (remember, that VAT-type code) that all other businesses need, although you can get one if you want one.

As a general rule you do not have to pay *IVA* if your business is small and has between two and five guest bedrooms.

Registering your B&B

Unlike most other procedures in Italy, registering your B&B is surprisingly straightforward. Visit your *Ufficio Turistico* (tourist office) in the town where you have your *residenza*. You will need to fill in the form for '*Dichiarazione d' Inizio Attività*' and make a formal communication to the authorities that you intend to open for business. Take along your *listino* (price list) which will then be date-stamped and approved by the council.

But if you live in Emilia Romagna, the rules are slightly different. You need to send the form detailing your prices to *Provincia*, *Ufficio del Turismo* before 30 September following the start of your business. Once the *Provincia* has checked the accuracy of the prices, it will send back the form with an embossed seal of approval, along with a chart to hang in the guests' room.

Under new laws you do not need to wait for approval to start running your B&B. It starts from the moment your form has been stamped. If the authorities believe your business is illegal, then it is up to them to contact you within 60 days.

Prices

You are free to set your own prices but it is best to keep in line with the prices in your area. Be warned: once you have fixed your minimum and maximum prices, you will not be able to change them unless the following applies:

- you have a group booking of ten people or more;
- your guests are staying for a continuous period of two weeks or more;
- guests include childen aged six and under or are guides or interpreters for group bookings of ten or more people.

Figure 22.1 below gives you an idea of the average prices of a double room in different Italian regions.

Figure 22.1

Regione	*Tarriff in euros*	*Regione*	*Tarriff in euros*
Veneto	85	Sicily	63
Trentino	50	Sardinia	70
Emilia-Romagna	65	Tuscany	69
Lazio	77	Umbria	53
Lombardy	63	Abruzzo	64
Source: Annba.			

As you do not have a *Partita Iva,* you will not be able to accept credit or debit cards, unless your guests pay in advance using PayPal.

Bedrooms

Under Italian legislation, B&Bs must have a maximum of three rooms but if you want to have more rooms move to the region of Emilia Romagna where you can have four rooms, or Tuscany where you can have five.

Room size

There is strict legislation on the minimum size of the rooms and this must be respected. The measurements given exclude ensuite bathrooms:

- double bedroom: 14 square metres (excluding bathroom);
- single room: 8 square metres (excluding bathroom);
- family room with additional single beds: 14 square metres + 6 square metres for each additional 80x190cm bed;
- family room with additional bunk beds: 14 square metres + 1 square metre for the bunk bed.

Furnishings

The minimum requirements (apart from the bed, of course!) for the rooms are:

- *comodino* (bedside cabinet) per person;
- *abatjour* (bedside lamp) per person;
- *sedia* (chair) per person;
- *armadio* (wardrobe);
- *specchio* (mirror);
- *presa* (electric socket);
- *cestino* (wastepaper bin).

Also remember that if you plan to open your home to Italian guests, forget the carpet. However nice it is to feel the fluffy wool under your feet when you wake up, Italians believe they are unhygienic. And whether you agree with them or not, there's another reason to get rid of them – in the summer, when temperatures reach 40 degrees, feeling a smooth parquet, stone or marble floor is much more refreshing.

Cleaning the rooms

Rooms must be cleaned daily. It goes without saying that bedding must be changed when guests leave. That aside, linen must be changed every three days. However, in Lazio they have a more lax attitude and it is acceptable for bedding to be changed weekly.

Prices of rooms

These must be displayed on the back of the bedroom door.

Bathrooms

In theory, you only need one bathroom to be shared between all guests. However, these days not many people like the idea of sharing with strangers and if you have ensuite bathrooms you will be much more popular.

In the bathroom, you will need a:

- *water* (toilet);
- *bidet* (bidet) yes, this is a must despite the amusement of most nationalities;
- *lavandino* (washbasin);
- *doccia* (shower);
- *specchio* (mirror);
- *presa* (electric socket) – yes, we know the dangers of water splashing into electric sockets but it's standard practice in Italy so make sure you include one near the mirror for hairdryers, electric shavers etc.

The kitchen

Again, there is strict legislation on the size of the kitchen. If guests will be eating elsewhere and the kitchen is only the place for you to prepare breakfast and drinks for the guests, it must be at least six square metres. The separate breakfast room for guests needs to allow one square metre per person. So, if you have one double room, one family room with an extra bed and one family room with bunk beds, your breakfast room will need to measure at least nine square metres.

If guests will be eating in the kitchen, then it must be at least six square metres plus an extra 0.5 square metres per guest. So, if you have one double room, one family room with an extra bed and one family room with bunk beds, your kitchen will need to measure at least 10.5 square metres. If space is at a premium, then clearly a combined kitchen/diner is the way to go. We know the owners of Lu Pastruccialeddu in Sardinia. They have an open plan kitchen and dining area and it works well.

Breakfast

Italians are very strict about fresh food and health regulations. So, if you're dreaming of serving guests home-baked cakes, the jam you made from the fruit in your orchard or even just a good old fry-up, stop right there. As a general rule, you must only serve shop-bought food which has been sealed in a bag or container. These rules are to ensure that the origins are easily traceable should there be any problem with the food for whatever reason.

Any food offered to guests must either be individually wrapped or a larger pack opened and consumed the same day. If any food-stuffs, such as croissants, are left over, these must not be offered to guests the next day. You can normally get round this by buying cakes, croissants etc. from your local *pasticceria* and only buying what you need.

Eating fresh food is of utmost importance to Italians and street markets are still of major importance in daily life. If this food has been produced locally, it is even better. Buying fresh unwrapped food such as *salami*, *prosciutto* and cheese and offering it to your guests is perfectly acceptable as long as it is consumed that day.

Of course, these rules don't apply to fruit, bread or milk as you can easily tell from the appearance or smell whether or not the produce is fresh and safe to consume.

Drinks

Milk must be pasteurised. Coffee needs to be freshly ground so forget the instant stuff. Invest in a good coffee machine (Gaggia is widely reputed to be the best) and learn how to make *caffe macchiato*, *caffelatte* and *cappuccinos*. The tea bags you find in Italian shops are often weak as Italians don't like their tea strong. They also take tea with a a slice of lemon and without milk.

However, rules vary from *regione* to *regione* so it's a good idea to check with your local *comune* (you need to go there to register your business, remember) what the current laws are as the mayor has the right to set his own rules as to what can and cannot be served for breakfast.

B&B Associations

Anbba, the national association of B&Bs in Italy (www.anbba.it), has a sliding scale of membership fees depending on how much you want to rely on them for publicising your business. Prices start from €29 per annum and go up to €299 for ratings and for inclusion in five internet sites dedicated to B&Bs in Italy.

Anbba is also available for telephone consultations and will also come to your B&B to work with you on a one-to-one basis. It also runs day courses on all aspects of running a B&B.

Case study

Sylvie Michelotti-Leder is Swiss. She lives with her Italian husband Michele and their two children in Montecatini Terme, in Tuscany, where she runs the B&B La Tartaruga.

Emma: Sylvie, what gave you the idea of setting up a B&B?

Sylvie: I was reading a financial magazine, and the article was on part-time jobs. One of the suggested jobs was a bed and breakfast.

Emma: What came first: your house or the idea for the B&B?

Sylvie: I already had a nice, large house. For the four of us, it was almost too big. I was born in Switzerland where my parents ran a hotel. I grew up in the hotel. So this type of work was like going back to childhood, and I already had quite a lot of know-how in this field since I used to help in the hotel during my holidays.

Emma: How important is location when it comes to running a successful B&B?

Sylvie: The location should satisfy at least one condition: it should either be strategically located so that people can easily travel to all the nearby places of interest or it should be centrally located in a tourist town. Failing that, it needs to offer something different, such as stunning views over countryside or have some kind of detail in the house that you can't find elsewhere.

Emma: What about attention to detail and beautiful furnishings?

Sylvie: Beautiful furnishings aren't necessary. What is really important is that guests feel welcome and at home. Your house needs to be clean and you need to provide guests with the information they need. They want to

▶

feel like a person not a number so attention to detail is important. In the bedrooms, I put a bowl of food and bottle of water in the rooms when guests arrive.

Emma: What sort of prices can you charge?

Sylvie: It depends on the region. What you need to remember is that there is a lot of competition these days so unless you have a really beautiful home, you need to make your prices slightly lower than your competitors to bring in the guests.

Emma: Italian bureaucracy is legendary. Are B&Bs affected by this in the same way as other businesses?

Sylvie: No, not at all. All you need is your **codice fiscale** and then you have to go to your comune and fill in the **Dichiarazione Inizio Attività**. As soon as you have filled it in, you can open your B&B.

Emma: Can you do all the tax returns yourself?

Sylvie: No. You need a **commercialista** who has experience in the sector. The **commercialista** can work out your income while you look after the B&B.

Emma: Is it time consuming?

Sylvie: Well, you need to always answer emails that guests send and then when they arrive you need to give them breakfast, clean the rooms and talk to them.

Emma: I know of several expats who dream of running a B&B in Italy on a full-time basis. What would you say to them? Is it even possible?

Sylvie: You really need to be in a main town like Florence, Milan, Pisa, Lucca or Rome where you will have guests all year round. Otherwise, you will need more than five rooms because your B&B will only be open during the tourist season from March through to October. If you only have two rooms, you can't really make enough money to make a full living for a family. Another thing I would say, is limit the amount of outside help you have. If you are a couple, split the tasks between you: one of you does breakfast, while the other one cleans the rooms.

Mario's Pearl of Wisdom

If you are planning on setting up a B&B but haven't yet purchased a property, think carefully about the location. Buying in an already saturated property market like Umbria or Tuscany means your initial outlay will be high. You will also have to compete with other B&Bs and guest houses in the area which have repeat business and high Google rankings/good press coverage. Why not think about a pretty but lesser-known area that is near a budget airline base? Your property will probably cost less and you'll have fewer competitors so it will be easier for you to make a name for yourself. The downside is the onus will be on you to publicise the area of Italy you live in.

(23)

Marketing

Your business is up and running in Italy but, unfortunately, you can't just sit back and relax otherwise the window of opportunity will pass you by. You need to actively market your company so that clients come to you rather than a competitor and so that your business is a success and doesn't go the way of so many start-ups in Italy which close before they have even got going.

Don't worry if your budget doesn't allow for slick marketing campaigns or back page adverts in the national press. There are much cheaper – and much more effective – ways of getting your name known among your prospective clients.

Cheap, marketing-on-a-shoestring methods include:

- becoming an expert in your chosen field;
- publishing a free newsletter which goes out on a monthly basis;
- being profiled in the press;
- joining trade and professional associations and then becoming active in them;
- writing articles and books on your area of expertise;
- becoming a keynote speaker;
- running seminars and workshops.

When you are starting out, make sure you are realistic and don't expect a deluge of phone calls from the press and customers on your first day. Remember that even though you know what your wow factor is and what makes your company so special, no one else does so you need to let them know. The best way to do this is with a PR campaign. This doesn't have to be expensive and you don't need to hire a PR guru to run a flashy campaign. If you are genuinely enthusiastic about your business, the chances are that other people will pick up on this.

When How to Italy launched, what we didn't do was start scrabbling around for PR ideas on our first day. Even before we set up the company, Emma was working away building contacts across the media and the expat world so that she could promote the business easily once it was up and running. Of course, the whole process creates a domino effect: the more publicity you have, the more people want to profile you, the more people profile you, the more clients you get, the more clients you get, the more people want to profile you.

Before you set out to build yourself a distinctive reputation, make sure you know what it is you want to promote. Instead of trying to promote all areas of the business, concentrate on a few areas initially and build up from there. It is always easier to make a name for yourself in one area and then branch out, than going for the jack-of-all-trades approach and not being an expert on anything at all.

NEWSLETTER AND BLOGGING

Sending out a newsletter is a good way to build your reputation and your potential client base – especially if the newsletter is free and inspirational. Don't make it too long – remember many people open it at work. It is better to keep it short and useful as that way people will return to it time and time again. Blogging is a similar method except your blog can be read by anyone and, if read, helps enormously in upping your Google ranking. When blogging, try to write little and frequently (every day if possible) rather than huge waffly diatribes on a weekly or monthly basis, and remember your readers and what they are after. With How to Italy, Emma tries to maintain a balance between practical information relating to job opportunities and news, the inspirational and a little bit of what she is up to.

TALKS

If you want to give talks, your local British or American Chamber of Commerce in Italy is often a good starting point as they are always on the lookout for speakers for their events. Similarly, contact other networking organisations to see if your free talk would be of interest to them. If you don't have any experience in public speaking, these small and often informal talks are a great way of improving your skills. From there, you can move on to larger audiences and start commanding a fee for your time. That way, not only do you get paid, you are also gaining valuable exposure for your business. You never know how many potential customers or friends of potential customers there are listening to you.

WRITING ARTICLES AND BOOKS

If you have never written an article before, or are just one of those people who are far better at getting across the message verbally rather than down on paper, then consider writing an article for the internet. Most pieces are short because people don't want to be wading through pages and pages of text on the internet. The advantage of writing for the internet is that the article will include a link to your company website so readers don't have to try to remember all the details. Once you have written quite a few short articles and have had good feedback from them, consider approaching an editor with an idea for a regular column. At worst, they can only say no. At best, you will be getting paid to promote yourself.

Writing books is another good way of getting valuable publicity, but if the idea of sitting down at the laptop and bashing out 60,000 words fills you with fear, consider hiring a ghostwriter to work with you. That way, clients can still get to read about your expertise.

CONTACT THE MEDIA

Set aside at least one hour per week and make sure you use that time to work out how you can become a news item in your local, national or trade press. Don't worry if you don't get a response straight away, it doesn't mean your company doesn't interest the journalist. You need to keep plugging away, sending the same person information on a monthly basis. Sooner or later, they will sit up and take interest in what you are telling them. Set aside a couple of hours per month to work on your media strategy.

Done properly, your marketing campaign should boost your business profile pretty quickly and that means only one thing: you truly have joined the *imprenditori* of Italy.

Conclusion

Complimenti for staying the course. You are well on your way to joining Emma, Graham and Lin, Sam, Dave, Max, Simon, Valerie, Tracy, Sally, Aimie and Silvie who have all set up their own businesses in Italy for different reasons.

Let's get one thing clear living in Italy and running your own business is incredibly rewarding, but it also requires grit, determination and hard work. We know, we've been there and so have all the other expats we've interviewed. At the beginning, we were putting in a lot of hours to build up the How to Italy name and market it. Add to that answering all the emails that arrived, preparing consultations, working with clients, networking and writing, and Emma didn't know what had hit her. The laidback lifestyle she had imagined wasn't anywhere to be seen initially.

The expats we know who are successful aren't lounging around under the Tuscan sun all day long. Instead of doing nothing but eating olives and sipping a few glasses of red wine, they work long hours, often meeting people and helping other expats who have queries of one kind or another, while also keeping the business afloat.

Of course, there are bad days when you end up questioning your sanity and wondering quite what made you decide to pack up your home, move thousands of miles away to a new country and set up a business in Italy where red tape rules. When that happens, it is a good idea to surround yourself with some optimistic expats who really are living *La Dolce Vita* and wouldn't go back to their old way of life.

Remember Graham Lane who runs the La Porta Verde in Umbria? He had this to say: 'I often arrive home completely exhausted after coping with Italian drivers, finding my way between the various properties and answering an endless stream of questions about properties and what life is like here. However, what I like about my business is helping people to realise a dream and sharing their excitement. I love driving, especially through the beautiful and ever–changing countryside. Add to that the opportunity to look round other people's houses and it must be the best job in the world!'

What more can we say, except *in bocca al lupo* (good luck)?

STAY IN TOUCH

We run workshops and seminars on setting up a business in Italy and Mario can work with you on your business plan and help turn it into reality.

In any case, write to us with your plans for Italy and let us know how you get on. We'd love to hear your story and progress reports and if we can help we will. Email Emma at: emma.bird@howtoitaly.com and Mario at: mario.berri@howtoitaly.com. Our website is: www.howtoitaly.com.

Appendix 1
General information

- ◆ Capital city: Rome
- ◆ Official name: Repubblica Italiana
- ◆ Head of government: Presidente del Consiglio (Prime Minister)
- ◆ Area: 301,262 square km
- ◆ Bordering countries: France, Switzerland, Austria, Slovenia
- ◆ Surrounding seas: Ionian Sea (south), Tyrrhenian Sea (west),
- ◆ Ligurian Sea (west), Adriatic (east)
- ◆ Religion: Laic state but Catholicism religion most widely practised
- ◆ Population: 57.6m
- ◆ Population growth: −0.08%
- ◆ Population density (people per sq. km): 196
- ◆ Gross national income (current US$): $1243.0bn (2003)
- ◆ Gross national income per capita: $21,560
- ◆ PPP (purchasing power partity) Gross national income: $1,542.5bn
- ◆ PPP Gross national income per capita: $26,760
- ◆ GDP growth: 0.4% (2003)
- ◆ GDP breakdown: agriculture: 2.7%, industry: 28.5%, services: 68.7% (this adds up to 99% due to rounding)
- ◆ Inflation (12–month average): 2.9 (2003)
- ◆ Gross capital formation as % of GDP: 19.9%

- Final consumption expenditure as % of GDP (growth): 79.0% (0.7%)
- Exports of goods and services as % of GDP: 27.0%
- Top 3 export markets: Germany, France, US
- Local industries: tourism, machinery, iron and steel, chemicals, food processing, textiles, motor vehicles, clothing, footwear, ceramics
- Languages : Italian (official), German and French

Appendix 2
Regional divisions

For administrative purposes, Italy is divided into 20 regions, five of which are autonomous or semi–autonomous. These regions have been given special powers because of their cultural distance from Rome. Each region (regardless of whether it has standard or special autonomy) is broken down into *province* (provinces) and each province is divided into *comuni* (towns). Outlying villages or hamlets are known as *frazioni*. As a foreigner, you'll spend a lot of time in and out of the public offices at *comune* and *provincia* level.

5 REGIONS WITH SPECIAL AUTONOMY
Below is a list of the Italian regions, followed by their provinces.
* Friuili–Venezia Giulia Gorizia, Pordenone, Trieste, Udine
* Trentino–Alto Adige Bolzen, Trento
* Val D'Aosta – Aosta
* Sardinia Cagliari, Nuoro, Oristano, Sassari (several more provinces are due to be added but the new borders are still being defined)
* Sicily Palermo, Ragusa, Syracuse, Trapini

15 REGIONS WITH STANDARD AUTONOMY
* Abruzzo Chieti, L'Aquila, Pescara, Teramo
* Basilicata Matera, Potenza
* Calabria Cantazaro, Cosenza, Reggio di Calabria

- Campania Avellino, Benevento, Caserta, Naples
- Emilia Romagna Bologna, Ferrara, Forlì, Modena, Piacenza, Parma, Ravenna, Rimini, Reggio nell'Emilia
- Lazio Frosinone, Latina, Rieti, Rome, Viterbo
- Liguria Genoa, Imperia, La Spezia, Savona
- Lombardy Bergamo, Brescia, Como, Cremona, Lecco, Lodi Manta, Milan, Pavia, Sondrio, Varese
- Marche Ancona, Ascoli Piceno, Macerata, Pesaro, Urbino
- Molise Campobasso, Isernia
- Piedmont Alessandria, Asti, Biella, Cuneo, Novara, Turin, Verbena, Vercelli
- Puglia Bari, Brindisi, Foggia, Lecce, Taranto
- Tuscany Arezzo, Florence, Grosetto, Livorno, Lucca, Massa–Carrara, Pisa, Pistoia, Prato, Siena
- Umbria Perugia, Terni
- Veneto Belluno, Padua, Rovigo, Treviso, Venice, Verona, Vicenza

Lombardy

Lombardy is the richest, most developed and most densely populated region of Italy. It is the backbone of the country's financial, banking and fashion industries and multinationals, such as Proctor & Gamble, Unilever and Shell have their Italian headquarters there. Milan oozes culture and glamour: think the Scala Opera House, the Castello Sforzesco, the Brera picture gallery and the Duomo. But despite the hoards of tourists, Lombardy has a strong work ethic more in line with Northern Europe than the rest of Italy. It is also geared up to the needs of expats. Consequently, you should find it fairly easy to register your business and go about everyday life.

Piedmont

Turin became the regional capital of Piedmont in the thirteenth century and, after playing a key role in Italy's unification, became the country's capital between 1860 and 1865. In 1861, it also enjoyed the accolade of being home to the first Italian parliament. Turin is steeped in culture: according to tradition, the Holy Shroud, the linen sheet Christ was supposedly wrapped in after his crucifixion, is kept in the city's cathedral.

These days, Turin has become one of the most important industrial centres in Italy. Car–maker FIAT and IT leader Olivetti are based here. The surrounding area is famed for its winemaking and produces some of the country's best–known wines: the Barolo and Barbaresco reds are known worldwide.

Turin doesn't have the same high levels of pollution as Milan and is only a few hours away from the Alps, France and the Italian Riviera, making it ideal for weekends away and for transporting goods through Europe.

Val D'Aosta

Tucked between Switzerland and France, the Val D'Aosta is, to some extent, off the beaten track. But that doesn't mean you should underestimate what this bilingual (French and Italian) region has to offer. In the third century BC, African general, Hannibal, drove his elephants along the steep mountainous routes (Mont Blanc is the highest mountain in Europe, standing at 4,807 metres) and the Romans built roads, bridges and a theatre that you can still see today. Val D'Aosta remained an important centre of commercial traffic right up to the Middle Ages.

Cormayeur and Breuil–Cervinia are the region's major ski resorts and holiday towns and the area quickly fills up with tourists in winter and at the height of the summer season.

Veneto

Say the name Veneto and the region's capital Venice, which is located approximately 4km from the Italian mainland, immediately springs to mind. It conjures up images of St Mark's Square, the Grand Canal and the gondolas, the Carnival and the international film festival. But, of course, there is a lot more to Veneto and Venice than that.

As early as the eighth century, Venice was an important power and trading centre within the Mediterranean and had its heyday between 1000 and the mid–1400s when it became one of the main thoroughfares for trade between Europe and the East. Vicenza, Verona (the city of Romeo and Juliet) and Padua are also important cities in the region.

Prices in the region are beginning to shoot upwards as foreign homeowners realise its potential.

Trentino–Alto Adige

Part of the Austrian empire until 1918, Italian and German are both spoken in this deeply divided region where racial tensions run high. Nevertheless, in Bolzen, the two cultures run seamlessly side by side. Trentino is the Italian–speaking area and Alto Adige the German speaking area. In 1939, Italian dictator Benito Mussolini told the German speakers they could either become Italian citizens or leave. Most left. The region is sparsely populated and isolated and you're more likely to find sauerkraut and schnitzels on the table than pizza and pasta. Nevertheless, if you're the sporty type and you love spending time in the big outdoors, then it's worth spending time in the region. Madonna di Campiglio and Cortona D'Ampezza are two ski resorts to be found in the Dolomites which bridge Austria and Italy.

Friuili–Venezia Giulia

The region has only officially been part of Italy since the 1970s. After the second world war, both Yugoslavia and Italy fought for the territory. However, the close ties with Eastern Europe remain. The region's main town, Trieste, is the most middle European of Italian cities and runs along the Slovenian border. The metal fence separating Gorizia from its Slovenian neighbour Nova Gorica was only pulled down in 2004. Grado, in the province of Gorizia, is loved by many tourists who regularly return for its mild climate and good beaches.

The region has a small, but thriving, winemaking industry and is best known for its aromatic white grapes.

Liguria

Liguria is one of Italy's smallest regions and is clouded in the same high–octane glamour as the French Riviera which follows on westwards. Between France and Genoa the area is known as the Riviera di Ponente. From Genoa down to northern Tuscany, it is known as the Riviera di Levante. Liguria stages an annual pop concert in glitzy San Remo, with Hollywood film stars in attendance. In 2005, Bruce Willis made a guest appearance and in 2006, Arnold Schwarzenegger was asked to appear but was rumoured to have turned it down because of a conflict of interests now that he is an American senator. Liguria has a thriving tourist industry and lots of Italians retire to the region.

Genoa is the regional capital and the birthplace of Christopher Columbus. It was an ancient marine trading centre and is still one of Italy's largest commercial and naval ports. From Genoa, ferries leave for Olbia, Porto Torres and Cagliari in Sardinia, for Palermo in Sicily, for Barcelona and Palma in Spain, for the Canary Islands and for Tunisia.

Emilia Romagna

Emilia Romagna is one of Italy's wealthiest regions and takes its name from Via Emilia, the Roman road leading to Rome, and from Romagna, the name for the former Papal state on the Adriatic Coast where Forlì and Ravenna are located.

The region has been dubbed the gastronomic heart of Italy and it's easy to see why. Parma ham (*prosciutto*), Parmesan cheese (*parmiggiano*), mortadella and Balsamic vinegar (*acetto balsamico di Modena*) are all produced here, as are *tortellini* (small stuffed pasta shapes), *tortelloni* (large stuffed pasta shapes) and *ragù*. Wash it down with a glass of the region's red Sangiovese wine and you won't go far wrong.

As well as being the gastronomic heart of Italy, it has also been nicknamed the *cuore rosso* (red heart) on account of its strong socialist leanings. The socialist newspaper *L'Unità* (once the Communist's official newspaper) is still based in the regional capital Bologna.

Bologna is also home to the oldest university in Europe and even today, the university is widely regarded as one of the best in Italy, with a tradition of turning out philosophers, political thinkers and economists. The Bolognesi are friendly and welcoming and there is a small but unified expat community in the city meaning integration is relatively easy. However, house prices are high and the cost of living is much like that of Milan and Tuscany.

Umbria

Commonly known as the green lungs of Italy, the landlocked region is a popular place for foreigners buying abroad. Although it tends to be overshadowed by its larger neighbour,Tuscany, the region has various attractions. Assisi is an important destination for pilgrims paying homage to Saint Francis, Italy's patron saint; Perugia has an annual chocolate festival and one of Italy's best known universities for foreigners (*Università Italiana per gli Stranieri*) where you can take courses in Italian art, culture and language; Spoletto has an annual musical festival, and just outside the industrial city of Terni are spectular waterfalls where you can go white–water rafting. Todi, Spello, Orvieto and Città di Castello are also pretty medieval towns.

Tuscany

Modern Italian was born in Tuscany between the fourteenth and sixteenth century and became part of the Austrian Empire in the eighteenth century. It only became a part of Italy during the *Risorgimento* in 1859. Frances Maye made the region famous in her book *Under the Tuscan sun* and property prices in Chiantishire have rocketed as foreign buyers try to buy a piece of this land for themselves. Tourists flock to the area all year round to soak up the culture and history. But Tuscany is more than the chic city of Florence, which was once a republic ruled by the Medici family. Siena is famous for its Piazza del Campo, its summer Palio and its winemaking (Chianti, Brunello, Montepulciano and Pienza all come from the province) and San Gimignano is renowned for its towers and turreted houses. Of course, there is also Pisa with its leaning tower. Arezzo was made famous in Roberto Begnini's Oscar–winning film *La Vita è Bella* (Life is Beautiful) and ancient Prato combines picturesque streets with a strong textile heritage. But be aware that the tourist industry has hiked up prices. A *panino*, *cappuccino* and a bottle of water now costs more than double what it would do in Sardinia.

Le Marche

Once firmly off the tourist map, Le Marche has now been discovered by foreigners who have fallen in love with the flat and sandy coastline, rugged rocky precipices, mysterious caves and the sparse Sibiliani mountain range mixed in with Renaissance architecture. If that wasn't enough, the region is immersed in legends. The town of Loreto boasts of angels having delivered the Virgin Mary's house on December 10 1294 and the body of Roman governor Pontius Pilot, who sentenced Jesus to the Cross, is said to be dumped in Lake Pilato near the town of Montecassino.

The regional capital is Ancona and means 'elbow' in Greek. It was given its name by Greek refugees from Siracusa because of the way it juts out from the Italian mainland and into the Adriatic sea. Other major towns in Le Marche are Ascoli Piceno, Urbino, Macerata and the coastal resort of Pesaro. In summer, the picturesque town comes to life and mixes beach fun with serious culture the Rossini Opera festival is held in the town every year.

Its relative isolation and lack of industry means few expats live in the region though this is slowly beginning to change as they realise property is much cheaper than it is in Tuscany and Umbria.

Abruzzo

Abruzzo, with its three national parks, a regional park and protected sites and nature reserves, is known as the region of parks. The size of this area cannot be underestimated the Parco Nazionale dell Abruzzo is 518 sq km alone. As much as 30 per cent of its territory is protected by environmental legislation more than any other region in Europe. The craggy mountain range used to be isolated but, thanks to new roads making the region easily accessible from Rome, it has become a popular ski resort in winter and a relaxing retreat in summer. The region has a number of folk traditions, the most famous of which is the *Festa degli Serpenti* (Festival of Snakes) in the tiny village of Cocullo. It attracts thousands of visitors on the first Sunday of May every year.

The regional capital L'Aquila ('The Eagle') has an impressive view of the Gran Sasso mountain and is dominated by an imposing sixteenth–century castle. Pescara, on the Adriatic coast, is a popular summer resort and on a clear day can be seen by skiers on the mountain peaks.

Molise

Until 1963, Molise and Abruzzo used to form one region, Abruzzi. But whereas Abruzzo has grown wealthy by taking advantage of Government and EU incentives schemes, Molise has remained underdeveloped and is where southern Italy is now said to really begin. The entire area is an earthquake zone and some buildings in the town of Isernia (worth a visit for its fourteenth century fountain and beautiful cathedral) are still held together by scaffolding after the earthquake in 1984.

Don't dismiss Molise, out of hand, however. In Sepino, you can see the remains of an ancient Roman colony and near Pietrabbondante there is an archeological site which proves the existence of the Sannites, an ancient Italic people who challenged and fought the powers of Rome.

Lazio

With its architecture and monuments, Rome is undisputedly elegant and timeless. But it is also noisy, chaotic and polluted. If you don't fancy the idea of living in Italy's capital city but it is essential to the success of your business, don't despair. There are other alternatives.

The Latin word for Lazio is 'Latium', meaning 'abundant territory' and the region certainly lives up to expectations. Once you leave the Eternal City behind you, the urban scenery gives way to wide beaches, great pinewoods, mountains, hills and vast plains. But just as it is rich in scenery, the region is also rich in history and culture. Necropolises and museums in Tarquinia, Cerveteri and Tuscania date back to the Etruscans. Rieti, Viterbo, Latina and Frosinone also have Roman ruins which rival those in Rome. And just forty minutes from the capital, you can find the stunning Villa Adriana and the Renaissance Villa D'Este.

Calabria

Calabria is the 'toe' of Italy and boasts some of the most stunning coastline in Italy. However, the region is one of the poorest in the country and constant corruption means there is little show for the huge amount of Government resources which have been poured into the region's infrastructure, tourism and modern communications. A lot of the allocated money has ended up in the pockets of Calabria's mafia the '*ndrangheta*'.

Whilst the comical side of the mafia is often played up in TV commercials and films, the reality is much more sinister and a part of everyday life in the region. In the '*ndrangheta*' (courage or loyalty) strongholds, the probability of mafia interference is high and so you should seriously think twice about whether or not you really want to set up business in the region.

Puglia

Puglia is the sun–drenched region that makes up Italy's 'heel' and is becoming increasingly popular with expats who have fallen for the charms of the *truili* circular, dry stone houses with conical roofs. You can find a whole town of them in Alberobello.

Other popular areas are Gargano, which juts into the Adriatic, and Lecce, known as the architectural jewel of southern Italy. Bari residents make the claim that 'If Paris was by the sea, it would be like a small Bari'. The city's golden age was during medieval times and the old quarter (*Bari vecchia*) is a shrine to Byzantine and Romanesque architecture. It now blends history and culture with high–tech and service industries.

Campania

Naples is the regional capital of Campania and draws visitors like flies to the honey pot. Despite its infamous rubbish problem, the overcrowded slums, the chaotic driving, alarming levels of petty crime and organised crime (Naples is under the thumb of the Campania mafia, the *Camorra*), Naples leaves an indelible print on your heart.

The Romans built palatial villas along the Bay of Naples and the area is still sought after today Sorrento, Amalfi, Positano and Ravello are beautiful seaside towns and many expats, running their own businesses, have settled there. The nearby islands of Capri, Ischia and Procida are popular with the rich and famous.

Basilicata

Basilicata is boarded by the Tyrrhenian and the Ionian seas and is a beautiful but barren region, with most of its inhabitants living in abject poverty. The regional capital Potenza doesn't have much going for it and recent earthquakes have seriously damaged the centro storico.

UNESCO has declared Matera, the region's second city, as the 'heritage of humanity'. The town is cut off from the rest of the region without any railway connecting it to the outside world. Houses were dug out of Tufa rock and hundreds of adults and children lived in the damp caves until the regional government moved them into *case popolari* (housing provided by the state). You can now visit the caves which have been restored.

If you are willing to venture into the wilderness, you will be rewarded with Greek ruins in Metaponto, medieval churches and castles in Melfi and Lagopesole and unspoilt countryside else-where.

Sardinia

Sardinia has special statutory powers and you can see why. Few Italians come to the island except for their summer holidays and as a result the Sardi view their Italian cousins with distrust. The Italian mainland is known as 'the continent' and Italians as 'continentals'.

Sardinia has a history of being invaded and you can still see the evidence today. The coastal towns are built away from the beach to protect the inhabitants from invasion; on the island of San Pietro off Sardinia's south–west coast, the cuisine is influenced by Tunisia, and in Alghero a fifteenth century form of Catalan is still spoken.

It is the second largest island in the Mediterranean and a region of contrasts. The Costa Smeralda on the north–east coast is a series of chic coastal villages, harbours and swish bars and restaurants loved by Hollywood actors, models and royalty. Naomi Campbell, Kate Moss, Denzel Washington and Diana, Princess of Wales, have all been spotted here over the years.

But the rest of the island is still relatively unknown and boasts shimmering turquoise sea, unspoilt beaches and the highest sand dunes in Europe. Inland, you can find isolated villages and ancient *nuraghi*, cone–shaped towers which date back thousands of years BC and are said to have special fertility powers.

There are lots of expats on the island but they are well integrated into Sardinian society. Expat–communities are rare.

Sicily

Sicily, which lies off the 'toe' of Italy, is the largest island in the Mediterranean. It is intrinsically linked to the mafia and it is estimated that 12 per cent of Italy's GDP comes from the criminal organisation. Palermo has been the island's capital since the Arabs and Frederic II and is a world centre of the drugs and gun trade.

But Sicily isn't just synonymous with the mafia. The island has beautiful scenery and its architecture is a fascinating mix of Arab, Baroque, Greek, Spanish and French styles. Syracuse was the second largest city of ancient Greek and still possesses some of the best–preserved Greek ruins in the Mediterranean.

Sicily has had a cash injection to the tune of millions of euros and tourism experts have been brought in from other Italian cities in a bid to revamp the island.

There is a lively expat community on the island, especially in Palermo, Gela, Messina and Syracuse. If you do settle on the island, bear in mind that Mount Etna erupted in 1983 and 2001 and another major eruption is forecast for the future, though no one is quite sure when.

Figure A2.1 Largest Italian cities

Position	Town	Population	Density per square km
1	Rome	2,459,776	1,913.8
2	Milan	1,182,693	6,495.8
3	Naples	993,386	8,470.9
4	Turin	857,433	6,587.0
5	Palermo	652,640	4,107.8
6	Genoa	603,560	2,477.7
7	Bologna	369,955	2,628.8
8	Florence	352,227	3,439.4
9	Bari	312,452	2,688.9
10	Catania	306,464	1,694.3
11	Venice	266,181	645.2
12	Verona	243,474	1,178.3
13	Messina	236,621	1,120.2
14	Trieste	209,520	2,479.8
15	Padua	203,350	2,190.1
16	Taranto	201,349	925.7
17	Brescia	187,865	2,071.7
18	Reggio Calabria	179,384	760.0
19	Modena	175,442	960.1
20	Prato	170,388	1,746.0

Appendix 3
Postal codes, provincial codes and telephone numbers

PHONE CALLS

When making *chiamate urbane* and *interurbane* (local and national calls), always remember to dial the full number, including the area dialling code (*prefisso*). Even if you're phoning the office next door, you will still need the area dialling code. When you give out your telephone number to friends and family and international clients, remind them that the zero at the beginning of the area dialling code must always be dialled.

POSTAL ADDRESS

The area postcode and the abbreviation for the province must always be included on correspondence. So if you were sending a letter to Sally Smith who lives at 5, Piazza Centrale, the address on the envelope would look like this:

Sally Smith
Piazza Centrale, 5
05100 Terni TR

You will need to write the abbreviation of the province where you live and where your business is registered on just about every document going, so consign it to memory.

Town	Area postcode	Dialling code	Province abbreviation
Agrigento	92100	0922	AG
Alessandria	15100	0131	AL
Ancona	60100	071	AN
Aosta	11100	0165	AO
Aquila (L')	67100	0862	AQ
Arezzo	52100	0575	AR
Ascoli Piceno	63100	0736	AP
Asti	14100	0141	AT
Avellino	83100	0825	AV
Bari	70100	080	BA
Belluno	32100	0437	BL
Benevento	82100	0824	BN
Bergamo	24100	035	BG
Biella	13051	035	BI
Bologna	40100	051	BO
Bolzano	39100	0471	BZ
Brescia	25100	030	BS
Brindisi	72100	0831	BR
Cagliari	09100	070	CA
Caltanisseta	93100	0934	CL
Campobasso	86100	0874	CB
Caserta	81100	0823	CE
Catania	95100	095	CT
Catanzaro	88100	0961	CZ
Chieti	66100	0871	CH
Como	22100	031	CO
Cosenza	87100	0984	CS

Town	Area postcode	Dialling code	Province abbreviation
Crotone	88074	0962	KR
Cuneo	12100	0171	CN
Enna	94100	0935	EN
Ferrara	44100	0532	FE
Firenze	50100	055	FI
Foggia	71100	0881	FG
Forlì	47100	0543	FO
Frosinone	03100	0775	FR
Genova	16100	010	GE
Gorizia	34170	0481	GO
Grosseto	58100	0564	GR
Imperia	18100	0183	IM
Isernia	86170	0865	IS
Latina	04100	0773	LT
Lecce	73100	0832	LE
Lecco	22053	0341	LC
Livorno	57100	0586	LI
Lodi	26900	0371	LO
Lucca	55100	0583	LU
Macerata	62100	0733	MC
Mantova	46100	0376	MN
Massa	54100	0585	MS
Matera	75100	0835	MT
Messina	98100	090	ME
Milano	20100	02	MI
Modena	41100	059	MO
Napoli	80100	081	NA

Town	Area postcode	Dialling code	Province abbreviation
Novara	28100	0321	NO
Nuoro	08100	0784	NU
Oristano	09170	0783	OR
Padova	35100	049	PD
Palermo	90100	091	PA
Parma	43100	0521	PR
Pavia	27100	0382	PV
Perugia	06100	075	PG
Pesaro	61100	0721	PS
Pescara	65100	085	PE
Piacenza	29100	0523	PC
Pisa	56100	050	PI
Pistoia	51100	0573	PT
Pordenone	33170	0434	PN
Potenza	85100	0971	PZ
Prato	59100	0574	PO
Ragusa	97100	0932	RG
Ravenna	48100	0544	RA
Reggio Calabria	89100	0965	RC
Reggio Emilia	42100	0522	RE
Rieti	02100	0746	RI
Rimini	47037	0541	RN
Roma	00100	06	ROMA
Rovigo	45100	0425	RO
Salerno	84100	089	SA
Sassari	07100	079	SS
Savona	17100	019	SV

Town	Area postcode	Dialling code	Province abbreviation
Siena	53100	0577	SI
Siracusa	96100	0931	SR
Sondrio	23100	0342	SO
Spezia (La)	19100	0187	SP
Taranto	74100	099	TA
Teramo	64100	0861	TE
Terni	05100	0744	TR
Torino	10100	011	TO
Trapani	91100	0923	TP
Trento	38100	0461	TN
Treviso	31100	0422	TV
Trieste	34100	040	TS
Udine	33100	0432	UD
Varese	21100	0332	VA
Venezia	30100	041	VE
Verbano	28048	0323	VB
Vercelli	13100	016	VC
Verona	37100	045	VR
Vibo Valentia	88018	0963	VV
Vicenza	36100	0444	VI
Viterbo	01100	0761	VT

Appendix 4
Spellings and numbers

SPELLINGS

When Italians spell anything, they always use a precise set of place names (see below). They don't say 'A per Ancona, B per Bologna' but simply Ancona, Bologna. Say Emma was spelling her surname. She would say: 'Bologna, Imola, Roma, Domodossola'. Be warned that your surname will undergo a change in pronunciation. Emma is known in Italy as Emma 'Beard' and not Emma 'Bird'.

A   Ancona
B   Bologna
C   Como
D   Domodossola
E   Empoli
F   Firenze
G   Genova
H   Hotel
I   Imola
J   Jolly
K   Kappa
L   Livorno
M   Milan
N   Napoli

O	Otranto
P	Perugia
Q	Quarto
R	Roma
S	Savona
T	Torino
U	Udine
V	Venezia
W	Washington
X	Ics
Y	York
Z	Zara

NUMBERS

Italians use full stops where we use commas and commas where we use full stops. For example, Italians would write 'two thousand, four hundred and ninety three euros 50' as €2.493,50 and not €2,493.50. Similarly, four and a half, would be written in Italian as 4,5 and not 4.5.

EURO AND THE LIRE

The Euro became Italy's official currency in January 2002. Nevertheless, even young people still think in the '*vecchie lire*', the country's former currency. When someone comes up with a price in Lire, remember the conversion is Lire 1,936.27 to one euro. In more approximate terms, knock off three zeros and divide by two.

Appendix 5
National holidays and Saints' Days

Nothing characterises the Italians' laid–back attitude to life more than the taking of public holidays. If a bank holiday falls on a Thursday or a Tuesday, there will inevitably be a '*ponte*' (literally, 'a bridge') and offices and shops will shut on either the Friday (if the holiday is on a Thursday) or the Monday (if the holiday is on a Tuesday) to take advantage of the long weekend. If you plan on hiring employees and don't shut on the day of the *ponte*, expect some of your workers to mysteriously fall ill. If, however, the public holiday falls on a weekend, the following Monday is never declared a holiday. 2003 was something of a bonus year because most of the bank holidays fell on week days, meaning lots of *ponti* were taken.

The main holiday dates are shown below:

- 1 January *Capodanno* (New Year)
- 6 January *Epifania* (Epiphany the witch Befana leaves children sweets or coal, depending on whether they've been good or bad)
- March/April *Pasqua/Pasquetta* (Easter Sunday and Easter Monday. Good Friday isn't a public holiday. *La Colomba*

pasquale a dove–shaped cake is eaten and Easter Eggs given as presents)
- 25 April *Anniversario della Liberazione* (Anniversary of Liberation from Nazis in 1945)
- 1 May *Primo Maggio* (May Day)
- 2 June *Festa della Repubblica* (Celebration of the Formation of the Republic)
- 15 August *Assunzione/Ferragosto* (Most Italians are on their summer holidays, taking a week either side of Ferragosto)
- 1 November *Ognissanto* (All Saints)
- 2 November *Tutti i Morti* (All Souls' Day. People visit graves of loved ones and lay flowers)
- 8 December *L'immaculata concezione* (Immaculate Conception)
- 25 December *Natale* (Christmas)
- 26 December *Santo Stefano* (Boxing Day)

In addition, each town has its own Patron Saint and businesses often close on its Saints' Day. The further south you go, the more likely this is to hold true. Celebrations in the south are also more likely to be religious in nature.

The main Saints' Days are shown below:

- 25 April San Marco (Venice)
- 1 May Sant'Efisio (Cagliari)
- 13 June Sant'Antonio (Padua)
- 24 June San Giovanni (Turin, Genoa, Florence)
- 29 June San Pietro (Rome)
- 10–15 July Santa Rosalia (Palermo)
- 23–25 July Caltagirone, San Giacomo (Sicily)

- ◆ 26 July Santa Anna (Ischia)
- ◆ 19 September San Gennaro (Naples)
- ◆ 4 October San Petronio (Bologna)
- ◆ 4 October San Francesco (Assisi)
- ◆ 7 December Sant'Ambrogio (Milan)

Appendix 6
Visas and permits

EU citizens do not need a visa to set up a business in Italy, but you will require a *permesso di soggiorno* (permit to stay) from the *Questura* (police headquarters) when you arrive. There are several different types of permits so request the *permesso di soggiorno per lavoro autonomo* (a work permit for the self–employed). To apply for the permit, you will need your passport, an application form for the *permesso* available in advance from the *Questura*, a *marca da bollo* (tax stamp) and four passport photos.

Non–EU citizens married to EU citizens will need a visa for a foreign spouse. If you wish to establish residency in Italy with your spouse, you will need your flight itinerary, identity document and declaration by the Italian/EU spouse requesting that you be issued with a visa, certificate of *stato di famiglia* or a certified copy of your marriage certificate bearing the *apostille* of your country. Once you are in Italy, you will need to apply for a *permesso di soggiorno per coesione familiare*.

Non–EU citizens not married to EU citizens will need a visa for business purposes. These are rare in Italy and there are no quotas because most expats are looking for paid employment. Employ an international immigration lawyer to help deal with the Italian embassy on your behalf. When you apply for a business visa, have copies of your business plan in both Italian and English that you can hand over to prove you are serious about your intentions. When you arrive in Italy, you will need the *permesso di soggiorno per lavoro autonomo.*

RESIDENZA

Once you have your *permesso di soggiorno* and have found a home, you will need to request *residenza* at the *comune* (town) where you live. The police will come to your new home to check that you do actually live there and that the size of the property is the same as you declared in your request for residency. A few weeks later, you will receive a letter telling you that your residency has been approved. You will need this to open your bank account and to start your business.

Appendix 7
Legislative process

Italy has a complicated legislative process. The main laws are shown below:

1. *Leggi Ordinarie* (abbreviated D.P.R.)   Ordinary laws
                                               (Presidential Decree)
2. *Decreti Legge* (abbreviated D.L.)   Ordinary laws
                                               (Executive Decree)
3. *Decreti Legislativi* (abbreviated D.Lgs)   Ordinary laws
                                               (Legislative Decree)
4. *Leggi Regionali*   Counties' laws
5. *Codice Civile*   Civil code

ORDINARY LAWS (*PRESIDENTIAL DECREES*)

Ordinary laws can be found with the abbreviation of 'D.P.R.' (Presidential Decree) followed by the number and the year. So, for instance, the Law n. 78 promulgated by the President of the Repubblic in 2001 will be found as D.P.R. 78/01.

DECRETI LEGGE (EXECUTIVE DECREES)

The *Decreti Legge* are considered Ordinary laws once they have been approved by the parliament. They are created by the government when there is an urgent situation that requires immediate action and the Parliament must approve them or overturn them within 60 days. However, you need to bear in mind that the effect of the *Decreti Legge* is immediate.

When you are looking for a *Decreto Legge*, the rules are the same as for the Ordinary laws, with the difference that you have to look for the abbreviation D.L. instead of D.P.R. So, if we take the first example, the correct abbreviation is D.L.78/01. When approved by the Parliament, the Decree becomes Ordinary Law and then you can find it with the abbreviation of 'L' that means *Legge* followed by the number and the year. Be careful: the law which has converted the D.L. can also modify it.

DECRETI LEGISLATIVI (LEGISLATIVE DECREES)

The *Decreto Legislativo* is another type of law brought into effect by the Italian government after a specific request has been made by Parliament. In this case, the government promulgates the laws by itself following the instructions given by the Parliament. We have a very important example with the D.Lgs. 6/2003 (now you know the meaning of it), which has been promulgated by the government in order to regulate the company law.

LEGGI REGIONALI (REGIONAL LAWS)

The counties also have the power to put a law in place. This happens for the subjects listed in art. 117 of the constitution. As far as we are concerned, the economic matter is regulated by the counties' law especially for the *leggi agevolative* (financial grants) which give contributions to the companies.

CODICE CIVILE

The *Codice civile* which can be translated as 'the Civil Law code' is the basic list of laws that everybody should know about when working in Italy because it regulates matters relating to companies, the labour market and properties. Most laws regarding business in Italy can be found in the *Codice civile*. The relevant articles are 2247 to 2510.

Appendix 8
Double taxation

Under Italian rules and those of other countries, you could end up being a tax resident both in Italy and the country you lived in prior to starting your business in Italy. To avoid citizens paying the same tax twice over, many countries have signed double taxation treaties. The Italian law also establishes a so–called *credito d'imposta* by which the taxpayer can deduct the amount of taxes already paid in another country from the amount due.

AGREEMENTS AGAINST DOUBLE TAXATION

Agreements are made with the purpose of concluding '*a convention for the avoidance of double taxation with respect to taxes on income and the prevention of fraud or fiscal evasion*'. The countries which have signed the agreement with Italy are:

Albania	Lithuania
Algeria	Luxembourg
Arab Emirates	Macedonia
Argentina	Malaysia
Armenia	Mauritius
Australia	Morocco
Austria	Mexico
Azerbaijan	Montenegro
Bangladesh	Morocco

Belgium	Mozambique
Brazil	New Zealand
Bulgaria	Norway
Byelorussia	Oman
Canada	Pakistan
Croatia	Poland
China	Portugal
Cyprus	Romania
Czech Republic	Russia
Ivory Coast	Senegal
Denmark	Serbia
Ecuador	Singapore
Egypt	Slovenia
Emirates Arabs	South Africa
Estonia	South Korea
Ethiopia	Spain
Philippines	Sri Lanka
Finland	Sweden
France	Syria
Georgia	Tajikistan
Germany	Tanzania
Greece	Thailand
Holland	Trinidad
Hungary	Tunisia
India	Turkey
Indonesia	Turkmenistan
Ireland	UK
Israel	Ukraine
Japan	US
Kazakhstan	Uzbekistan

Kenya   Venezuela

Kyrgyzstan   Vietnam

Kuwait

Given that double taxation treaties are detailed and depend on your own personal circumstances we suggest you speak to an international accountant or financial advisor who can best advise you on how to manage your non–Italian assets and the taxes you are likely to incur.

Appendix 9
Glossary   economic words, Italian words, Italian institutions, public holidays

Abbonamento	Season ticket
Abbuono	Allowance, discount
Abilità	Skill
Abilitazione	Qualification
Abitazione	House, residence
Abolizione	Abolition
Abrogare	To abrogate
Abuso	Abuse
Accertamento tributario	Assessment on income
Accettare	To accept
Accoglienza	Reception
Accomandante	Limited partner
Acconto	Payment in advance
Accordo	Agreement
Accreditare	To credit
Acquistare	To buy
Acquisto	Purchase
Addebitare	To charge
Addizionale	Additional, supplementary
Affermare	To state
Affidare	To entrust
Affittare	To rent

Agente	Agent
Agente di commercio	Sales representative
Agente immobiliare	Estate agent
Agenzia delle Entrate	Tax Office
Agricoltore	Farmer
Aiutare	To help
Albergo	Hotel
Albo (dei commercialisti, avvocati, ecc)	Professional association (of accountants, lawyers, etc.)
Aliquota	Tax rate
Amministratori	Directors
Ammortamento	Depreciation
Anagrafe	Register Office
Anagrafe tributaria	Tax register
Anno fiscale	Tax Year
Annullamento	Write–off
Anticipo	Payment in advance
Approvare	To approve
Arbitraggio	Arbitration
A.S.L.	Local Health Authority
Assegno	Cheque
Assegno a vuoto	Bounced cheque
Assegno non girato	Unendorsed cheque
Assegno senza copertura	Uncovered cheque
Assemblea	Meeting
Assemblea Ordinaria	General Meeting
Assicurazione	Insurance
Assumere	To recruit
Attività	Assets
Attivo netto	Net assets
Atto costitutivo	Article of incorporation
Attrezzatura	Equipment
Aumentare	To increase
Autenticazione	Authentication, legalisation

Auto aziendale	Company car
Autorizzazione	Authorisation
Avallo	Guarantee
Avviare un'impresa	To start up a business
Avviso di accertamento	Summons
Avvocato	Lawyer
Azienda	Business
Azione	Share
Azionista	Shareholder
Bagaglio	Luggage
Bagno	Bathroom
Banca	Bank
Bancarotta	Bankruptcy
Banconota	Banknote, Bill
Basso	Low
Basso tenore di vita	Low quality of life
Beneficiario	Beneficiary, payee
Beni	Goods
Beni di investimento	Investment goods
Biglietto	Ticket
Bilancio	Balance sheet
Bolla	Delivery note
Bonifico	Bank transfer
Borsa di studio	Student grant
Brevetto	Patent, licence
Buoni del Tesoro	Government bonds
Burocrazia	Bureaucracy
Busta paga	Payslip
Bustarella	Bribe
Buttare	To throw
Cabina telefonica	Telephone box
CAF	Fiscal Assistance Centre

Caffè	Coffee
Cambiale	Draft Bill of Exchange
Cambio	Change
Camera	Room
Camera di Commercio	Chamber of Commerce
Cameriere	Waiter
Campagna	Countryside
Canale di distribuzione	Trade channel
Cancellare	To delete
Cantiere	Building or engineering site
Capacità	Abilities
Capitale	Capital
Capire	To understand
Capitale d'esercizio	Working capital
Capitale interamente versato	Fully paid up capital
Capodanno	New Year
Carabinieri	Police
Carcere	Prison
Carica	Office
Carta	Paper
Carta bollata	Stamped paper
Carta da lettere	Notepaper
Carta intestata	Headed letter
Carta stradale	Road map
Cartella esattoriale	Tax assessment
Cartolina	Postcard
Casa	House
Casellario giudiziale	Judicial register
Casellario penale	Criminal records
Cassa	Petty Cash
Cassaforte	Safe
Castelletto	Fluctuating overdraft
Cellulare	Mobile phone
Centro	Centre

Certificato	Certificate
Certificato di deposito	Deposit warrant
Certificato di nascita	Birth certificate
Cessione	Transfer
Chiamare	To call
Chiedere	To ask
Chilogrammo	Kilogram
Chiusura	Closing
Circolante	Currency
Circoscrizione	District, small entity of Municipality
Città	Town
Clausola	Clause, article
Clausola penale	Penal clause
Cliente	Customer
Codice Civile	Civil law
Codice Fiscale	Tax code
Cognome	Surname
Colazione	Breakfast
Collaborazione	Cooperation
Collega	Colleague
Collegamento	Connection
Collegio arbitrale	Arbitration board
Collegio sindacale	Auditors
Colpa	Fault
Commercialista	Chartered Accountant
Commerciante	Trader
Comparire in giudizio	To appear before the court
Compensazione	Offset
Compilare	To draw up
Comprare	To buy
Compromesso	Compromise
Compromettere	To jeopardise
Comune	Municipality, Council
Concessione	Grant

Concludere un accordo	To carry out an agreement
Concordare	To agree
Concorrente	Competitor
Concorso	State–run exam
Conferma	Confirmation
Congedo	Leave (paid or unpaid)
Congedo per maternità	Maternity leave
Conguaglio	Adjustment
Conoscenza	Knowledge
Consegna	Delivery
Consiglio	Advice
Consiglio di Amministrazione	Board of Directors
Consorzio	Pool
Consorzio industriale	Industrial consortium
Consulente del lavoro	Consultant specialised in employment issues
Contabilità	Accounting
Contante	Cash
Contenuto	Contents
Conto corrente bancario	Bank account
Conto economico	Profit and loss account/statement
Contrassegno	Countersign
Contrattazione	Negotiation
Contratto	Contract
Contratto preliminare	Preliminary contract
Contributo	Contribute
Contributi previdenziali	Social security payments
Controllo	Control, check
Convegno	Conference
Convocare un'assemblea	To call a meeting
Cooperative	Cooperatives
Copertura	Cover
Corruzione	Corruption

Corte	Court
Corte costituzionale	Constitutional Court
Corte dei conti	State Audit Court
Corte di Cassazione	High Court of Justice
Costituzione	Constitution
Costo	Cost
Costi amministrativi	Overheads
Costi fissi	Fixed costs
Costi variabili	Variable costs
Costoso	Expensive
Costruire	To build
Crediti	Debtors Accounts receivable
Crisi	Crisis
Cucina	Kitchen
Curatore	Trustee, administrator
Curriculum	CV, resumè
Custodia	Custody
D.L.	Ordinary laws (Executive Decree)
D.Lgs	Ordinary laws (Legislative Decree)
D.P.R.	Ordinary laws (Presidential Decree)
Danno	Damage
Dare	To give
Dare le dimissioni	To resign
Data di nascita	Date of birth
Data di spedizione	Shipping date
Dazio	Customs
DDT (Documento di Trasporto)	Delivery Note
Debiti verso fornitori	Accounts payable
Decidere	To decide
Decisione	Decision
Decreti Legge (abbr. D.L.)	Ordinary laws (Executive Decree)

Decreti Legislativi (abbr. D.Lgs)	Ordinary laws (Legislative Decree)
Decreti ministeriali	Ministerial Decree
Deducibile	Deductible
Dedurre	To deduct
Delega	Proxy
Denaro	Money
Deposito	Deposit
Detrarre	To detract
Dichiarare	To declare
Dichiarazione dei redditi	Tax return
Differenza	Different
Differire un pagamento	To put off a payment
Difficile	Difficult
Difficoltà	Difficulty
Diminuzione	Decrease
Dipendente	Employee
Direttore	Director, senior manager
Direttore del Personale	HR Director
Direttore delle vendite	Sales Director
Dirigente	Senior Manager
Diritto	Right
Diritto (di fare)	Right (of doing something)
Disoccupazione	Unemployment
Disponibile	Available
Distinta di carico	Consignment note
Ditta	Business, firm
Ditta individuale	Sole trade business
Dividendo	Dividend
Divisa	Currency
Documento	Document
Domanda	Question, request
Domicilio	Domicile
Dovere	To have to, must (v), Duty (n)

Durata	Duration
Eccedenza	Excess
Eccedenza di personale	Over–staffed
Economia	Economy
Economia sommersa	Hidden economy
Economico	Cheap
Effettivo	Actual
Effetto	Bill of Exchange
Efficiente	Efficient
Elenco	List
Elettricità	Electricity
Elusione fiscale	Tax evasion
Emettere fattura	To issue an invoice
Emissione	Issue
Ente locale	Local authority
Ente pubblico	State organisation
Ente senza fine di lucro	Non–profit organisation
Entrata (ricavo)	Income, revenue
Epifania	Epiphany
Equilibrio	Balance
Equo	Fair
Erario	Inland Revenue
Erede	Heir
Eredità	Inheritance
Errore	Mistake
Esame	Exam
Esattore	Collector
Esecuzione	Fulfilment
Esente	Exempt
Esente dale imposte	Exempt from taxation
Esercizio commerciale	Business, shop
Esigibile	Collectable, payable
Esperto	Expert

Esportare	To export
Estero	Abroad
Estinguere un credito	To pay off a credit
Estratto conto	Bank statement
Evasione	Evasion
Eventuale	Possible
Fabbricato	Building
Fallimento	Bankruptcy
Falsificare	To counterfeit
Falso	False
Fare	To do
Fare affari con qualcuno	To trade with somebody
Fare appello	To appeal
Fare concorrenza	To compete
Fare credito	To give credit
Fare un'offerta	To make an offer
Fare parte del Consiglio di Amministrazione	To sit on the Board of Directors
Fascicolo	File
Fattura	Invoice
Fatturato	Turnover
Ferragosto	Bank holiday on 15 August
Ferrovia	Railway
Fidarsi	To trust
Fido	Credit line
Fiducia	Confidence
Fila	Queue
Finanza	Finance
Finanziamento	Financing
Firma	Signature
Fissare un prezzo	To set a price
Flessibilità	Flexibility
Flusso finanziario	Cash flow

Fondatore	Founder
Fondersi	To merge
Fondo	Fund
Fondo Comune di Investimento	Investment trust
Fondo d'ammortamento	Depreciation fund
Fondo di previdenza	Pension fund
Fondo Monetario Internazionale	International Monetary Fund
Formalità	Formality
Fornitore	Supplier
Franchigia	Franchise
Frodare	To commit a fraud
Funzionario	Officer
Funzionario di banca	Bank manager
Garanzia	Security
Garanzia bancaria	Bank guarantee
Gente	People
Gestione	Management
Giacenza	Cash in hand
Giacenza iniziale/finale	Opening/closing stock
Giacenza minima	Minimum stock
Giornale	Newspaper
Giornale di cassa	Cash Journal
Giornata lavorativa	Working day
Giorno di valuta	Value day
Girata	Endorsement
Giudice	Judge
Giudizio arbitrale	Award
Giuramento	Oath
Giustificare	To justify
Giusto	Fair
Governo	Government

Gradimento	Acceptance
Gratis	Free
Gravare d'ipoteca	To mortgage
Gruppo finanziario	Holding
Guadagnare	To earn
Guadagno netto	Net profit, net income
Guardia di Finanza	Tax Police
ICI	Tax in residential property
Igiene	Hygiene
Illecito	Unlawful
Imballaggio	Package
Immagine	Image
Immatricolare	To register
Immediato	Immediate
Immobilizzazioni	Fixed assets
Impegno	Undertaking
Impianti	Equipment
Impiegato	Employee
Importazione	Import
Imposta di registro	Registry tax
Imposta sul reddito	Income tax
Imposta sul valore aggiunto (IVA)	Value Added Tax
Imprenditore, imprenditrice	Entrepreneur
Impresa	Business, company
Incontrare	To meet
Incontro	Meeting
Incorporare	To merge
Indebitamento	Borrowing
Indennità di buonuscita	Severance pay
Indennizzo	Compensation
Indice dei prezzi	Price index

Indice di disoccupazione	Unemployment rate
Indirizzo	Address
Industria	Industry
Inflazione	Inflation
Informazione	Information
Informazioni commerciali	Business report
Infortunio	Accident
Infrazione	Breach
Ingiunzione	Precept
Iniziativa	Initiative
Inoltrare	To submit
INPS	National Institute of Social Security
Insegnante	Teacher
Interessi	Interests
Interessi di mora	Overdue interests
Interessi legali	Legal interests (calculated on legal rate)
Intervallo	Break
Intestazione	Heading
Inventario	Inventory
Investimento	Investment
Inviare	To send
Ipoteca	Mortgage
Ipoteca di primo grado	First mortgage
IRAP	Company Tax
IRE	Personal Tax on income
IRES	Company Tax
Istanza	Request
Istanza fallimentare	Petition in Bankruptcy
Istituto	Institute
Istruzione professionale	Professional training
Lanciare un nuovo prodotto	To launch new product
Lavorare	To work

Lavorare in nero	Black market
Lavorare part time	To work part–time
Lavoratore autonomo	Self–employed worker
Lavoro	Job
Lavoro dipendente	Employment salary
Legalizzare	To legalise
Legalizzare un atto	To legalise a deed
Leggi Costituzionali	Constitutional laws
Leggi Ordinarie	Ordinary laws (Presidential Decree)
(abbr. D.P.R.)	
Leggi Regionali	Counties' laws
Legislazione	Legislation
Lettera di	
accompagnamento	Covering letter
Lettera di reclamo	Complaint letter
Lezione	Lesson
Libero	Free
Libro	Book
Licenza	Permission
Licenza di fabbricazione	Manufacturing licence
Licenziare	To fire, to sack
Licitazione	Bid
Linea di prodotti	Product line
Liquidare un azienda	To wind up a company
Listino prezzi	Price list
Locali	Premises
Locazione	Rent
Lotto	Lot
Luogo di consegna	Place of delivery
Luogo di nascita	Place of birth
Macchinari	Equipment
Magazzino	Warehouse
Maggioranza	Majority

Mandato	Order
Manodopera	Labour
Mansione	Task
Manutenzione	Maintenance
Marca da bollo	Tax stamp
Marchio	Brand
Marchio di fabbrica	Trademark
Margine	Margin
Massimo	Maximum
Mastro	Ledger
Medico	Doctor
Membro	Member
Mercato	Market
Mercato del lavoro	Labour market
Merci	Goods
Merci contraffatte	Counterfeited goods
Mezzo di pagamento	Mean of payment
Mezzogiorno (d'Italia)	Southern Italy with the islands
Migliorare	To improve
Migliorare la qualità	To improve on quality
Ministro	Minister
Minuta	Draft
Mobili e arredi	Furniture and fittings
Modificare	To change
Modulo	Form
Moneta	Coin
Moneta europea	European currency
Monopolio	Monopoly
Movimento di merci	Good traffic
Movimento di prezzo	Cash adjustment
Multa	Fine, penalty
Mutuo	Loan, mortgage
Natale	Christmas

Nazionalità	Nationality
Nazione	Country
Necessità	Necessity
Negoziabile	Negotiable
Negoziare	To trade
Negozio	Shop
Netto	Net
Noleggiare	To hire, to rent
Nominare	To appoint
Norma	Rule
Nota di consegna	Delivery note
Nota di Credito	Credit note
Notaio	Notary
Notifica	Notification
Notificare	To notify
Notizia confidenziale	Confidential information
Notizie	News, information
Noto	Well known
Nullaosta	Permit
Numero	Number
Numero di riferimento	Reference number
Numero di targa	Plate number
Numero legale	Quorum
Obbligare	To oblige
Obbligatorio	Compulsory
Obbligazione di Stato	Government Bond
Obiettivo	Objective
Obsoleto	Out of date
Occupazione	Employment
Offerta	Offer
Offerta di lavoro	Job offer
Omaggi	Free goods
Omologazione	Approval, confirmation

Onere previdenziale	Social security cost
Oneri finanziari	Borrowing costs, financial charges
ONLUS	Organisations without any profit aim
Opzione	Option
Orario d'ufficio	Office hours
Ordine	Order
Organizzare	To organise
Ottenere	To obtain
Pacco	Parcel
Paese (città)	Village
Paese (nazione)	Country
Paga	Wage
Pagamento	Payment
Pagamento a rate	Payment in instalments
Pagamento alla consegna	Payment on delivery
Pagamento arretrato	Payment overdue
Pagamento in anticipo	Payment in advance
Pagamento in contanti	Cash payment
Pagamento mediante assegno	Payment by cheque
Pagherò	Promissory note
Parcella	Fee
Parere	Opinion, advice
Partecipare	To participate
Partecipare agli utili	To share profits
Partecipazione	Share
Partita doppia	Double entry
Partita Iva	VAT number
Partitario fornitori/clienti	Creditors/debtors ledger
Pasqua	Easter Sunday
Pasquetta	Easter Monday
Passività	Liabilities
Passività a breve	Current liabilities

Passività a medio/lungo termine	Medium/long–term liabilities
Passo	Step
Patente	Driving licence
Patrimonio Netto	Equity
Patto	Agreement
Penale	Criminal
Pensione	Pension
Percentuale	Percentage
Perdita	Loss
Perdita non deducibile	Non-deductible loss
Periodo d'imposta	Fiscal year
Perizia	Estimate, appraisal
Permesso di soggiorno	Permit to stay
Permettere	To allow
Persona giuridica	Legal person, company
Personale	Personnel, staff
Peso	Weight
Peso fiscale	Tax burden
Pianificazione	Planning
Piano (di palazzo)	Floor
Piano (progetto)	Plan
Piano dei conti	Chart of accounts
Piazza di pagamento	Place of payment
Pignorare	To repossess
PIL	GDP
Polizia	Police
Polizza	Policy
Polizza assicurativa	Insurance policy
Ponte	Day added on to bank holiday
Portafoglio	Portfolio
Posizione finanziaria	Financial standing
Possesso	Ownership
Possessore	Holder

Possibilità di carriera	Career opportunities
Posto di polizia	Police station
Potere	Power
Prassi	Standard practice
Praticante	Apprentice
Preavviso	Notice
Prelevamento	Withdrawal
Premio	Prize
Premio d'assicurazione	Insurance premium
Premio di produzione	Bonus
Prendere accordi	To negotiate
Prendere contatto	To contact
Presidente	Chairman
Prestito	Loan
Previsione	Forecast
Prezzo	Price
Prezzo di listino	List price
Prezzo di mercato	Market price
Prezzo IVA inclusa	VAT–inclusive price
Priorità	Priority
Privilegio	Lien
Procedura	Procedure
Procura	Proxy
Prodotto	Product
Produttività	Productivity
Produttore	Manufacturer
Professionista	Professional
Profitto	Profit
Progetto	Project
Programma	Plan
Promozione	Promotion
Proporre	To suggest
Proprietà	Property, ownership
Proprietà immobiliare	Real estate

Proprietà privata	Private property
Proprietario	Owner
Protesto (spese)	Protest (charges)
Provvedimento	Measure
Provvigione	Commision
Pubblicità	Advertising
Quadro	Picture
Quadro direttivo	Junior manager
Qualità	Quality
Querela	Lawsuit
Questura	Italian Police Headquarters
Quietanza	Receipt of payment
Raccomandata	Registered letter
Ragione sociale	Business name
Ragioniere commercialista	Certified Accountant
Rappresentanti	Salespeople
Rata	Instalment
Reato	Crime, offence
Recapito	Business address
Reclamare	To make a complaint
Redditi di capitale	Capital gains
Redditizio	Profitable
Reddito	Income
Reddito imponibile	Taxable income
Regione	County
Registrare	To register
Registro contabile	Account book
Registro delle imprese	National Business Registry
Regola	Rule
Relazione	Report
Rendiconto	Statement
Rendimento	Performance

Rendita vitalizia	Life income annuity
Reparto	Department
Residenza	Residency
Respingere indietro	To send back
Respingere una richiesta	To reject a request
Responsabilità limitata	Limited liability
Retribuzione	Remuneration, salary
Revisione contabile	Audit
Riassumere	Summarise
Ricavi	Revenues
Ricerca di mercato	Market research
Ricevuta	Receipt
Richiesta	Request
Ricorso	Appeal
Ridurre	To reduce
Riduzione delle spese	Cost reduction
Rifiutare	To refuse
Rimanenze	Inventories
Rimborso	Refund
Rinviare	To postpone
Rischio	Risk
Riscuotere	To collect
Riserva	Fund
Risparmiare	To save
Risposta	Reply
Ritardo	Delay
Ritenuta d'acconto	Withholding tax
Riunione	Meeting
Salario	Wage
Saldo	Settlement, balance
Sbagliato	Wrong
Scadenza	Deadline
Scadere	To fall due

Scelta	Choice
Scheda carburante	Petrol form
Sciogliere un'assemblea	To break up a meeting
Sciopero	Strike
Sconto	Discount
Scoperto di banca	Bank overdraft
Scoperto di conto	Overdraft
Scrittura contabile	Book entries
Scuola	School
Sede legale	Registered Office
Segretario comunale	Town clerk
Sentenza	Judgement
Servizio Sanitario Nazionale	Italian National Health Service
Sigillo	Seal
Sindacato	Trade Union
Società	Company
Società controllante	Holding
Società di capitali	Joint Stock Corporations
Società di persone	Partnerships
Socio	Partner
Socio accomandante	Limited partner
Soldi	Money
Sollecitare	To dun
Soluzione	Solution
Somma	Sum
Sottoscritto	Undersigned
Speculare	To speculate
Spedire	To send, to consign
Spesa	Expense
Spese bancarie	Bank charges
Stampa	Print
Stanza	Room
Statali	Public sector employees

Stato Patrimoniale	Balance Sheet
Statuto	Memorandum
Stipendio	Salary
Stipulare	To stipulate
Straordinario	Extraordinary
Studente	Student
Successione	Succession
Sviluppo	Development
Tariffa	Tariff, price
Tassa	Tax
Tassa Rifiuti (TARSU)	Refuse tax
Tassa sulla pubblicità	Tax on advertisement
Tassazione	Taxation
Tecnica	Technique
Tecnologia	Technology
Telefono	Telephone
Telegramma	Telegram
Televisione	Television
Tendenza	Tendency
Termine	Expiration, limit
Termine di preavviso	Notice period
Terreno	Land
Terziario	Service sector
Terzo	Third party
Testamento	Will
Testimone	Witness
Titolare	Owner (of the business)
Titolo	Security
Transazione commerciale	Business transaction
Trarre una cambiale	To draw a Bill of Exchange
Trasferimento bancario	Bank transfer
Trasferirsi	To move
Trasmettere un ordine	To pass an order

Trasportare	To transport
Tratta	Bill of exchange
Trattenuta	Deduction
Tribunale	Court
Trovare	To find
Truffa	Fraud
Udienza	Hearing
Udienza del tribunale	Sitting of the court
Ufficiale	Official
Ufficio	Department Office
Ufficio pubblico	Public Office
Università	University
Usare	To use
Utile (di bilancio)	Profit (P&L Account)
Utile (vantaggio)	Advantage
Vacanza	Holiday
Vaglia cambiario	Promissory note
Vaglia postale	Postal money order
Valore Catastale	National rent value
Valore di mercato	Market value
Valore imponibile	Taxable amount
Valuta	Currency
Valuta estera	Foreign currency
Valutare	To estimate
Valutazione del credito	Rating
Vantaggio	Advantage
Variazione	Change
Vendere	To sell
Vendere al dettaglio	To retail
Vendere in nero	To sell on the black market
Verifica fiscale	Tax inspection
Versare	To pay

Vettore	Carrier
Vigili del fuoco	Firefighters
Volume	Volume

DON'T GET CAUGHT OUT WHEN MAKING REGULAR FOREIGN CURRENCY TRANSFERS

Even once you have started your business in Italy it's important that you don't forget about foreign exchange. If you find yourself in the position where you need to make regular foreign currency transfers from the UK you may not realise that using your bank to arrange these transfers isn't always the best option. Low exchange rates, high fees and commission charges all eat away at your money and mean that each time you use your bank you lose out. However, by using Currencies Direct's Overseas Regular Transfer Plan you can get more of your money time after time.

Exchange Rates

Your bank is likely to only offer you a tourist rate of exchange due to the small amounts being transferred. However, Currencies Direct is able to offer you a commercial rate of exchange regardless of the amount that you transfer.

Transfer Charges

Most banks will charge between £10 and £40 for every transfer. Currencies Direct is able to offer free transfers, which will save you a considerable amount of money over time

Commission Charges

When made through a bank, transfers are usually liable for a commission charge of around 2%. By using Currencies Direct you can avoid commission charges altogether.

How does it work?

It's very easy to use Currencies Direct. Firstly you need to open an account with them. Once this is done all you need to do is set up a direct debit with your bank and confirm with Currencies Direct the amount you would like to transfer and how often (monthly or quarterly). The money will be taken from your account on a specified day, and once cleared funds are received, transferred to Italy at the best possible rate available.

Information provided by Currencies Direct
www.currenciesdirect.com
Tel: 0845 389 1729   Email: info@currenciesdirect.com

Index

Bold numbers refer to headed sections or chapters referring directly to the entry.